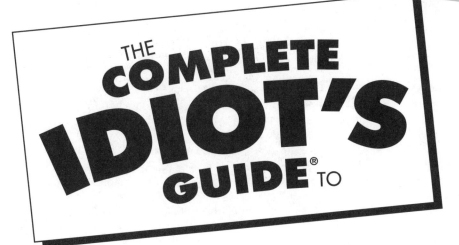

THE COMPLETE IDIOT'S GUIDE® TO

Music Composition

by Michael Miller

ALPHA

A member of Penguin Group (USA) Inc.

This book is dedicated to my fellow participants in the original Free University Songwriter's Workshop, 20-some years ago, who had to suffer through my very first attempts at teaching this stuff. I hope it's a lot clearer now than it was then.

ALPHA BOOKS

Published by the Penguin Group

Penguin Group (USA) Inc., 375 Hudson Street, New York, New York 10014, U.S.A.

Penguin Group (Canada), 10 Alcorn Avenue, Toronto, Ontario, Canada M4V 3B2 (a division of Pearson Penguin Canada Inc.)

Penguin Books Ltd, 80 Strand, London WC2R 0RL, England

Penguin Ireland, 25 St Stephen's Green, Dublin 2, Ireland (a division of Penguin Books Ltd)

Penguin Group (Australia), 250 Camberwell Road, Camberwell, Victoria 3124, Australia (a division of Pearson Australia Group Pty Ltd)

Penguin Books India Pvt Ltd, 11 Community Centre, Panchsheel Park, New Delhi—110 017, India

Penguin Group (NZ), cnr Airborne and Rosedale Roads, Albany, Auckland 1310, New Zealand (a division of Pearson New Zealand Ltd)

Penguin Books (South Africa) (Pty) Ltd, 24 Sturdee Avenue, Rosebank, Johannesburg 2196, South Africa

Penguin Books Ltd, Registered Offices: 80 Strand, London WC2R 0RL, England

Publisher: *Marie Butler-Knight*
Product Manager: *Phil Kitchel*
Senior Managing Editor: *Jennifer Bowles*
Senior Acquisitions Editor: *Renee Wilmeth*
Development Editor: *Ginny Bess Munroe*
Senior Production Editor: *Billy Fields*
Copy Editor: *Krista Hansing*
Cartoonist: *Shannon Wheeler*
Cover/Book Designer: *Trina Wurst*
Indexer: *Angie Bess*
Layout: *Ayanna Lacey*
Proofreading: *Mary Hunt*

Contents at a Glance

Contents

Foreword

When I tell people that I compose music, the most common response I get is, "I can't even begin to understand how someone could do that." Composing seems mysterious partly because it apparently involves creating something out of nothing—there's no block of stone, lump of clay, or troupe of dancers to mold. Although composing music is by no means the only art that doesn't involve working directly with physical objects, most if not all of the rest of them (poetry, fiction, scriptwriting, and so on) are verbal, and people understand the concept of composing with words because they do it every time they speak. But music is different. A B♭ below middle C doesn't have a relation to the real world like the word "bucket" does; it's a blank slate, waiting for the composer to give it meaning through the way it's sounded as well as through its relationships to other sounds. Furthermore, the end product of a composer's work is invisible and ephemeral—vibrations of the air. No wonder, to those who haven't done it, composing can seem like wrestling smoke in the dark.

I usually reply to people's befuddlement in one of two ways. The first is to admit that the longer I compose, the more mysterious and out of my hands the whole business seems. I titled one of my compositions *Signals* in recognition of this; often while I'm composing I feel like I'm a radio antenna receiving messages from who knows where, which (as long as I like them) I then figure out how to write down. (Other artists call this channeling; it's the same idea.) Part of the beauty of creating art comes from getting comfortable with opening yourself up to such signals. But, although they may be mysterious, they're also democratic. Twenty years of teaching composition has taught me that we're all capable of receiving them, and that includes you, gentle reader.

My other reply is to tell people that, like any other complex tasks, composing can be broken down into a series of manageable steps. As Mike Miller describes in these pages, melody and harmony rarely emerge simultaneously as a composer works; it's much more common to work on one and then the other. Likewise, if you're composing a contrapuntal piece (with two or more melodies taking place at the same time), you will most likely switch back and forth between the two, working on the melodic parts one at a time and listening to how they fit together—alternating between seeing the forest and the trees, as it were.

Composing is a constant search for one's individual musical voice. As you gain experience in composing, you may find that your voice speaks most clearly in pop tunes, country songs, jazz charts, church hymns, contemporary classical music, or any of a million other realms of sound—classifiable and unclassifiable. Maybe you know the direction you're heading already, or maybe you don't. Rather than force the issue prematurely, this book wisely starts you out composing on terra firma; in what's called functional tonality, the common musical language in which Mozart, the Beatles, and Alan Jackson are all rooted. As you gain more experience and confidence being creative within this safe harbor, you can then get ready to set sail for wherever your inner light pulls you. Or if you decide to stay a landlubber, that's fine, too; as the old saying goes, there's still plenty of good music to be written in C major.

Have fun. Don't force things. Listen carefully to your inner ear. Run everything past the filter of your taste, but at the same time don't be too quick to judge and reject. Oh, and one more thing. Don't believe Mike when he disses himself— I've played some of his handwritten music, and it's not nearly as messy as he says.

—David Vayo

David Vayo is Professor and head of the composition department at Illinois Wesleyan University, where he teaches composition and contemporary music and coordinates the Symposium of Contemporary Music and the New Music Café concert series. David has received numerous awards and commissions for his work; more than two hundred performances and broadcasts of his compositions have taken place in Mexico, Japan, the Netherlands, Finland, France, and throughout the United States. You can read more about David and his work at www.iwu.edu/~music/faculty/vayo.html.

Introduction

I love good music. It doesn't matter whether it's a major symphony or a simple song: music that is well written and inspired touches my soul, makes me think, and inspires me to do better in my own efforts. I respect anyone who has the desire to write music, and I admire those who do it well.

Good compositions are borne from a combination of inspiration and perspiration, as the saying goes, as well as some specific skills. The inspiration comes in the form of the musical ideas you hear in your head, the perspiration is the hard work you have to do to develop those ideas, and the skills are what you'll learn in this book.

I've found that there are a large number of aspiring and self-taught composers who want and need to learn these basic skills. If you're reading these words, you're probably one of that group; you have the inspiration and are willing to put forth the perspiration, but you're not quite sure how to proceed.

Fortunately, you've just taken a good first step toward acquiring the proper skills. *The Complete Idiot's Guide to Music Composition* introduces you to the logic and the tools you need to create your own musical compositions. Chords, melody, structure, it's all here—presented in an easy-to-follow, step-by-step fashion. Follow the instructions and advice presented here, and you'll be well on your way to creating your own musical compositions.

Before you proceed, however, a few caveats. First, this book presents just one approach to composition. You might find that some of the ideas here don't always work for you, personally, or you might discover a totally different approach that does. That's okay. You should take out of this book those aspects that help you improve your writing, and if you find a better way to proceed, all power to you.

In addition, this book can't tell you everything you need to know to become a great composer; no book can. If you're serious about writing your own music, you'll want to supplement the information in this book with some formal training with an experienced teacher or mentor, someone who can listen to and critique your compositions. You'll also want to find some venue for your compositions so you can hear what you write performed in the real world. And, finally, you'll want to write as much and as often as you can; practice might not make perfect, but it will help you develop your musical skills.

This book can teach you a lot, but it can take you only so far; it's your own desire and talent that will determine how good you get.

Who This Book Is For

The Complete Idiot's Guide to Music Composition is for anyone who wants to learn how to compose or to become a better composer. This book doesn't focus on any one particular musical genre; the techniques presented here can be applied equally well to songs and symphonies, and every type of music in between.

As to prior experience, it doesn't matter if you've never written a note in your life; this book starts at the very beginning. And if you've already tried your hand at writing music, the beginning is still a good place to start—you'll probably learn some techniques you might have skipped over on your own.

What You Need to Know Before You Start

Although I don't assume that you've written anything before, I do assume that you have some musical training. I assume that you can play an instrument, and hope that you know your way around a piano keyboard. It also helps if you have access to a piano or other keyboard instrument, to work through the examples and the exercises in this book—which require you to play chords and melody at the same time, something you can't do on a flute, trumpet, or violin.

I also assume that you know some basic music theory—scales, intervals, chords, and the like. If you get into the book and find that you're a little behind the learning curve, do yourself a favor and take some time to refresh your knowledge of music theory before you continue. For a good guide to music theory, I recommend my companion book, *The Complete Idiot's Guide to Music Theory, Second Edition* (Alpha Books, 2005). It should be available at the same place you purchased this book.

In addition, it's helpful if you have some knowledge of the particular musical genre in which you want to write. That means studying a little music history, as appropriate. If you're interested in composing concert music, make sure you know the music of the Baroque, Classical, and Romantic periods, as well as some of the trends and composers in twentieth-century music. If you want to be a songwriter, brush up on the best of the breed—Berlin, Gershwin, and Porter from the first half of the twentieth century, and Bacharach, Webb, Lennon/McCartney, and others from the second half. And if you're interested in composing television and film music, familiarize yourself with the works of Elmer Bernstein, Bernard Herrman, John Williams, and the like.

Bottom line? You need to be fluent in the musical language, immerse yourself in the great works, and have a sense both of history and of contemporary trends in the field. Doing a little homework now will help you be a better composer in the future.

What You'll Find in This Book

The Complete Idiot's Guide to Music Composition contains 18 chapters that lead you step by step through the process of musical composition. The chapters are organized into five general parts, as follows:

Part 1, "Before You Start," helps you prepare for your first compositions and describes the tools you need to assemble before you start writing.

Part 2, "Harmonic Composition," addresses the art of composing music, chords-first. You'll learn how to create a harmonious chord progression, how to use both standard and extended chords, and how to employ chord substation to create more sophisticated compositions.

Part 3, "Melodic Composition," is all about the melody—to me, the most important part of the composition. You'll learn various techniques for creating great-sounding melodies, including the use of scales and modes, structural tones and embellishments, rhythm and syncopation, melodic contour and flow, and tension and release. You'll also learn how to fit chords to a melody—and reharmonize an existing chord progression.

Part 4, "Developing the Composition," shows you how to turn a basic composition into something more substantial. You'll learn how to turn a short melody into a full-length work, how to use repetition and variation, and techniques for creating multiple-voice compositions.

Part 5, "Advanced Techniques," moves beyond basic composition into more specific—and more sophisticated—musical areas. You'll be introduced to the topics of orchestration, chromaticism and atonality, contemporary composition, and that unique type of composition we call songwriting.

The Complete Idiot's Guide to Music Composition concludes with a glossary of musical terms and the answers to selected exercises presented at the end of each chapter in the book.

How to Get the Most Out of This Book

To get the most out of this book, you should know how it is designed. I've tried to put things together to make reading the book and learning how to compose both rewarding and fun.

This book mixes information and instruction. The information you can handle on your own—just read the text and look at the musical examples. The instruction is in the form of musical examples and exercises. You should play through the examples as they appear in the text, and when you get to the end of each chapter, work through each of the exercises. The exercises are particularly important because they both reinforce the techniques introduced in the chapter and enable you to write your own compositions based on those techniques. Some of the exercises have specific answers (which are presented in Appendix B); others simply encourage you to flex your musical muscles and compose. (I like these exercises best!) For these latter exercises, there are no correct answers—let your ears judge your success.

In addition to the musical examples sprinkled throughout each chapter, you'll find a number of little text boxes (what we in publishing call *sidebars* and *margin notes*) that present additional advice and information. These elements enhance your knowledge or point out important pitfalls to avoid, and they look like this:

> **Note**
>
> These boxes contain additional information about the topic at hand.

Warning

These boxes warn you of common mistakes to avoid.

Tip

These boxes contain tips and hints on how to improve your compositional skills.

And, just in case a few mistakes happen to creep into the printed book, you can find a list of any corrections or clarifications on my website (www. molehillgroup.com/composing.htm). That's also where you can find a list of my other books, so feel free to look around—and maybe do a little online shopping!

Let Me Know What You Think

I always love to hear from my readers. Feel free to e-mail me at composing@molehillgroup.com. I can't promise that I'll answer every e-mail, but I will promise that I'll read each one!

Acknowledgments

Thanks to the usual suspects at Alpha Books, including but not limited to Marie Butler-Knight, Renee Wilmeth, Ginny Bess Munroe, Billy Fields, Jennifer Bowles, and Krista Hansing for helping to turn my manuscript into a printed book.

Special thanks go to my old friend and well-known composer/educator David Vayo, who wrote the foreword to this book. In addition to his written words, David offered insight and advice that informed the content throughout this book, and I thank him for that. If you ever have the opportunity to listen to one of David's compositions, you're in for a real treat. His stuff is good.

Special Thanks to the Technical Reviewer

The Complete Idiot's Guide to Music Composition was reviewed by an expert who double-checked the accuracy of what you'll learn here, to help us ensure that this book gives you everything you need to know about composing music. Special thanks are extended to Peter Gilbert for his review and comments in this regard.

Peter holds music degrees from the Cleveland Institute of Music and Illinois Wesleyan University, and is currently a doctoral fellow at Harvard University. His compositions have been performed by the American Classic Quartet, Cleveland Chamber Symphony, Dallas Wind Symphony, Indianapolis Brass Choir, and New York City's One World Symphony Chamber Players, among others. You can read more about Peter and his work at his website, www. petergilbert.net.

My heartfelt thanks to Peter for his assistance and advice—and for helping to make this a better book.

Trademarks

All terms mentioned in this book that are known to be or are suspected of being trademarks or service marks have been appropriately capitalized. Alpha Books and Penguin Group (USA) Inc. cannot attest to the accuracy of this information. Use of a term in this book should not be regarded as affecting the validity of any trademark or service mark.

Part 1

Before You Start

Before you put notes on paper, you need to do a little homework. Read on to discover how the art of composition works and what things you need to assemble for your own personal composer's toolkit.

So You Want to Write Your Own Music ...

In This Chapter

◆ What is composition?

◆ Different approaches to composition

◆ Learning how to write your own music

◆ Exploring composition-related careers

The desire to compose your own music is admirable. Composing lets you express yourself musically as well as entertain and inform those who listen to your compositions. Beautiful and interesting sounds can be made, assuming you know how to make them—or, more precisely, how to make other musicians make them. Getting those sounds in your head down on paper, and then into the instruments and voices of performers, is what requires skill.

Fortunately, composition can be learned. Although I can't teach you creativity or inspiration, I can show you how composition works—the nuts and the bolts behind the sounds and the colors of musical compositions. But before we delve into the mechanics of composition, we need to examine the art of composition itself. Just what is music composition—and how do you go about becoming a composer?

What Is Composition?

Put simply, composition is the art of creating a piece of music. That piece of music can be as short as an advertising jingle or as long as an opera. It can be instrumental or vocal; it can be "serious" or commercial, popular or avant garde, classical or contemporary. A composition can be an unadorned melody or a complex work for a full orchestra and chorus. In short, a musical composition can be anything you can hum, sing, or play. There are no boundaries to what you can create.

That said, you can't just jot down a bunch of random notes and call it a composition. A good composition has form and meaning; it tells a story, or invokes a mood, or takes you from one place to another. The best compositions create their own self-contained realities, where individual components relate to and with each other within the whole. There is a reason for each phrase and individual note, all of which combine to create a whole that is more than the sum of the parts.

I like to think of writing a composition as being similar to telling a story. Just as you can tell many different types of stories, you can create many different types of compositions. Some stories relate a specific set of facts, others convey a general mood, and still others exist merely to entertain. A good story takes you from point A to point B in a relatively efficient fashion, while containing enough extraneous elements to make the journey entertaining; there are often characters, places, or other elements that provide both color and context. And when the story is over, there's typically a point to the whole thing, something to remember and reflect upon.

You can see how all of these elements are also important to a musical composition. A piece of music can do many different things; it can literally tell a story, convey a mood, express a point of view, or just entertain. A composition moves from the beginning to the end in a logical fashion, while maintaining some type of musical interest along the route. Different elements within the composition provide color, and at the end the composition makes some sort of statement. It doesn't matter whether you write a three-minute pop song or an hour-long tone poem: a good composition has a point of view and has something to say.

Different Approaches to Composition

As you learn how to write your own music, you'll discover that there are several different ways to approach a composition. They all start with a blank sheet of staff paper, so to speak, but require you to look at your pending composition in different ways.

Note that there is no one "correct" way to begin a composition. Some composers take one approach, some another, some work both ways—often by creating the chords and melody simultaneously. Which method you choose is a personal decision. And you're not limited to just one approach; you can use different approaches for different pieces. Whichever way you start, the goal should be the same: to create an artistically viable piece of music. How you create each piece of music is a personal choice.

Harmonic Composition

Facing the blank page is always difficult. If you're writing a piece that is constructed from a combination of chords and melodies (and, in the case of songwriting, lyrics), there are two common ways to get started. You can start by creating a chord progression and fitting a melody to your chords, or you can start by creating a melody and then fitting chords to that melody. The first approach is called *harmonic composition;* the latter is called *melodic composition.*

When you compose in a chords-first fashion, you are defining the harmonic structure for your composition. Everything else you write—melody, accompaniment, counterpoint, and the like—is based on that initial harmonic structure that you define.

Know, however, that even if you start with a chord progression, the melody is still the most important part of a composition—and a good melody is more than just a few notes hummed over a series of chords. A melody should have form, shape, and color, as well as its own harmonic integrity. It shouldn't be a simple motif that is dragged from place to place by whichever chord is being played. It's unfortunate that many untrained composers take the easy route of strumming and humming rather than working diligently with all the tools at hand to create well-formed, logical, and highly musical melodies.

This, then, is the chief drawback of chord-based composition. It doesn't have to be a fatal drawback, but it is something you have to watch out for. If you decide to compose chords-first, use the chord progressions you create to establish the harmonic framework of your composition. Then work equally hard on the piece's melody; don't let the melody be driven solely by the notes contained in the individual chords.

Tip

The chords-first approach is popular among many composers, especially those working within the framework of the popular song. That's because after you've created a chord progression, you essentially have a harmonic roadmap for the entire composition that helps to guide the melodies you create. A little structure can be good.

Melodic Composition

As popular as chord-based composition is, some purists insist that the only way to compose is from a melodic viewpoint. By crafting a melody on its own, that melody isn't subject to the harmonic constraints of an arbitrary chord progression. The melody is allowed to flow wherever it needs to; there are no chords to dictate that the melody go here or there (or not here or there). You can even let the melody go outside the key, if that's where it needs to go. This approach gives melody the front seat, with all other aspects of the composition taking a subsidiary role.

The freedom of writing the melody first is also one of this approach's biggest challenges. With no chord progression to serve as a guide, the seemingly limitless number of possibilities can be somewhat daunting. In addition, when a melody can go anywhere, it often does—sometimes to the exclusion of melodic and harmonic integrity and listenability. It takes a skilled and disciplined composer to construct a solid melody out of whole cloth; many composers need the framework of a chord progression to serve as a guide.

And even when you start with the melody first, you still have to employ a thorough knowledge of chord theory and harmony. The chords you choose will affect how the melody will sound within your piece.

Tip

If you choose to create the melody first, you'll need knowledge of harmony to fit a chord progression to the melody. Since any given melody can be harmonized in a number of different ways, which chords you choose should be influenced by the harmonic tendencies of your melody—but also used to expand the harmonic structure of your composition.

Holistic Composition

If you can approach composition with a chords-first or melody-first approach, why not combine both approaches and compose everything at once? That's the nature of holistic composition, where you progress measure by measure, creating the melodies and harmonies simultaneously. Because melodies and chords are intrinsically related, it makes sense to write them together—if you can.

Not all composers possess the facility to work melodically and harmonically in a concurrent fashion. It really takes a thorough understanding of music theory, a very good ear, and a good feel for where you want your composition to go. The difficulty behind this approach might not make it the first choice for beginning composers; then again, the fact that you get to create the entire picture, one measure at a time, might make it easier for you to grasp the entirety of your composition. As with all approaches, it's a personal choice.

Tip

Composing holistically doesn't necessarily mean that you have to write all the parts of a complex orchestration at the same time. Holistic composition can involve just the basic harmonies (chords) and melodies, perhaps with some important parts and counterpoint sketched in. Don't feel as if you have to orchestrate an entire symphony from scratch; it's perfectly acceptable to create the harmonic/melodic framework and then go back and create the final instrumental or vocal arrangement.

Layering

There's one other approach to composition that you should consider—that of *layering*. With layered composition, you start by creating one vocal or instrumental part, and then you layer additional parts on top of that. The composition builds piece by piece, until you've built a layered whole.

The layering approach is used to good effect in certain contemporary idioms, such as minimalism (listen to any Philip Glass composition) and various electronic music styles. It's also the approach used in loop-based music, in which you build a composition by layering different musical loops on top of each other. Depending on what type of music you want to create, it may be worth looking at.

Learning How to Write Your Own Music

To be an accomplished composer, you need a certain set of skills. In particular, you need to be able to manipulate the building blocks of any composition— the notes, rhythms, and chords that combine to create a piece of music. To this end, you will benefit from a thorough grounding in music theory and a cultivated ear. It also helps to have some innate sense of melody and harmony, although this can be developed with proper training.

Note

Learn more about essential compositional skills in Chapter 2.

Assuming that you have (or learn) these basic skills, learning how to compose involves fitting the various building blocks together to express your musical vision. It's kind of like learning how to write prose or poetry; once you know the building blocks of written language, you then have to learn how to use those building blocks to tell your stories in print.

Imitation Is More Than Flattery—It's a Learning Tool!

As you explore your own personal creativity, one way to proceed is to learn from what you listen to. There's nothing at all wrong with—and a lot to be gained by—examining and emulating individual compositions that you're particularly fond of. Not that you want to base your emerging style on someone else's sound, of course; rather, you can learn useful techniques by discovering how other composers create particular types of music. Once you learn how others do it, you can use those tools in service to your own compositional goals.

One way to approach this type of examination is to transcribe a particular work. Write it down, note by note, as you hear it. This process will help you get "inside the head" of the original composer; you'll discover which chords are used to produce different sounds, and how particular melody notes fit to those chords and combine with one another to create the melodic line. You'll learn structure, you'll learn form, you'll learn how different sounds are created. When you dissect a composition with your own hands, you really learn what makes it tick.

And take the time to examine more than one type of music. Dissect some popular songs (from different eras), some movie scores, some jazz compositions, and some classical works. Learn what makes the soundtrack to *The Magnificent Seven* sound like a Western, or a particular folk song sound Irish, or a particular composition sound Classical or Romantic. Learn the techniques used to impart various moods and feels.

Then, once you've figured some of this out, try composing something of your own that sounds the same way. Listen to a Bach piece and try to replicate the feel on your own. Try to emulate that Western movie theme, or Irish folk song, or big band chart. Do your best to replicate the original sound and feel, using the techniques you picked up. You don't want to copy the originals; what you want to do is practice the technique so you can employ it later when you create your own original compositions.

Learning in the Real World

The next step, and it's a vital one, is to put pen to paper and start writing. It's a simple fact that the best way to learn composition is to simply do it. The way life works, the more you do something, the better you get at it. That's certainly the case with composition; the more you write, the better you'll become. You need to create as many compositions as you can—write and write and write some more—in order to learn from the process. Don't try to make every composition a masterpiece; write as a method of learning, a way to experiment with different forms and approaches.

And, beyond just writing, you need to hear what you've written. You can do some of this yourself, using various computer devices and programs, but there's no substitute for hearing your work played by real-life musicians. If that means imposing on friends and colleagues for a one-time run-through, so be it. You'll learn only when you hear your notes played out loud—even the bad ones.

It's also important to have your work heard by trained and critical ears. That means finding a composition teacher or mentor to help guide your progress. Check out the music program at your local school or college, and don't shy away from approaching professional musicians in your area. Even occasional contact with (and criticism from) a professional composer can pay enormous dividends in your development.

Further Reading

You should also seek out contrasting viewpoints presented by other educators and writers. I don't pretend for this book to offer the final word on the subject; many other fine books are available that can be quite useful to any budding composer.

Here is a short list of books that can help you hone your skills, presented in alphabetical order:

- *Composing Music: A New Approach* (William Russo, The University of Chicago Press, 1980). A book filled with exercises to help you develop your compositional skills; the focus is on doing rather than reading.

- *Jazz Composition: Theory and Practice* (Ted Pease, Berklee Press, 2003). A guide to composing in the jazz idiom. Based on the jazz composition and arranging curriculum at the renowned Berklee College of Music.

- *Melody in Songwriting: Tools and Techniques for Writing Hit Songs* (Jack Perricone, Berklee Press, 2000). An excellent hands-on guide for writing melodies in any type of composition, focusing on but not limited to popular songs. This is the textbook used in songwriting classes at the Berklee College of Music.

- *Musical Composition* (Reginald Smith Brindle, Oxford University Press, 1986). A compact guide to the principles of serious composition.

- *Techniques of the Contemporary Composer* (David Cope, Wadsworth Publishing, 1997). An essential guide to serious contemporary composition, focusing on a broad spectrum of modernist techniques such as serial music, indeterminacy, pitch-class sets, musique concrete, and electronic music.

- *Tunesmith: Inside the Art of Songwriting* (Jimmy Webb, Hyperion, 1998). This is one of the finest and most entertaining books available on the art of popular songwriting, by one of the master songwriters of our age. Jimmy Webb leads you through basic music theory and the art of musical and lyrical composition, while imparting numerous pearls of wisdom (and interesting stories) garnered from his many years in the business.

♦ *What to Listen for in Music* (Aaron Copland, Mentor, 1939). A classic, not necessary a composition book, per se, but rather a general guide to music theory and analysis. Eminently readable and thoroughly informing; a must-have for any serious composer.

Beyond these and other books, the most important thing you can do is to practice your art. As I said before, you have to learn by doing. The more you write, the more you'll learn—and the better you'll become. And make sure you work through all the studies and exercises in this book!

Careers in Music Composition

For most composers, art precedes commerce, but there will always be bills to pay. How, then, can you apply your composing skills in the real world?

Fortunately, there are many career opportunities for a skilled composer. Some of the most popular composition-related careers include:

♦ **Songwriter.** A songwriter is a composer who writes popular songs—that is, both music and lyrics. So-called singer/songwriters write for themselves or their own musical groups; professional songwriters are those who don't perform their own songs, instead providing pieces (often through a publishing company) for others to perform.

Today's popular songwriters, even if they don't perform their own songs, tend to produce the music they compose for others. These producer/songwriters need to have arranging, producing, and recording skills, in addition to their songwriting skills.

♦ **Jingle writer.** A jingle writer is a composer who specializes in writing music for radio and television commercials. Successful jingle writers must be able to create short, memorable melodies with a recognizable hook, and to write fluently in a variety of musical styles.

Many jingle writers freelance for a variety of advertising agencies; others are employed directly by one of the many large agencies. Although some jingles are written on a royalty basis (you get paid every time the commercial airs), it's more common today to be paid a flat fee for your freelance work. If you're employed by an agency, your compensation is your weekly paycheck.

♦ **Jazz composer.** A jazz composer writes specifically for jazz orchestras, ensembles, and big bands. Work is typically found on a local level (writing for local musicians) and on the educational level (writing scores for high school and college jazz bands). Writing for big bands and jazz orchestras requires extensive arranging skills—in particular, the ability to work with brass and woodwind instruments and a jazz rhythm section. Not surprisingly, many (but not all, by any means) jazz composers are also players, so your writing can take into account the personalities of particular musicians.

◆ **Publishing composer.** We'll call someone who composes music that publishing companies sell to school bands and choirs a publishing composer. Music publishing is a thriving industry, with a decent appetite for both original compositions and arrangements of popular songs. For this type of work, you need to have a good feel for the musical abilities of students at specific grade levels; you're often composing for seventh-grade choir or high school band or something similar.

You can create original works on spec or write compositions to fill specific needs of the music publishers; you'll typically be paid by the piece. Obviously, excellent arranging and orchestration skills are also necessary to be successful in this area.

◆ **Religious composer.** A related music-publishing field is that of church music. Several large music publishers specialize in religious compositions and arrangements, typically vocal music for church choirs. As with traditional music publishing, a religious composer must have good working relationships with the appropriate music-publishing companies. In addition, many large churches across the country commission original compositions from time to time, so some direct work is available.

◆ **Film and television composer.** A film composer creates soundtracks for motion pictures and television series. Today's film composers must be able to create both memorable theme songs and relevant background music to play underneath the entire film; the film's score should also comment on particular passages of the movie. As you might expect, strong orchestration skills are also necessary because many movie scores involve large orchestras, as well as other smaller combinations of instruments.

◆ **Video game composer.** One of the newest venues for composers is the video game soundtrack. Many state-of-the-art video games have scores no less sophisticated than that found in the average film, complete with "theme songs" and incidental music. One factor that distinguishes video game composing from film or television composing is that, in many cases, you're working exclusively with digital instruments rather than with live performers. Look for this type of composing to become more important over time.

◆ **Broadway composer.** As the name implies, this type of composer writes musicals for the Broadway or off-Broadway stage, or for the increasingly rare original film or television musical. Composing a Broadway musical is long and involved work, requiring dozens of original songs and a variety of incidental music. You should be prepared to devote several years to a single project, and be willing to add, delete, and edit songs as the musical evolves. You'll typically be working with a "book" writer, who writes all the nonmusical parts of the production. You'll also be working in partnership with the musical's producer and director to bring the project to fruition.

Tip

In most cases, the scoring of a film takes place in a short period of time after the filming and editing have been completed, which means that the ability to write quickly and efficiently is necessary. Although the rise of independent films has somewhat decentralized the industry, most major films are still produced in Hollywood; for this reason, most serious film composers are based on the West Coast.

Note

Working with digital instruments isn't unique to video game composing. Many television scores today are performed with high-end synthesizers and sequencers, as a cost-cutting measure.

◆ **Serious composer.** Let's not neglect the art of composing artistic, non-commercial music for concert performance—what we'll call, for lack of a better term, "serious" or "classical" composing. Today's serious composers are more likely to create contemporary works for various combinations of instruments and voices, from solo pieces and chamber works to full orchestral pieces—often including a variety of electronic instruments.

Most serious composers get their works performed in one of two ways. The first approach is the personal contact—that is, you write for musicians you know. For example, you might write a piece for a soloist to perform at an upcoming recital. The second approach is the professional request, where an individual or organization commissions you to write a piece for an upcoming concert or event. In both cases, it helps to build a network of contacts, as well as to establish your reputation in the field.

However you choose to proceed, you'll need to hone your compositional skills—which means learning how to create music in a wide variety of genres and then developing your own unique voice. The better you are, the more options will be available to you.

> **Note**
>
> Unfortunately, in today's commercially oriented society, composing concert music seldom provides a steady income; some venues for serious compositions don't even pay for the use of the work. This is why many serious composers become educators or music administrators; their day jobs pay the bills, allowing them the freedom to pursue their artistic endeavors without having to commercialize their work.

The Least You Need to Know

◆ A musical composition is any piece of written music—including everything from advertising jingles to symphonies.

◆ To create a composition, you can employ one of a number of approaches—harmonic (chords-first), melodic (melody-first), holistic (chords and melody together), and layering (building the composition one part at a time).

◆ To become a successful composer, you need a good grounding in music theory, as well as training in orchestration.

◆ The best way to improve your compositional skills is to write as much as possible—and then listen to your work performed by other musicians.

◆ There are many different careers for a professional composer, including songwriting, writing advertising jingles, composing for jazz ensembles and school bands and choirs, creating film and television scores, writing soundtracks for video games, creating Broadway musicals, and composing serious noncommercial works.

> **Tip**
>
> There are many entities that commission serious compositions, and others that offer grants, prizes, and awards for composers. You should seek out those organizations with a history of commissioning musical works, as well as enter as many composing contests and competitions as you're comfortable with.

Chapter 2

The Composer's Toolkit

In This Chapter

- All the tools you need to start composing
- Learn the proper skills, including music theory, conducting, transposition, and orchestration
- Assemble the necessary devices, including an electronic keyboard, computer, and music-notation software

Every composer needs a set of practical tools at his or her disposal. Some of these tools are physical (pencil, staff paper, and so on) and some are skills-based (chord theory, orchestration, and the like), but all are necessary to help create musical compositions. It will take time to assemble your own personal composer's toolkit, but this chapter shows you what to look for.

Essential Music Theory

The first component of your composer's toolkit—and the one that requires the most work on your part—is an essential grounding in music theory. To create full-blown compositions, you need to know all the pieces and parts that are involved—what they do, how they work, and how to use them. The knowledge of all those pieces and parts is the basis of music theory, which is something you need to learn.

Here are the main elements of music theory essential to the art of music composition:

- **Notes.** It might seem somewhat basic, but there are many songwriters who have little or no formal music training. Although it's possible to compose without knowing how to read music, being able to "talk the language" makes it a lot easier to communicate with other musicians and share your compositions with others. The first concept that any budding musician must learn, then, is where each note falls on the musical staff and, ideally, where each note falls on the piano keyboard. (Yes, even guitarists need to have a working knowledge of the piano keyboard.)

◆ **Intervals.** Knowing which notes are which isn't quite enough, however. You also need to learn the relationship between different tones, or what we call *intervals.* The interval is the distance from one tone to another, measured either in half-steps or annotated whole steps. Intervals are important because they're used to create and describe the progress of a melody, as well as the individual notes within a chord.

◆ **Rhythm.** Music is more than just pitch; it is also space in time. The duration of any given note is specified by rhythmic notation, and you need to be familiar with all forms of such notation—from simple note values to dotted notes, triplets, and syncopation.

◆ **Key signatures and time signatures.** In order to notate a composition, you need to tell the performers what key and meter it's in. You do this via the key signature and the time signature that are placed at the very beginning of a piece.

◆ **Scales and modes.** A series of eight ascending or descending notes is called a scale. It's a little more complicated than that, but, essentially, when you play from one A to the next (or one B to the next, or one C to the next), you're playing a scale. Different types of scales are determined by specific intervals between the adjacent notes. You should be familiar with the major scale, the three types of minor scales (natural, harmonic, and melodic), and the seven so-called church modes, which are like scales but with different intervals.

◆ **Chords and harmony.** When you put one note on top of another, you create *harmony.* And when you play three or more notes together—typically spaced a third apart—then you have a *chord.* A simple three-note chord (with the notes spaced in thirds) is called a *triad,* and there are four different types—major, minor, diminished, and augmented. A series of chords is called a *chord progression,* which can be notated either with the chords themselves (C, Am, B♭7, and so on) or using Roman numeral notation (I, ii, iii, IV, V7, and so on.) Confused? If so, you need to go back and revisit basic chord theory because this is an integral part of the composition process.

> **Note**
>
> I wish it were otherwise, but I can't present all there is to know about music theory in just a few pages of text. If you want a more thorough grounding in theory, you should read my companion book, *The Complete Idiot's Guide to Music Theory, Second Edition* (Alpha Books, 2005).

These elements, the key components of music theory, comprise the language of trained musicians. You need to know not only how to read and write the language (to read and write music), but also how the language works. A knowledge of the musical language will take you far; scales and intervals and rhythms and chords are the building blocks you use to create your compositions. If you *don't* have a thorough grounding in music theory, *get one!*

A Trained Ear

Music theory is important, but knowing the theory and being able to *hear* the theory are two different things.

The ability to hear specific intervals and chords and know what you're hearing requires a well-trained ear. Experienced musicians can hear two notes played sequentially and be able to tell the interval between them—whether it's a minor third or a perfect fifth or whatever. They can also listen to a scale and tell whether it's major or minor, or listen to a chord and tell you what type of chord it is and whether there are any extensions employed.

To develop your ears, you need to engage in *ear training*. What you do, essentially, is listen to various groups of notes until you can determine what you're listening to. It's somewhat repetitious, but it's the only way to train your ears.

And why, exactly, are good ears necessary? Because you need to know what your music will sound like, even as you're writing it. Or, put another way, the better your ears, the easier it will be for you to translate the sounds you hear inside your head into the corresponding notes on paper. If you hear a major third in your melody, you'll know to write a major third—even if you're nowhere near a piano or guitar. Experienced composers can write music without the use of any instrument because they know what they're hearing internally. It's a skill you have to develop, but it's also a skill you *can* develop.

> **Note**
>
> One way to start training your ears is with my *Complete Idiot's Ear Training Course* CD, available for purchase from my website (www. molehillgroup.com) or included free with the second edition of *The Complete Idiot's Guide to Music Theory.*

Performance Skills

Why, you ask, does a composer need to perform? Isn't it enough that the composer creates the music—don't other musicians do the actual performing?

Well, yes and no. Certainly, your final work will be performed by others, at least in most instances. (This is different if you're a singer/songwriter, of course, or if you're producing your entire piece in your home recording studio.) But even when you're writing for other performers, it's quite helpful to understand the way a performer thinks. Learning the challenges that performer face will help you better utilize their skills and avoid writing in a way that makes their jobs needlessly difficult.

Even more common is the need to play your music at an audition or on a demo recording. If you're trying to sell a song to a singer, you'll need to play (and probably sing) that song either live or on a demo. Not that you have to exhibit virtuoso skills, of course; you just have to play well enough to get the point across. If you can't play … well, then you'll have to engage an accompanist to do the work for you.

Some rudimentary performance skills are also necessary if you record your own demos in your home studio or on your computer. Even using various MIDI instruments or samples, you may have to hit the keyboard every now and then in proper rhythm. It's hard to go far as a composer if you have zero performance skills.

Conducting Skills

Related to performance skills are conducting skills—especially if you're composing for concert ensembles. Even if a professional conductor is engaged for the concert, you may need to lead the ensemble through one or more rehearsals. And if you're composing for film or television it's you, the composer, who's typically expected to pick up the baton and lead the way. It's your work and you're expected to conduct it, so you'd better learn how to wave the baton.

Penmanship

This next tool in your toolkit is one that was more necessary in the past than it is today—even though it's still important. Put simply, you need to be able to write notes on staff paper in a legible fashion—good enough for others to read clearly, in any case. Not that you have to become a professional music engraver, but you want to write well enough that the lead trumpet player won't have to guess whether the second note in the third measure is an A, B, or C—and whether that chicken scratch in front of the note is a sharp, a natural, or just a squished bug.

The need for good penmanship was especially pronounced in that ancient era before computers invaded the rehearsal space. In those olden days (up to 1990 or so, actually), you actually had to write out all your parts by hand. This led to most music schools requiring students to take at least one semester of calligraphy—a requirement that is now seldom seen.

Today most composers use computerized notation programs to create all their scores. These programs, which I'll discuss later in this chapter, produce perfect note heads every time—and much faster than you can write them manually. This has led to the expected decline in manual penmanship, as most musicians simply don't get the practice writing that they used to. This is unfortunate, for several reasons.

First, you don't always have your computer nearby when the muse hits. If you're sitting on your piano bench or on your couch with your guitar, do you really want to rush to the other side of the house, fire up your computer, load a blank notation template, and start punching the keys? It's a lot easier to jot down musical ideas on a blank sheet of staff paper than it is to go through this entire routine. A piano (or guitar), a piece of staff paper, and a pencil is all you need to start composing; why complicate things?

Second, even though you use a notation program to create your score (and all individual parts), you still may need to make manual changes when you're out in the real world. What do you do, during the first rehearsal of your magnum opus, when the French horn part in the seventh measure doesn't sound quite right? You change it, that's what. That doesn't mean running to the computer and printing out a complete new set of parts; what you do is take out your pencil, cross out the original note, and write in a new one. If your penmanship is too sloppy, the French horn player won't be able to read what you just wrote. You need decent calligraphy skills to make it through this type of real-life scenario—which you'll encounter quite frequently, trust me.

> **Note**
>
> My personal penmanship is so bad that I can't even read my own scores. Without the advent of computerized notation programs, I wouldn't have been able to create the examples and exercises in this book—let alone produce legible compositions!

Blank Staff Paper

While we're on the topic of writing out music by hand, make sure you have something to write on. You should always have on hand a good supply of blank staff paper, along with a nice pen or pencil. I prefer spiral-bound books of staff paper and a good mechanical pencil, along with a heavy-duty eraser. Other composers prefer individual sheets of staff paper, although I find this approach more difficult to keep organized. Some composers swear by a quality ball-point or fountain pen, but that's too final for me; I'm always editing what I've written, and you can't erase ink!

Transposition Skills

Here's another one that is becoming a lost skill: the ability to transpose music. In the precomputer days, you composed your score in concert key and then transposed the music as necessary as you wrote out the individual parts. (For example, you write the trumpet part up a major second from concert key.) Today, however, notation programs do the transposition automatically, depriving you of the ability to hone your transposition skills. This can be bad when you *have* to transpose something—say, when you've written a song in F but the singer needs to sing it in G, or when you need to jot off a quick tenor sax part on the spot. There is real value in knowing how different instruments transpose and also in being able to perform that transposition automatically, without having to think too hard about it. Like most skills, this one can be learned—but it's easier the more often you do it.

> **Note**
>
> For what it's worth, I used to write my scores with each part transposed from scratch. Other composers prefer to compose in concert key and do the transposition later.

Orchestration Skills

While we're on the subject of transposing instruments, you'll also need to develop your orchestration skills—that is, the ability to write for a variety of instruments and voices. Unless you're composing strictly for a single instrument or voice, your compositions will include parts for a number of different instruments. You need to learn not only how these instruments transpose, but also how they sound and how they play. That is, you should learn the technical and practical ranges of each instrument, which notes or passages are particularly difficult to play (and should thus be avoided), and how various instruments sound in combination with others. It's the orchestration that creates the sound of your composition; the same melody will sound different orchestrated for different groupings of instruments.

> **Note**
>
> Learn more about orchestration in Chapter 15.

Computers and Other Hardware

Today's composer relies on more than just a piano or guitar. Composition today involves a variety of "hardware," in the form of computers, synthesizers, mixers, and the like. Although learning how to use all these devices takes some time (and technical skills), once you're up and running, you have a lot more options available to you.

Perhaps the most important piece of hardware in your arsenal is a personal computer. This can be either a desktop or a laptop (more expensive but more portable), either PC (Windows) or Macintosh—it really doesn't matter. What matters are the programs you install on the computer; these programs will help you more easily create your compositions. (We'll examine the various types of music software in the following sections.)

You may want to connect your computer to an electronic keyboard. You can use a relatively simple keyboard (typically called a *keyboard workstation*) or a full-featured synthesizer. If you use a keyboard workstation, you rely on so-called "soft synth" software on your computer to create various instrumental sounds. If you use a synthesizer, the sounds are created in the keyboard itself. In either instance, you connect the keyboard to your computer via a MIDI interface; once connected, you can use the keyboard to create music in your notation program or record directly to mixing/recording software.

If you're not only composing music but also recording it, you may want to invest in an outboard MIDI mixing console. Most recording programs have their own "soft" mixers included, which you control with your mouse and display onscreen; an outboard mixer lets you twiddle physical knobs and sliders in that old-school way that many musicians prefer.

Finally, if you're creating vocal works, don't forget a microphone. Because microphones don't have MIDI connections, you'll definitely need a MIDI mixer or some sort of interface box if you want to connect your mic to your computer. And remember, you can use that mic not only to sing into, but also to record any acoustic instrument.

Tip

To listen to your composition, you might want to invest in a good set of powered monitor speakers. The speakers that typically come with a computer system are of uniformly mediocre quality; a good set of studio monitors (not as expensive as you think) will make a world of difference.

Tip

You can also use the notation software to play back your work-in-progress. Most programs have a MIDI playback option so you can hear the complete orchestra with either MIDI instruments or plug-ins with digital samples. It's a whole lot easier to hit the Play button to hear your work than it is to assemble an orchestra for practice!

Music-Notation Software

Now let's talk about the music software you can use with your personal computer. For composers, the most important piece of software is the music-notation program.

A music-notation program lets you compose directly on your computer. You can enter notes via your computer keyboard or mouse, or via a MIDI keyboard connected to your computer. Most programs let you play music on your electronic keyboard and then translate what you play into notes and rhythms on a staff. You can then edit the notes with your mouse or computer keyboard, directly from the program.

And that's not all these programs do. You can create full scores for any combination of instruments and voices, often using predesigned score templates. You can embellish your score with all manner of notation marks, from decrescendos to trills, to grace notes. You can even have the notation program automatically transpose parts for specific instruments.

When your composition is complete, you don't have to bother with transposing and writing out all the individual parts. Press a button, and the program will print out your score (using one of a number of professional notation fonts) and even create individual parts for each instrument or voice—transposed to the correct key. The notation is high quality, with professional note spacing and such, often with your choice of fonts. You can also output your music in Adobe PDF files, to send to other musicians electronically.

The two most popular notation programs today are Finale (www.finalemusic. com) and Sibelius (www.sibelius.com). Both programs offer similar features and work in similar ways. If I had to characterize the two, I'd say that Finale offers more notation options, while Sibelius has an easier-to-use interface. That said, which program you choose depends on your own personal needs or (most likely) what others around you use. For example, if your music school uses Finale, you should probably become a Finale user, too. Both programs should be able to do what you need them to do.

> **Warning**
>
> Music notation software isn't perfect; individual parts often require some degree of manual cleaning up after they're automatically generated by the program. Still, using one of these programs is a great deal faster than writing each part out by hand!

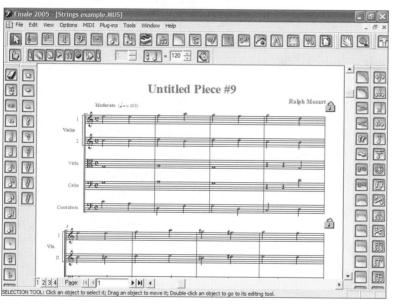

The Finale music-notation program.

You can find more information about these programs at each company's website. Know that several versions of each program are available; for example, Sibelius offers Home, Education, and Professional versions, each with slightly different feature sets. Finale also offers Finale NotePad, a reduced-functionality version that you can download for free from its website. It's a good way to try out the program before you invest in the full version.

> **Note**
>
> Personally, I've been a Finale user for five years now. I used Finale to create all the examples you see in this book.

The Sibelius music-notation program.

Other Music Software

Music-notation software is essential for any composer, but you might want to consider adding other music programs to your setup:

◆ **Virtual instruments.** These are programs that plug into other programs (such as your notation or recording program) and provide high-quality digital samples of different instruments. Some of the more popular of these plug-ins are so-called orchestral libraries that include surprisingly good reproductions of symphonic orchestral sounds. Plug-ins are available from East West Samples (www.eastwestsamples.com), Garritan Orchestral Libraries (www.garritan.com), and Vienna Symphonic Library (www.vsl.co.at).

◆ **Digital audio workstations.** A digital audio workstation (DAW) is a software-based recording studio that runs inside your computer. You use DAW software to record live performances, layer electronic or MIDI-based performances, and mix all the instruments into a final recording. Popular programs include Cakewalk Studio and SONAR (www.cakewalk.com), MOTU Digital Performer (www.motu.com), Steinberg Cubase (www.steinberg.net), and the industry standard Pro Tools (www.digidesign.com).

◆ **Loop-based music production.** These programs are sequencers of a sort that let you create recordings by building up a series of sampled musical "loops." It's a different way to compose—not necessarily one I endorse, but still widely used in certain genres, such as hip-hop. Popular programs include Apple GarageBand (www.apple.com/ilife/garageband/), Propellerhead Recycle (www.propellerheads.se), and Sony ACID (mediasoftware.sonypictures.com/products/acidfamily.asp).

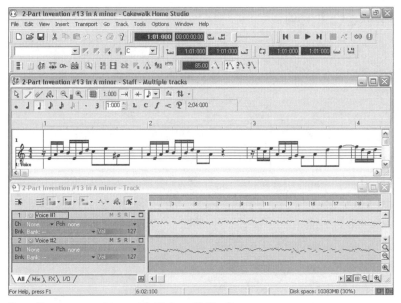

Recording a composition with Cakewalk Studio.

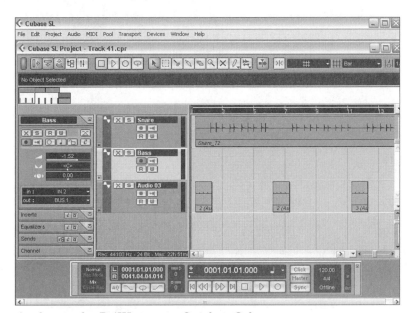

Another popular DAW program, Steinberg Cubase.

The key thing with any of these software tools is to use them to supplement the creative process, not to drive it. It's too easy to start playing with a program—especially a loop program—and fall in love with some new sound you've clicked on. Linking together a bunch of sound loops is *not* music composition!

The Least You Need to Know

◆ Your composer's toolkit should include the following items:

  ◆ A thorough understanding of music theory

  ◆ A trained ear

  ◆ Performance skills

  ◆ Conducting skills

  ◆ Penmanship

  ◆ Blank staff paper

  ◆ Transposition skills

  ◆ Orchestration skills

  ◆ Electronic keyboard or synthesizer

  ◆ Personal computer

  ◆ Music-notation software, such as Finale or Sibelius

  ◆ Other music software, such as virtual instruments, a digital audio workstation, and perhaps some sort of loop-based music-production program

Part 2

Harmonic Composition

You can start a composition with the chords first or the melody first; this section starts with the chords. Read on to learn all about chords and chord progressions and how to create a memorable harmonic structure for your music.

Composing with Chords

In This Chapter

- ◆ Constructing your own chord progressions with chord leading
- ◆ Ending phrases with cadences
- ◆ Choosing the right key
- ◆ Establishing a harmonic rhythm
- ◆ Applying chord progressions to musical structures
- ◆ Putting melody to chords

It's a chicken-and-egg type of question: which do you write first, the chords or the melody? After all, they're both equally important and both dependent on the other. There's no single correct approach, of course, but you have to start a new composition somehow, and either of these ways can work.

Many composers find it easier to start with a harmonic framework—that is, to write the chords first and then to fit a melody to those chords. Because of the popularity (and, for many, the relative ease) of this approach, that's how we'll start our composition studies.

Of course, a successful chord-based compositional approach depends on your knowledge of chords and harmony—which chords to use to convey specific colors and moods, and which chords lead to one another in a logical progression. If you can strum only three chords on a guitar, your choices are going to be limited—as are your resulting compositions. The more advanced your knowledge of harmony, the more room you have to express your creativity and individuality.

So read on to learn how to create the underlying harmonic structure of a composition—the chord progression.

Which Chords Can You Work With?

When you're working with harmonic composition, you can work with any number and type of chords. You don't have to limit yourself to the natural chords within a scale or key (the *diatonic chords*) or with simple three-note triads, especially when you're working in more contemporary forms. You can explore all manner of chromatic chords, extended chords, and the like, even chords that don't really look or sound like traditional chords—two-note harmonies, or note clusters with no discernable tonal center. In other words, the entire harmonic spectrum is available for your use.

That said, when you're first starting out, it's a good idea to work within some sort of structure, to help guide your creativity. Once you've learned how to compose within a traditional harmonic structure, you can begin to explore nontraditional harmonies; you use the structure to help hone your craft.

The traditional harmonic structure is that contained within a standard major or minor key. You can create chords from each of the seven tones of the corresponding scale; these seven diatonic chords form the basis of the harmonic structure and become the base chords you work with to create your compositions.

To refresh your knowledge of basic chord theory, here are the diatonic triads that are formed from the seven tones of the major scale, shown here in the key of C major:

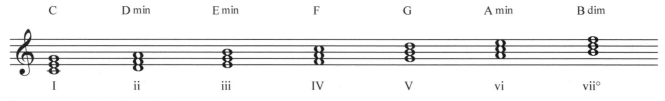

C	D min	E min	F	G	A min	B dim
I	ii	iii	IV	V	vi	vii°

The seven diatonic triads (in C major).

For ease of use, we'll use Roman numeral chord notation throughout much of this book. This way, you can apply the chord types to any key you choose to work in.

Using Chord Leading to Create Chord Progressions

Although you can create a composition using any combination of chords that sounds good to your ears—even chromatic chords or chords from other keys—most chord progressions are based on a few simple rules. These rules come from a concept called *chord leading*, which says that certain chords naturally lead to other chords.

You can hear chord leading for yourself by playing some chords on the piano or guitar. We'll work in the key of C major.

Start by playing a C major chord. This is the I chord in the scale, which doesn't necessarily lead anywhere because, based on chord-leading rules, the I chord can be followed by any chord in the scale.

Now play a G major chord. This is the V chord in the scale, and it definitely wants to go somewhere. But where? You could follow it with an F major (IV), D minor (ii), E minor (iii), or even A minor (vi) chord, all valid chords in the key of C major. But none of these chords sounds quite as satisfying after the V chord than the I chord (C major). This is one of Western music's most important traditions, the natural leading of the V chord back to the I chord. Although you *can* write another chord after a V, the best resolution—especially at the end of a phrase—is to follow the V with the I.

Which Chords Lead to Which

All chords within a scale have related chords that they naturally lead to. Some chords can even lead to more than one chord. To learn which chords lead where, take a look at the following table:

Chord Leading Reference

These Chords ...	Lead to These Chords ...
I	Any chord
ii	IV, V, vii°
iii	ii, IV, vi
IV	I, iii, V, vii°
V	I
vi	ii, IV, V, I
vii°	I, iii

This means that if you have a iii chord, you can follow it with either a ii, IV, or vi chord. Or if you have a vi chord, you can follow it with either a ii, IV, V, or I chord, and so on. Although you don't have to follow these chord-leading rules, doing so is a relatively safe and easy way to create a pleasant-sounding chord progression.

Creating Chord Progressions with Chord Leading

Let's use the chord-leading rules to create some simple chord progressions. In our first example, we'll start with the I chord. Because I leads to any chord, let's go up one scale note and insert the ii chord after the I. According to our chart, ii can lead to either IV, V, or vii°. We'll pick V. Then, because V generally leads to I, the next chord is a return to the tonic.

The entire progression looks like this:

        I   ii   V   I

When you play this progression in the key of C, you get the following chords:

        C   Dm   G   C

A rather simple progression, but one that feels right.

Note

You should recognize the I-vi-IV-V-I progression as the chords that drove thousands of doo-wop tunes in the 1950s and 1960s.

Let's try another example. Again, we'll start with the tonic (I), but this time we'll use the vi chord as the second chord. According to the chord-leading chart, vi can lead to either ii, IV, V, or I; let's pick IV. Then, because IV can lead to either I, iii, V, or vii°, we'll pick V as the next chord—which leads us back to I as our final chord. The entire progression looks like this:

| I | vi | IV | V | I |

When you play this progression in the key of C, you get the following chords:

| C | Am | F | G | C |

Let's return to this progression and make an alternate choice for the third chord—ii instead of IV. Because ii also leads to IV, we can leave the rest of the progression intact, which creates the following alternate progression:

| I | vi | ii | V | I |

When played in the key of C, this results in these chords:

| C | Am | Dm | G | C |

It's another familiar-sounding chord progression that can be used in many different situations.

Working Backward from the Final Chord

You can also use chord leading to work backward from where you want to end up—your final chord. In most cases, you want the final chord to be the tonic (I), so all you have to do is work through the various options that lead to that chord. You can then continue to work back through the chords that lead to the penultimate chord, and the chords that lead to that chord, and so on until you come to an appropriate starting chord.

Let's do an example. Consulting the chord-leading table, you find that four chords can lead to the I: IV, V, vi, and vii°. The obvious choice is the V chord, which traditionally has the most final-sounding resolution, so we'll put a V before the I.

Now we have to pick a chord to lead to V; the choices are ii, IV, vi, and I. Let's pick ii. Now we pick a chord that leads to the ii; the choices are I, iii, IV, and vi. Let's pick iii. Now we pick a chord that leads to the iii; the choices are I, vi, and vii°. Let's pick I, which is also a good chord with which to start the phrase. When you put all of these chords together, you get the following progression:

| I | iii | ii | V | I |

Play this progression in the key of C, and you use these chords:

| C | Em | Dm | G | C |

Pretty easy, isn't it?

Common Chord Progressions

With all this talk of chord leading, it would seem that creating a harmonious chord progression is a simple matter of applying a few hard-and-fast rules. It isn't quite as simple as that—there are a lot of choices available, and the rules aren't always hard and fast—but following the rules *can* help you create some familiar and overtly listenable chord progressions.

To whit, the following table presents some of the more common chord progressions found in both popular songs and other types of compositions. Although it's not a good idea to limit yourself to only these progressions, they're a good place to start.

Note

Obviously, all these progressions cycle back around to end/start again with the I chord. So the I-IV-V progression actually follows through to end on the I, like this: I-IV-V-I.

Common Chord Progressions

Progression	Example (in the key of C)	Comments
I-IV	C F	It doesn't get much simpler than this, just the tonic (I) and subdominant (IV) cycled over and over.
I-V	C G	If you can cycle between the tonic and the subdominant, why not the tonic and the dominant (V)? Like the first progression, the simplicity of this one makes it somewhat common in folk music and some forms of popular music.
I-IV-V	C F G	This is probably the most common chord progression in popular music. When people talk about "three-chord rock and roll," these are the three chords they're talking about.
I-IV-V7	C F G7	Similar to the previous progression, with increased tension from the dominant seventh chord.
I-IV-I-V	C F C G	A variation on the I-IV-V progression, but with an extra tonic (I) chord between the subdominant (IV) and dominant (V).
I-IV-I-V7	C F C G7	Same as the previous progression, but with increased tension from the dominant seventh chord.

continues

Common Chord Progressions (continued)

Progression	Example (in the key of C)	Comments
I-IV-V-IV	C F G F	A variation on the I-IV-V progression, in the form of a shift back to the subdominant (IV), which then forms a plagal cadence when it repeats back to the tonic. It's a nice rolling progression without a strong ending feeling to it, which makes it a good choice for pieces that repeat the main melody line again and again.
I-V-vi-IV	C G Am F	This progression is another rolling one, good for repeating again and again. (That's because of the ending plagal cadence—the IV repeating back to I.)
I-ii-IV-V	C Dm F G	This progression has a constant upward movement, resolved with a perfect cadence on the repeat back to I. It can also be played with a V7 instead of the standard V chord.
I-ii-IV	C Dm F	This is a variation of the previous progression, with a soft plagal cadence at the end (the IV going directly to the I, with no V involved). As with all progressions that end with a plagal cadence, this progression has a rolling feel and sounds as if it could go on and on and on, like a giant circle.
I-vi-ii-V	C Am Dm G	This was a very popular progression in the popular music of the 1950s, the basis of numerous doo-wop and jazz songs. It's also the chord progression behind the Gershwin song "I've Got Rhythm" and sometimes is referred to (especially in jazz circles) as the "I've Got Rhythm" progression.

Progression	Example (in the key of C)	Comments
I-vi-IV-V	C Am F G	This is a variation on the "I've Got Rhythm" progression, with a stronger lead to the V chord (IV instead of ii). This progression was also popular in the doo-wop era and in the early days of rock and roll. The defining factor of this progression is the descending bass line; it drops in thirds until it moves up a step for the dominant chord, like this: C-A-F-G. You've heard this progression (and that descending bass line) hundreds of times; it's a very serviceable progression. (You can also play it with a V7 at the end instead of a plain V chord.)
I-vi-ii-IV-V7	C Am Dm F G7	This variation on the "I've Got Rhythm" progression has more of a rolling feel because of the vi-ii-IV sequence in the middle.
I-vi-ii-V7-ii	C Am Dm G7 Dm	This is another variation on the "I've Got Rhythm" progression, with an extra ii chord squeezed in between the final V and the return to I, and with the V chord played as a dominant seventh. By adding the ii chord between the V7 and the I (at the start of the following progression), almost in passing, it takes the edge off the perfect cadence and makes the progression feel a little smoother.
IV-I-IV-V	F C F G	As this progression shows, you don't have to start your chord progression on the tonic. This progression has a bit of a rolling nature to it, but also a bit of an unresolved nature. You can keep repeating this progression (leading from the V back to the IV) or end the song by leading the progression home to a I chord.

continues

Common Chord Progressions (continued)

Progression	Example (in the key of C)	Comments
ii7-V7-I	Dm7 G7 C	This progression is quite popular in jazz, played either with or without the sevenths. Sometimes jazz tunes cycle through this progression in a variety of keys, often using the circle of fifths to modulate through the keys. This progression is also frequently played at the end of a phrase in many jazz tunes.
I-IV-I-V7-IV-I	C F C G7 F C	This 12-bar progression is called the blues progression. The blues progression isn't relegated solely to blues music, however; you'll find this form used in many jazz and popular tunes as well.
I-IV-vii°-iii-vi-ii-V-I	C F Bdim Em Am Dm G C	This is called the "circle of fifths" progression, because each chord is a diatonic fifth above the following chord. This makes each chord function kind of as a dominant for the next chord, but in a diatonic function. The progression circles back around on itself, always coming back to the tonic chord.

Of course, you don't have to limit yourself to these common chord progressions. You can use the chord-leading rules to create endless variety of chord progressions. You can even take several of these common chord progressions and link them to create longer and more complex progressions. You shouldn't feel constrained by length or by what sounds familiar. As the composer, you are in total control of the harmonic structure of your composition; think of chords as building blocks to create the sound you hear in your head.

Ending a Phrase

Building on the concept of chord leading, let's examine how this technique can help you create final-sounding endings in your compositions. When you come to the end of a musical phrase—which can be anywhere in a composition, not just at the very end—you use chords to set up a tension and then relieve that tension. This feeling of a natural ending is called *cadence*, and you can use some accepted chord progressions to provide this feeling of completion.

Perfect Cadence

The most common phrase-ending chord progression uses the V (dominant) chord to set up the tension, which is relieved when you move on to the I (tonic) chord. This progression is notated V-I and, in the key of C, looks like this:

G   C

You could probably see this cadence coming just by looking at our old friend, the chord-leading table. There simply is no better way to get back home (I) than through the dominant chord (V).

Tip

The V-I progression can be enhanced by using the dominant seventh chord (V7) instead of the straight V. This progression is notated V7-I.

Plagal Cadence

A slightly weaker but still satisfactory ending progression uses the IV (subdominant) chord in place of the V chord. This IV-I progression is called a *plagal cadence*; in the key of C, it looks like this:

F   C

Although this is an effective cadence, it isn't nearly as strong as the perfect V-I cadence. For that reason, you might want to use a plagal cadence in the middle of a composition or melody, and save the stronger perfect cadence for the big ending.

Imperfect Cadence

Sometimes, especially in the middle of a melody, you might want to end on a chord that isn't the tonic. In these instances, you set up an unresolved tension, typically by ending on the V (dominant) triad.

This type of ending progression is called an *imperfect cadence*, and you can get to the V chord any number of ways, with I-V, ii-V, IV-V, and vi-V being the most common. In the key of C, these progressions look like this:

I-V:	C	G
ii-V:	Dm	G
IV-V:	F	G
vi-V:	Am	G

Remember, the key point to the imperfect cadence is that you don't lead back to the tonic (I); you lead to the dominant (V) instead.

Note

The imperfect cadence is sometimes called a *half cadence*.

Interrupted Cadence

Even less final than an imperfect cadence is an ending progression called an *interrupted* or *deceptive cadence*. In this progression, you use a V chord to trick the listener into thinking that a perfect cadence is on its way, but then move to any type of chord *except* the tonic.

V-IV, V-vi, V-ii, and V-V7 progressions all are interrupted cadences—and, in the key of C, look like this:

V-IV:	G	F
V-vi:	G	Am
V-ii:	G	Dm
V-V7:	G	G7

The Key Matters

One important thing to note is that the same chord progression will probably sound different in different keys. That is, the underlying key influences the resonance and color of both individual chords and complete chord progressions. Even the I-IV-V progression sounds different in C than it does in A.

You can hear this phenomenon for yourself by simply playing the same chord progression in a number of keys. Try playing the I-vi-ii-IV-V progression (with the following I chord) and in the following keys: C, E♭, F, and A.

C:	C	Am	Dm	F	G	C
E♭:	E♭	Cm	Fm	A♭	B♭	E♭
F:	F	Dm	Gm	B♭	C	F
A:	A	F#m	Bm	D	E	A

The chords have the same harmonic relationship within each key, but still, the sound is subtly different. I particularly like the resonance of this progression in A; A is a very satisfying home key for a number of different chord progressions.

The point is that you have to give a lot of thought to the keys on which you base your compositions. Different keys have different feels, which will contribute to the overall effect of your composition.

Chord Progressions in a Minor Key

Up to this point we've discussed common chord progressions for use in major keys. But which chords do you use if you're composing in a minor key?

The diatonic chords of a natural minor scale follow a much different harmonic progression than those of the major scale. It's an odd sound; both the tonic and the dominant chords are minor instead of major. Here's what they look like, in the key of C natural minor:

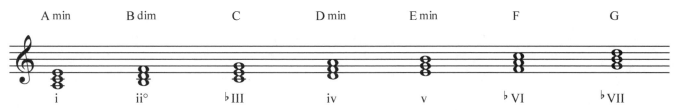

The seven diatonic natural minor chords (in A minor).

Obviously, the v chord leads to the i, but other traditional major-key chord-leading rules are less set. For example, you probably won't use the ii° chord much, if at all. Many composers stick to the minor chords (i, iv, and v) when composing in a minor key, using the major chords (♭III, ♭VI, and ♭VII) only sporadically.

Another option is to turn the v chord into a V or V7 chord. This requires an implicit shift from the natural minor to harmonic minor scale, which has a raised seventh. In this arrangement, the diatonic chords are somewhat different, as you can see here (in A harmonic minor):

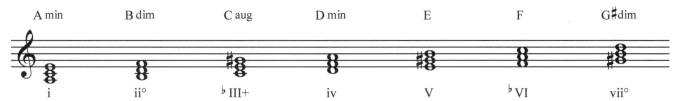

The seven diatonic chords of the harmonic minor scale (in A harmonic minor); note the raised seventh (G#) throughout.

Especially interesting here are the augmented ♭III chord (a major chord with a raised fifth), the major V chord, and the diminished vii chord based on the raised seventh of the harmonic minor scale. It's an odd combination of chords because of the odd nature of the harmonic minor scale.

Establishing a Harmonic Rhythm

Working with chord-based composition brings up an interesting question. Just how often should you change chords? The pace of a chord progression, or where the chords are placed within a phrase, is called *harmonic rhythm*. In other words, the harmonic rhythm dictates how often you change chords—and when.

Obviously, the number of beats or measures allotted to each chord isn't set in stone. For example, you could write the I-IV-V progression with a single measure for each chord. Or you could write two measures of I and a measure each of IV and V. Or you could write three measures of one, and then two beats each of IV and V in a fourth measure. Or you could write 16 measures of I, 16 measures of IV, and another 16 measures of V. It all depends on the nature of your composition and helps provide an almost infinite variety of possible chord combinations.

Tip

Many composers strike a middle ground by using the basic chords of the natural minor scale, with the exception of the major V and diminished vii° of the harmonic minor scale. Both a bit of a harmonic compromise, albeit easy on the ears.

There are no rules for harmonic rhythm. You can choose to extend a chord over any number of measures, or to change chords frequently within a single measure. You can set your chord changes on the first beat of each measure or on any subsidiary beat. You can even change chords on the upbeat, if you want.

That said, it's common to change chords more often at slower tempos than at faster ones. It's simply easier to fit two or four chords into one slower-moving measure than it is within a faster-paced tune. A fast-paced country song, for example, might have chord changes every two or four measures. A slower-tempo ballad, on the other hand, might change chords every two beats within a single measure. There's more space for each chord when the tempo is slower.

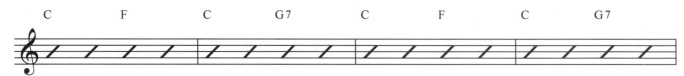

A fast-paced harmonic rhythm, with two chord changes a measure.

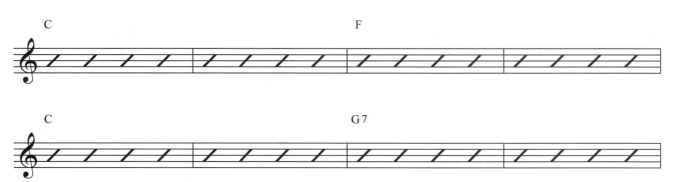

The same chord progression, but spread out with a slower-paced harmonic rhythm—two measures per chord.

Of course, your chords don't have to always change at the same pace throughout the entire composition. You might employ a different harmonic rhythm in the A section than in the B section, or even between different phrases within a section. You might use longer chord phrasing throughout the meat of a phrase and then switch to a shorter phrasing during the ending cadence.

Changing chords at different paces in different parts of the phrase—four beats per chord for the first three measures, and then two beats per chord in the final measure.

The harmonic rhythm is one factor that establishes the sound and feel of a particular composition. A rapid harmonic rhythm will dictate, more often than not, particular types of melodies—typically faster-moving melodies. A slower harmonic rhythm will let your piece breathe a little more. And varying the harmonic rhythm will provide contrast within your piece. Use harmonic rhythm to establish the mood and pace of your compositions.

Tip

Although there are many notable exceptions, I find that a somewhat rapid harmonic rhythm helps to create more interesting melodies. Whenever there's a chord change, there is impetus to make the melody move accordingly—and the more movement there is in a melody, the more interesting it is.

Applying Chord Progressions to Musical Structure

Let's say you create a musical phrase that uses a simple I-vi-IV-V7 chord progression. Does this mean that you're limited to using these same four chords throughout your entire composition?

The answer, of course, is no. As you'll learn in Chapter 12, most longer compositions are made up of numerous shorter sections. Each section in your composition can have its own harmonic structure—its own chord progression, in other words. In fact, that's one way to delineate one section from another, by giving each section its own signature chord progression.

Let's take the somewhat standard ABA form, which is composed of two separate musical sections (designated A and B), with the first section repeated after playing the second. In this structure (which in songwriting circles is called the verse-chorus form), you create different chord progressions for each section. For example, you might write a I-vi-IV-V7 progression for the A section of the piece, but then employ a IV-I-IV-V7 progression for the B section. This gives each section its own distinct sound—and also encourages you to create totally separate melodies for each section.

Other musical structures work the same way. The ABCA structure would use three different chord progressions (A, B, and C); the ABACADA structure would use four different chord progressions (A, B, C, and D). Of course, you don't *have* to use different chord progressions in each section; you can differentiate the sections purely melodically. But for the greatest contrast, it's best to use a different chord progression for each section of your composition.

Putting Melody to Your Chords

By employing a chord-based compositional approach, the chord progression you create becomes a framework on which you later construct a melody. But just how do you fit a melody to your chords?

We'll talk a lot more about melodies in Chapter 5, but for now, let's look at a few simple approaches, just to get you started.

One approach is to base your melody on the notes of the chords. That is, you use the chord tones to define the main notes of your melody. For example, if you're holding an A minor chord in a specific measure, you would work with the notes A, C, and E for your melody. You can then add passing and approach notes to connect these main chord tones.

A melody based on key chord tones.

You can also try to find a logical line between the main notes in different measures. For example, if your chord progression goes C-Am-F, realize that these chords have one note in common—the C. So you can base your melody around the C note. Conversely, if your chord progression goes C-F-G, you might want to pick three notes (one from each chord) that flow smoothly together, in a step-wise motion—E to F to G, for example, or G to F to D.

A melody based on tones that flow smoothly upward (E-F-G).

Another approach is to use notes that emphasize the key quality of the underlying chords. For example, when you're writing to a V7 chord, emphasize the tension by using either the root or the seventh of the chord in the melody. When shifting between major and minor chords, emphasize the changes by basing the melody on the thirds of each chord.

A melody that emphasizes the defining features of the underlying chords.

That's just a start, of course. You'll want to turn to Chapter 5 for more concrete melodic techniques—and to Chapter 4 to learn how to construct more sophisticated chord progressions.

The Least You Need to Know

- ◆ It's easy to create simple chord progressions by using the technique of chord leading, in which each chord within a scale always leads to the same chord (or chords).
- ◆ You bring a musical phrase to conclusion by using one of several different cadences—set chord progressions that always come back around to the tonic chord.
- ◆ The chord progressions you write will sound different in different keys.

◆ Another way to create your own unique sound is to vary the harmonic rhythm of a composition—that is, the pace and placement of the chord changes.

◆ When you work with longer compositions, you can differentiate between musical sections by using different chord progressions in each section.

Exercises

Starting with this chapter, I'm presenting several end-of-chapter exercises. Many of these exercises are open-ended—that is, there is no single correct solution. For those exercises that *do* have correct answers, you can find the answers in Appendix B.

Exercise 3-1

Fill in the blanks in the following chord progressions:

a: I	IV	?	V
b: I	?	IV	V
c: ii7	?	I	
d: I	?	IV	
e: I	?	V7	

Exercise 3-2

Write the following chord progressions in the keys of C, F, G, B♭, and A:

a: I	IV	V	IV	
b: I	IV	V		
c: I	V	vi	IV	
d: I	vi	IV	V	
e: I	vi	ii	IV	V7

Exercise 3-3

Write the following cadences in the keys of C, F, G, and B♭:

a: Perfect

b: Plagal

c: Imperfect (I-V)

d: Imperfect (IV-V)

e: Interrupted (V-ii)

Exercise 3-4

Using chord leading, finish the following chord progressions:

       a: I   vi   …

       b: I   IV   …

       c: I   ii   …

       d: I   vi   …

       e: ii   IV   …

Exercise 3-5

Using blank staff paper, write the "I've Got Rhythm" chord progression (C-Am-Dm-G in the key of C) in 4/4 time, with the following harmonic rhythms:

    a: One chord per measure

    b: Two chords per measure—two beats per chord

    c: Three beats apiece for the first and third chords, one beat for the second and fourth chords

    d: One full measure apiece for the first two chords, then two beats apiece for the second two chords

    e: Two beats apiece for the first and third chords, six beats apiece for the second and fourth chords

Chapter 4

Creating More Sophisticated Chord Progressions

In This Chapter

♦ How and when to ignore chord-leading conventions

♦ Creating richer harmonies with extended chords, chord inversions, altered bass chords, and compound chords

♦ Grounding a chord progression with a pedal point

♦ Altering progressions with chord substitutions and nonscale chords

♦ Using chords as tonal centers

When you employ the technique of chord leading, as you learned in the previous chapter, it's easy to create pleasant-sounding chord progressions. That's because these are the chords that listeners expect to hear—V leading to I, and so forth. You don't always want to give the listener something so obvious, however, which means it's okay sometimes to abandon chord-leading principles and go off in unexpected directions.

Breaking the Rules

What would be an unexpected chord choice? Simple—a chord that doesn't follow naturally from the established chord-leading conventions.

All you have to do is refer back to the chord-leading table in Chapter 3 and choose a chord that doesn't follow from the preceding chord. For example, the table tells us that the V chord naturally leads to the I; insert any other chord after the V, and you surprise the listener. For example, try playing V-vi (G-Am in the key of C) or V-ii (G-Dm) and see how unexpected these changes sound.

Tip

One fun exercise is to create a complete chord progression in which *none* of the chords flows naturally from any of the other chords—a chord progression in which every chord is unexpected. Although the results will likely be mostly theoretical, you might actually like some of what you hear.

Note

The seventh chord is so common that some music theorists categorize it as a basic chord type, not as an extension—they're that common.

Let's look at an example of a chord progression that breaks all the rules. Instead of starting on the tonic, we'll start on the seventh of the scale (with a diminished chord) and go from there. Every chord that follows is a chord that isn't dictated by chord-leading rules. Here's how it might look:

| vii° | IV | iii | V | vi | iii | V | ii | I |

Or in the key of C:

| Bdim | F | Em | G | Am | Em | G | Dm | C |

These are all the standard chords available within the C major scale, but they're put together in a totally unexpected way. Interesting sound, don't you think?

Extending the Chords

If you know your music theory, you know that chords can include more than three notes. When you get above the basic triad, the other notes you add to a chord are called *extensions*. One of the easiest ways to make your composition more interesting is to embrace the use of these extended chords.

As you know, chord extensions are typically added in thirds. The first type of extended chord, then, is called a *seventh chord* (because the seventh is a third above the fifth); next up is the *ninth chord* (which is a third above the seventh), then the *eleventh chord* (a third above the ninth), and so on.

Extended chords can be major, minor, or dominant, depending on the triads on which they're based. A *major seventh* chord takes a standard major chord and adds a major seventh on top of the existing three notes. A *minor seventh* chord takes a standard minor chord and adds a minor seventh on top of the existing three notes. A *dominant seventh* chord—sometimes just called the "seventh" chord, with no other designation—takes a major triad and adds a minor seventh on top; in other words, it's a major chord with a lowered seventh. The less-used diminished seventh chord takes a diminished triad and adds a minor seventh on top.

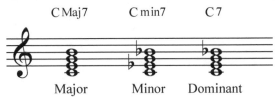

The different types of seventh chords, built from a root of C.

Even the simplest chord progression sounds slightly fuller and more sophisticated when you replace the standard triads with the diatonic seventh chords. Let's take the common I-IV-V progression and replace it with seventh chords:

| IM7 | IVM7 | V7 |

The I and IV chords become major seventh chords, and the V chord becomes a dominant seventh chord. In the key of C, it plays like this:

    CM7   FM7   G7

Sounds a bit more lush than the simple C-F-G progression, doesn't it?

Let's take another example, the similarly common I-vi-ii-V progression. Add sevenths to each chord, and you get this progression:

    IM7   vim7   iim7   V7

The I chord, of course, becomes a major seventh chord; the vi and ii chords become minor seventh chords, and the V becomes the expected dominant seventh chord. In the key of C, it plays like this:

    CM7   Am7   Dm7   G7

It gets even better when you add the ninths. Here's that last chord progression with ninths added, notated in C:

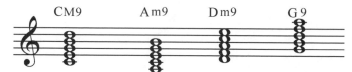

Playing the doo-wop chord progressions with ninth chords.

Inverting the Chords

As you progress in your compositional training, you'll learn that orchestration is a big part of the process. That is, a sophisticated composition is more than just chords and melody, but also about how those notes and harmonies are ordered and assigned to different instruments.

To that end, it's important to talk about chord inversions as a means to create a more sophisticated sound. Now, to some extent, a C major chord is a C major chord is a C major chord. But when you play the notes of the chord in a slightly different order, the chord takes on a slightly different quality. It's subtle but important.

The term *inversion* refers to the order in which the notes of a chord are stacked. The standard order is called the *root inversion* because the root's on the bottom, the third is in the middle, and the fifth is on top (1-3-5). When you take the root off the bottom and stick it on top, leaving the third on the bottom and the fifth in the middle, you have a *first inversion* chord (3-5-1). Take the third from the bottom and stick it on top, leaving the fifth on the bottom and the root in the middle, and you have a *second inversion* chord (5-1-3). If you have a seventh chord, you can create a *third inversion* by putting the seventh on the bottom, the fifth on top, and the root and the third in the middle (7-1-3-5). It's all a matter of order.

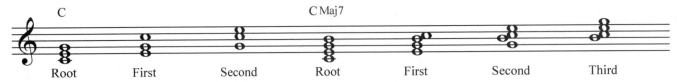

Different inversions of the C major and C major 7 chords.

The particular order of a chord's notes is also referred to as that chord's *voicing*. You can specify a voicing without writing all the notes by adding a bass note to the standard chord notation. You do this by adding a slash after the chord notation and then the name of the note that should be played on the bottom of the chord.

For example, if you want to indicate a first inversion of a C major chord (normally C-E-G, but E-G-C in the first inversion), you'd write this: C/E. This specifies a C major chord with an E in the bass—which just happens to be the first inversion of the chord. If you wanted to indicate a second inversion (G-C-E), you'd write this: C/G. This specifies a C major chord with a G in the bass.

> **Tip**
>
> The first and third inversions are equally jarring with extended chords. All of these inversions put the closest notes right next to each other, instead of spreading them out (as you have with a root inversion chord).

Chord inversions are important when you're orchestrating your composition because different voicings have different sounds. When you write a chord in the first inversion, you create an *open voicing*, where each chord tone is at least a third apart from the other notes. It's a nice sound but nothing special. If you want to emphasize the root of the chord, use the first inversion, where the root is on the top. If you want to create a bit more tension, write an extended chord in the second inversion (5-7-1-3, in the case of a seventh chord), which creates a *closed voicing* in the middle of the chord with the extended note right next to the root; it's a bit jarring but quite interesting to the ear.

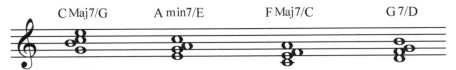

The IM7-vim7-IVM7-V7 progression, written with closed voicings—second-position inversions, in the key of C.

Using Altered Bass Chords

The same slash notation you use to indicate chord inversions can be used to indicate other nonchord tones to be played in the bass part—another way to produce more sophisticated chord sounds. For example, the notation Am7/D signifies an A minor seventh chord, but with a D added in the bass—a note that doesn't exist within the A minor seventh chord proper.

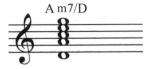

Notating an altered bass chord.

Chords of this type are called *altered bass* chords. By adding a nonchord note in the bass, you create a different chord with a different harmonic structure. Slash chords are used a lot in jazz and other contemporary music, and also in more sophisticated popular music.

You can, in theory, use this technique to stick any note in the bass. In practice, however, you'll find that not all bass notes sound good when played against a given chord. You should let your ear be the guide, of course, but know that seconds and fourths of the chord typically sound better than sixths and sevenths.

Using Compound Chords

An altered bass chord uses a diagonal slash mark to separate the chord from the bass note. When you see a chord with a horizontal line between two different notes, like a fraction, you're dealing with a much different beast, called a *compound chord*.

This type of notation indicates that two chords are to be played simultaneously. The chord on top of the fraction is placed on top of the pile; the chord on the bottom is played underneath. For example, when you see $\frac{A}{D}$, this signifies that an A major chord is to be played on top of a full D major chord. This is a harmonically complex sound—and yet another way to spice up your chord-based compositions.

Notating a compound chord.

Working with a Pedal Point

Another way to make any chord progression more interesting is to place it over a constantly repeating bass note—what we call a *pedal point*. The pedal point creates a steady harmonic anchor, while the chord progression creates color over this tonal center. You can end up with some interesting harmonic structures just by playing a chord over a bass note that isn't included as part of the chord.

> **Note**
>
> Some musicians call altered chords *slash chords* because the altered bass note is indicated after a diagonal slash mark, like this: A/B. You read the chord as "A over B," and you play it as an A chord with a B in the bass.

> **Note**
>
> Compound chords are often used to signify extremely complex harmonies—those that might otherwise be too complex to notate using traditional chord extensions.

For example, let's look at a standard I-IV-V7 progression over a tonic pedal point. The repeating bass note anchors the composition to the tonic and adds tension to a somewhat-clichéd progression.

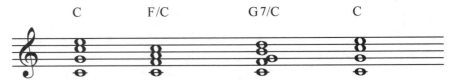

A simple chord progression enhanced with a pedal point.

Here's another example, with a circular IM7-iim7-iiim7-iim7 progression played over a tonic pedal point. In the key of C, it looks like this:

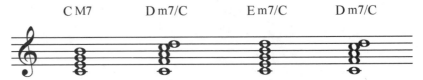

A circular chord progression grounded by a pedal point.

This is a chord progression that sounds somewhat airy while still remaining grounded. There's a constant root to it because of the pedal point, even as it circles around and around. Some of the individual chord progressions are quite interesting—in particular, the iim7/I (with the seventh in the bass) and iiim7/I (with the bass note existing totally outside the chord construction).

Employing Chord Substitutions

Our next approach to creating more complex chord progressions is called *chord substitution*. All you do is take a chord—any chord—from a chord progression and replace it with a related chord. The substitute chord should have a few things in common with the chord it replaces, not the least of which is its place in the song's underlying harmonic structure. So, for example, if you replace a dominant (V) chord, you want to use a substitute chord that also leads back to the tonic (I). Or if you replace a major chord, you want to replace it with another major chord, or at least a chord that uses some of the same notes as in the original chord.

Diatonic Substitutions

The easiest form of chord substitution replaces a chord with a related chord by either a diatonic third above or a diatonic third below the original. This type of substitution is called *diatonic substitution* because you're not altering any of the notes of the underlying scale; you're just using different notes from within the scale for the new chord. With diatonic substitution, the replacement chord has a clear relationship to the original chord—it sounds different but not wrong. That's because you keep two of the three notes of the original chord, which provides a strong harmonic basis for the new chord.

For example, the I chord in any scale can be replaced by the vi chord (the chord a diatonic third below) or the iii chord (the chord a diatonic third above). In the key of C, this means replacing the C major chord (C-E-G) with either Am (A-C-E) or Em (E-G-B). Both chords share two notes in common with the C chord, so the replacement isn't too jarring.

You can replace extended chords in the same manner, and because you have more notes to work with, substitute chords have more notes in common with the original chord. For example, you can replace C major 7 with either Am7 or Em7, both of which have three notes in common with the original chord.

You can also replace extended chords with chords a full fifth above or below the original chord (again, because you have more notes to work with). So that C major 7 chord can also be replaced by the F major 7 or G7 chords.

> **CAUTION**
>
> **Warning**
>
> The further away the replacement chord is from the original, the less likely it is to fulfill the same harmonic role in the composition.

Major Chord Substitutions

Now that you know the general theory behind diatonic chord substitution, how about some hard-and-fast rules you can use when creating your own compositions?

Let's start with major chords. The following table presents four different substitutions you can make for a standard major chord. Remember that the root of the substitute chord must stay within the underlying scale, even if some of the chord notes occasionally wander about a bit.

Major Chord Substitutions

Substitution	Example (for the C Major Chord)
Minor chord a third below	Am
Minor 7 chord a third below	Am7
Minor chord a third above	Em
Minor 7 chord a third above	Em7

The first substitution in the table is the standard "down a third" diatonic substitution. The second substitution is the same thing, but it uses an extended chord (the minor seventh) for the substitution and is actually a more harmonically fulfilling replacement. (In other words, it sounds a little better.) The third substitution is the "up a third" diatonic substitution, as discussed previously. The fourth substitution is the same thing, but it uses an extended chord (the minor seventh).

Minor Chord Substitutions

Substituting a major chord is relatively easy. So, for that matter, is substituting a minor chord.

As you can see in the following table, some of the same substitution rules work with minor as well as major, especially the "up a third" and "down a third" diatonic substitutions.

Minor Chord Substitutions

Substitution	Example (for the C Minor Chord)
Major chord a third above	E♭ major
Major 7 chord a third above	E♭ major 7
Major chord a third below	A♭ major
Major 7 chord a third below	A♭ major 7
Diminished chord with same root	C dim

The last substitution falls into the "more of a good thing" category. That is, if a minor chord sounds good, let's flat another note and it'll sound even more minor. It's a particularly sophisticated substitution that sounds good in jazz-flavored compositions.

Dominant Seventh Substitutions

Okay, now you know how to substitute both major and minor chords. But what about dominant seventh chords? They're not really major and they're not really minor—what kind of chords can substitute for *that*?

The answer requires a little creativity. You *can* do a diatonic substitution (using the diminished chords a third above or below the dominant seventh), but there are more interesting possibilities, as you can see in the following table.

Dominant Seventh Chord Substitutions

Substitution	Example (for the C7 Chord)
Major chord a second below	B♭ major
Diminished chord a third below	A dim
Diminished chord a third above	E dim
Minor 7 chord a fourth below—over the same root	Gm7/C

The most interesting substitutions here are the first one and the last one. The first substitution replaces the V7 chord with a IVM7 chord; the use of the IV chord results in a softer lead back to the I chord. The last substitution uses an altered chord so that you're leading back to the I chord tonic with a iim7/V. It's a very pleasing sound.

Functional Substitutions

Related to the previous chord substitutions is the concept of functional sub-stitutions. Within the harmonic context of a composition, different chords serve different functions. The three basic harmonic functions are those of the tonic, subdominant, and dominant—typically served by the I, IV, and V chords, respectively. But other chords in the scale can serve these same functions, even if not as strongly as the I, IV, and V.

For example, the subdominant function can be served by either the ii, IV, or vi chords. The dominant function can be served by either the V or vii° chords. And the tonic function can be served by either the I, iii, or vi chords. All these functions are shown in the following table.

Functional Chord Substitutions

Chord Function	Chords
Tonic	I, iii, vi
Subdominant	ii, IV, vi
Dominant	V, vii°

When you have a chord serving a specific function in a composition, you can replace it with another chord of the same type. So if you have a IV chord, serv-ing a subdominant function, you can substitute any of the other subdominant-functioning chords—the ii or the vi. Along the same lines, if you have a ii chord, you can replace it with either the IV or the vi.

The same thing goes with the other functions. If you have a V chord, serving a dominant function, you can replace it with a vii° chord—or vice versa. And a I chord, serving a tonic function, can be replaced by either a iii or a vi chord—and also vice versa. It's actually a fairly easy way to make some simple chord substitutions.

> **Note**
>
> Just in case you think you found a mistake in the preceding table, the vi chord can serve both the tonic and subdominant functions. It's a very versa-tile chord!

Using Nonscale Chords

Another approach is to use nonscale chords—that is, chromatic chords that don't appear naturally in the underlying scale. This might mean playing a minor chord where a major one should be, or playing a chord on a flatted or sharped scale tone.

For example, in the key of C, the vi chord should be A minor. If instead you play an A major chord (VI), it's something totally unexpected, as in the follow-ing progression:

| I | VI | IV | V |

Or in the key of C:

| C | A | F | G |

Let's look at another example, this time using chords based on nonscale tones. In this instance, we'll play a chord based on the flatted sixth (♭vi) instead of the natural sixth (vi). Again, the result is startling:

I	♭vi	IV	V

Or in the key of C:

C	A♭m	F	G

The result is particularly striking if you build on the unexpected chord harmonically, using it as the tonal basis for the rest of the progression. Using the current example, if we take the A♭ minor chord to be the new sixth, it would lead not to an F-major chord, but rather to an E major chord (the same half-step down as the ♭vi) and then to a G♭ major chord (instead of the expected G major):

I	♭vi	♭IV	♭V

This produces a somewhat unsettling sound, especially if you cycle from the G♭ back to the original C:

C	A♭m	E	G♭	(C)

The point of these exercises is that you don't have to limit yourself to the chords suggested by the chord-leading technique. To create harmonic interest, spice it up—and lead your listener somewhere unexpected.

> **Note**
>
> Technically, the A♭ major chord actually leads to an F♭-major chord—which is enharmonically the same an E major chord. Since E major is more common (and easier to work with) than F♭ major, that's the better way to write it, as I did in the example.

Using Chords as Tonal Centers

Although traditional chord progressions are used in many different types of compositions, you don't have to use chords in a traditional manner. So-called *modal music* uses chords to create shifting tonal centers within a composition. In this fashion, a single chord is extended over multiple measures and used to define a specific scale or mode.

> **Note**
>
> A mode is like a scale, in that it contains eight consecutive tones in a specific order. There are seven modes that date back to ancient Greece, each starting on a specific note of the traditional major scale. For example, the Aeolian mode consists of all the notes of a major scale but starts on the sixth of the scale instead of the tonic. (You play the A Aeolian mode by using the notes of the C major scale, but going from A to A.)

A modal composition might use only two or three chords throughout the entire piece. For example, the A section of the piece might center on one chord, with the B section centering on a second chord. During each section, the tonal center is defined by that section's chord.

Let's look at an example in which the first section of a composition is centered on the D minor chord and the second section is centered on the E minor chord. The underlying key signature might be C major, but this composition would not use traditional C major harmony—that is, you wouldn't create melodies based on the C major scale. Instead, you might base the melody in the first section (the one with the D minor chord) on the D Dorian mode—which happens to use the same notes as the C major scale, but in a different order (starting on D instead of C). When you switch to the second section (based on the E minor chord), the tonal center might switch from D Dorian to E Phrygian—which also uses the underlying notes of the C major scale, but starting on E this time. Even though the same notes are used in each section, the entire sound of the piece changes.

And you don't have to limit yourself to chords that use the same underlying notes. Another approach is to totally shift underlying scales when you shift from one chord to another. Consider a piece in which the first section is based on the C major chord, but the second section is based on the B♭ major chord. In this instance, the tonal center of the first section might use the C major scale, while the tonal center of the second section might use the B♭ major scale. It's pretty much like changing keys, but, in this instance, dictated by which chords are selected.

Trust Your Ears!

As you can see, the chordal structure of a composition can become quite complex. It doesn't have to be grounded in diatonic chords or simple chord-leading rules; the chords you use can go off into all manner of unexpected directions. This is especially true if you explore jazz or serious contemporary music, where traditional harmonic structure is replaced by chromatic and even atonal approaches.

In classical and popular music forms, a more traditional approach to harmony is expected. Here you get lots of good use out of diatonic chords and chord-leading rules—although you can still spice up traditional harmonies with extensions, pedal points, and the like.

After all, the "rules" for chord-based composition are only suggestions, tools for you to use to express the colors and sounds you hear inside your head. You can use these tools as you see fit; they exist to serve your creative instincts, not the other way around. In other words, when you're creating any type of chord progression, trust your ears! You're the best judge of what sounds good and what doesn't; don't let any arbitrary rule constrain your creativity.

The Least You Need to Know

- One way to make your chord progression more interesting is to move to a chord not indicated by chord-leading conventions.
- You can create richer harmonies by adding chord extensions—sevenths, ninths, and the like.

◆ Another way to create more sophisticated harmonies is to use altered bass and compound chords, as well as a repeating pedal point bass note.

◆ Chord substitutions let you alter a chord progression by substituting harmonically similar chords.

◆ For a more dramatic effect, replace existing chords with chords constructed from or based on nonscale tones.

◆ You can also shift the tonal center of your composition as you move from chord to chord, rather than remaining in the original scale or key.

Exercises

Exercise 4-1

Using unexpected chords (that is, nonchord-leading chords), complete the following chord progressions:

a: I   IV   …

b: I   ii   …

c: I   vi   …

d: I   V   …

e: I   iii   …

Exercise 4-2

Rewrite the following chord progressions (in the key of C) using extended chords:

a: C   G   Am   F

b: C   Am   Dm   G

c: C   F   C   G

d: C   Dm   F   G

e: F   C   F   G

Exercise 4-3

Using staff paper, write out the notes for the following altered bass and compound chords:

a: Am7/G   G/C   F/D   Em7/A

b: C/D   D/E   Em/F#   G/A

c: $\frac{C}{D}$ $\frac{D}{E}$ $\frac{Em}{F\#}$ $\frac{G}{A}$

d: Gm/C   Am/D   Bb/C   C7/G

e: $\frac{F7}{Bb}$ $\frac{EbM7}{Cm}$ $\frac{Gm7}{Dm}$ $\frac{BbM7}{F7}$

Exercise 4-4

Write two substitute chords for each of the chords in the following progressions (in the key of C):

      a: C   F   G

      b: CM7   Am7   Dm7   G7

      c: C   Am   F   G7

      d: Dm7   G7   C

      e: C   F   C   G7   F   C

Exercise 4-5

Alter the following chord progressions (in the key of C) with one or more non-scale chords:

      a: C   F   C   G7

      b: C   G   Am   F

      c: C   Dm   F   G

      d: C   Am   Dm   F   G7

      e: C   G   Dm   Am   Em   Bdim F C

Part 3

Melodic Composition

The melody's the most important part of a composition, so it deserves a lot of attention—which is what you get in this part. Start with a basic melodic outline, embellish it a little, set it to an interesting rhythm, and then give it a pleasing shape—along with a little tension (and release) along the way—and you'll have a melody you can work with.

Understanding Melody

In This Chapter

- ◆ Why melody is important
- ◆ What qualities contribute to making a memorable melody
- ◆ How to build a melody from motifs and short phrases

In the previous two chapters, we examined harmonic composition—the art of composing chords-first and then adding melodies to those chords. The opposing approach creates the melody first and then harmonizes that melody with the appropriate chords.

Personally, I believe that the melody is the most important part of the composition. Seldom do you hear someone humming a song's rhythm or chord changes; you do, however, hear people humming melodies. The melody is what most people remember from a composition, whether that's a popular song, a jazz piece, or a serious composition.

Something as important as melody should seldom be subservient to any other component of a composition. This begs for a melodic approach to composition—or, at the very least, an approach that treats melody as something other than that last bit you layer on top of a chord progression or fit to a stream of lyrics.

Melody—The Most Important Part of a Composition

I admit it; I'm a melody snob. I have trouble listening to music that has little or no melody, or to compositions with uninteresting, static melodies. To my ear, melodies need to be lively and interesting, distinctive and memorable, well-formed and logical, lyrical and expressive. In other words, melodies need to be … well, *melodic*.

That's not to say that there's only one acceptable type of melody, or that all melodies have to adhere to the same formulas or rules. Quite the opposite. Composers throughout the centuries have managed to compose innumerable melodies while still maintaining their own musical personalities. After all, there's no confusing a melody written by Bach with one written by Chopin, Beethoven, or Dvořák—or, for that matter, by Cole Porter, Richard Rodgers, or Burt Bacharach. Each of these composers worked with the same tools, the same 12 tones of the Western scale, but managed to create distinctly individual types of melodies. And all of them created music with memorable melodies. When you hear one of their works, whether it's a piano sonata, an operatic aria, a big band chart, or a popular ballad, you hear well-shaped, tightly constructed, eminently singable melodies. You remember their compositions because their melodies are memorable.

This is all prelude to the key question, of course: what makes a particular string of notes a memorable melody?

Defining Melody

Music theoreticians define melody as a logical progression of tones and rhythms—a tune set to a beat. But pay close attention to that word, *logical*. A melody isn't a random conglomeration of notes; the notes have to relate to and follow from each other. In other words, a melody has to make sense, or else it's just a bunch of noise.

This textbook definition of melody, however precise, doesn't go far enough for my tastes. A good melody packs an emotional punch; it can make us jump with joy or weep with sadness. When done right, a melody can tell a story without words or reinforce the meaning of a song's lyrics. It takes the listener from point A to point B and makes the journey both enjoyable and memorable.

What Makes a Melody Melodic?

Some musicians believe that great compositions are the result of divine inspiration. That is sometimes true, but just as often a composition results from careful construction. This is certainly the case with melodies, which are sometimes delivered from some other worldly plane but more often are built from some rather mundane compositional tools. Because I can't teach you how to become inspired, we'll concentrate on the tools and techniques instead.

A Good Melody Has Movement

A good melody doesn't just sit there; it goes someplace. You can propel a melody rhythmically, or tonally, through the "motion" of the tones. In this sense, *motion* refers to the progressive upward or downward direction of the pitches, or what some call the *contour* of a line of music.

A good way to think about the upward or downward motion of a melody is to look at the starting note and the ending note—while ignoring, for the time

Warning

Although it's perfectly acceptable to use the same note two or more times consecutively (George Gershwin did it a lot), you don't want to overdo it. An overreliance on repeated tones is lazy melody making, a trait unfortunately held by many untrained singer/songwriters who think that all they have to do is warble their lyrics over a chord progression.

being, all the notes in between. To create an upward-moving melody, make sure the ending note is at least a third (and, ideally, a fifth or more) higher than the starting note. Same thing with a downward-moving melody: force the last note to be lower than the first one.

All the notes between the first and last notes help you move to that final note. The notes don't all have to go in the same direction, but they do have to gradually move up or down to where you want to end.

A melody with upward motion.

Note that it's okay to have a melody that starts and ends on the same note. What you can do is make the midpoint of the melody higher or lower than the starting/ending pitch. If you choose a higher midpoint, the first half of the melody will have upward movement, and the last half will use downward movement to return to the home pitch.

And as you move from start to end, you want your melody to actually *move*. That means avoiding the overuse of repeated tones. Intelligent movement is what melody is all about; it's how a melody is constructed, moving from tone to tone with a purpose—and a certain amount of lyricism.

Two melodies, the first one rather static, the second with an interesting sense of movement.

A Good Melody Is Familiar—Yet Unexpected

The type of movement you employ in your melodies determines, to a great degree, the strength of your melody. In his book *Tunesmith*, songwriter Jimmy Webb says that the key to writing interesting melody is "to lead the ear on a path which is both *pleasant* and to some degree *unexpected*" (emphasis his). I agree wholeheartedly. The best melodies sound familiar yet still manage to surprise us somewhere along the line.

This is typically accomplished by employing a judicious mix of step-wise and skip-wise motion. We'll get into this more in the following chapters, but step-wise motion leads directly from one note of the underlying scale to the next adjacent note; skip-wise motion uses intervals of a third or larger between notes. Step-wise motion creates a familiar, expected sound, while skip-wise motion is less expected. A good melody leads the listener step-wise to an unexpected skip.

A melody that mixes step-wise and skip-wise movement.

It's this variety within the melody that's important. If a melody is all step-wise movement, it can quickly become mundane and a tad boring. On the other hand, if a melody is all large skips, every note is unexpected and the listener has nothing familiar to fall back on; too much unpredictability is tiring. Mix step-wise and skip-wise motion and you'll get that balance Jimmy Webb was talking about.

A Good Melody Sets Up—and Resolves—Tension

Another way to make a melody familiar yet unexpected is to use the technique of tension and resolution. A melody without any tension isn't terribly exciting; on the other hand, a melody with unresolved tension feels somehow uncomfortable. This is why many composers introduce some sort of tension into their melodies (to make things interesting) and then resolve that tension (to create a feeling of comfort and relief).

One of the most common melodic techniques is to divide your melody into two parts and set up a harmonic tension in the first part that is then resolved in the second part. This gives the melody a distinct form and its own internal logic; it also helps to propel the melody from the first part to the second. It's like taking a deep breath (the tension) and then releasing it (the resolution).

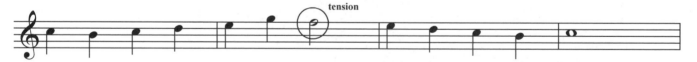

The half note in measure two creates tension; the next two bars resolve the tension.

A Good Melody Has a Center

The best melodies, while interesting, aren't so interesting that they have no form. You don't want your melodies wandering around all over the place, like a dog looking for a place to do his business. What you want is more of a hunting dog of a melody, one that knows where home is and, at the end of the day, finds its way back there.

The "home" of a melody needs to be a specific pitch. When you pick a home pitch, your melody can then revolve around the pitch. You can start on that pitch (although you don't have to), and you should end on that pitch. Equally important, the other notes in the melody can play around that pitch—and even land on it, occasionally.

For example, listen to the following melody. It's in the key of G but revolves around the home pitch of B—the third of the scale.

A four-measure melody in the key of G, which hovers around the third of the scale (B).

A Good Melody Repeats Itself

To make a melody memorable, it helps to know what to remember. To that end, most memorable melodies liberally repeat themselves. This may mean repetition of the entire melodic line, or may mean constructing a longer melodic line from shorter, repeating melodic snippets. (These snippets are called *motifs*, and we'll discuss them later in this chapter.) The point is, repetition within a melody is important, in that it helps the listener to remember the melodic line. It's like giving a speech, where a good speaker knows to repeat the main points to help the audience grasp what's important. It's the same thing in musical composition; repeat the important line(s) to establish the musical theme of your piece.

For example, here's a melody with a simple one-measure motif that is repeated in the second and third measures. This repetition of the motif creates a cohesive longer melody and helps the listener to remember it.

Tip

The home pitch of your melody doesn't have to be the tonic of the scale. You can make the third your home, or the fifth—but probably not the second, sixth, or seventh because they're less related to the tonic triad of 1-3-5.

A melody that employs liberal repetition of a motif.

A Good Melody Has Form

Part of making a melody memorable is to give it an easily comprehended form. Although melodies *can* wander as long and as far afield as you like, it's typically better if they're a little shorter and a little more organized. This calls for compartmentalizing the melody into easily digested phrases. In most Western music, melodic phrases are typically divisible by 2. That means creating a 2-, 4-, 8-, or 16-measure melody. Or it could mean constructing a 64-measure melody composed of four 16-measure phrases. Or a 16-measure melody composed of two 8-bar phrases, or four 4-measure phrases, or some other such mathematically correct construction.

Warning

You want to avoid having each measure of your melody center on a different pitch, or have your home pitch shift as the underlying chords change. The home pitch should be central for the entire melody, not central to each chord.

For example, the following 16-measure melody is constructed from four 4-measure units.

A 16-measure melody, consisting of four 4-measure phrases.

A Good Melody Stays in Range

The best melodies are not only centered, but they're also somewhat contained. That is, they're not overly broad in their range of notes. If the distance between the lowest note and the highest note is too wide, the melody starts to sound random and disjunctive, without a home.

You should strive, if at all possible, to keep the lowest and highest notes in a melody within an octave of each other (or, at most, within an octave and a third). Know, however, that this is one of those rules that is meant to be broken; many of the greatest melodies have had a fairly large range.

A melody with too wide a range.

A Good Melody Is Unique

All this said, a melody doesn't have to be harmonically or rhythmically complex to be memorable; it doesn't have to be long or short or any certain length. It does, however, have to be distinctive. A memorable melody might remind us of other melodies, but it can't duplicate them. The best melodies have something unique about them, some distinctive hook, motif, or rhythmic pattern that makes them stand out.

It's difficult (if not impossible) to tell you how to be unique, so this is something you'll have to address on your own. Does your melody stand on its own? Does it sound a little like something else you've heard? Does it sound a *lot* like something else you've heard? As with many aspects of composition, this is one area in which you'll have to trust your ears—and one that you definitely have to listen for.

The Building Blocks of Melodic Form

To end this introduction to melody, we'll take a quick look at how melodies are constructed. We briefly addressed melodic form earlier in this chapter; now let's see how this form business really works.

Note

Learn more about voice and instrument ranges in Chapter 15.

The Motif

For a melody to be truly memorable, there needs to be a piece of the melody that really reaches out and grabs the listener's attention. In pop music, this is called the *hook* because it's the part of the song that hooks the listener. In more traditional music, this piece of the song is known as the *motif* or *motive*. Whatever you call it, it should be memorable enough that you want to repeat it not only within a longer melodic phrase, but throughout the entire composition.

A motif is typically fairly short—a few notes (think of the five whistling notes in Sergio Leone's theme from the movie *The Good, the Bad and the Ugly*) or, at longest, one or two measures. You can reuse a motif throughout a composition by varying it in one way or another—repeating the same tones with a different rhythm, playing the tones up or down a specified interval, playing different tones to the same rhythm, and so on.

A simple four-note motif.

The Short Melodic Phrase

The motif is typically part of a more complete melodic phrase. This phrase is typically two or four measures long and contains a complete musical thought or statement. For want of a better term, we'll call this the short melodic phrase or the short melody.

A short melodic phrase typically defines itself by coming to some sort of easily identifiable endpoint. That might be a cadence (perfect or otherwise) or an extended note (after shorter rhythms). In essence, the endpoint of a melodic phrase is where the music breathes.

The short melody doesn't have to begin and end on the tonic or other stable tone or chord; in fact, short melodies often function within an even longer musical phrase to set up and resolve tension. To this end, some short melodies within your composition might end on an unstable harmony, while a following melody might end on a stable harmony to resolve the tension.

Tip

Of all the short melodies within a composition (and there should be more than one), one of them should be memorable enough to become the *theme* of the composition. The melodic theme defines the composition and is typically repeated several times throughout a piece.

The motif used within a two-measure short melodic phrase.

The Long Melodic Phrase

Short melodic phrases combine into longer melodic phrases. You typically put two or four short melodic phrases together into a single long melodic phrase. The end of a long melodic phrase is a major breathing (or resting) point; after all those short melodies, your composition needs to take a significant break.

Four short melodic phrases combined into a single longer melodic phrase.

Of course, you don't combine short melodic phrases haphazardly. You want one phrase to lead smoothly and logically into the next. This ultimately means thinking of the big picture as you put together the multiple small pictures. If one phrase ends on a tension, the next phrase should resolve the tension; if one phrase leads in a particular direction, the next phrase should continue in the same direction. It's a matter of hearing and then creating a logical flow throughout the entire long melodic phrase; the building blocks (the short melodic phrases) must be used to create something substantial (the long melodic phrase) that then stands on its own.

Longer Forms

Within longer compositions, you combine multiple long melodies into even larger forms. After all, few serious compositions are only 16 measures long!

For example, popular songs sometimes use a verse-chorus-verse form (sometimes notated as ABA), with two separate long melodies. The first long melody is the verse (section A), the second long melody is the chorus (section B), and then the first long melody is repeated for the second verse (the second section A). There are many variations to this form, including AABA (the first long melody is repeated once before the chorus) and ABCA (with a third long melody—now notated as the B section—serving as a "bridge" to the C-section chorus).

Serious compositions also employ a variety of larger forms. The concept of A, B, and C sections carries over into symphonies and chamber works, as well as more modern forms. The whole point is to create a series of building blocks (motifs, short, and long melodies) that you combine in various fashions to create a longer work.

Creating a Shape

In addition to (or in conjunction with) the structure of a melody, you need to be concerned with the shape of your melodic phrases. By *shape*, I mean the contour of the melody—how it rises and falls and generally travels from start to finish. Shape is so important that it deserves an entire chapter of coverage; turn to Chapter 9 to learn more.

The Least You Need to Know

- Melody is the most important part of a composition; it's the part that people remember.
- Melody is defined as a logical progression of notes and rhythms—a tune set to a beat.
- A good melody must have movement, be familiar yet unexpected (via the use of both step-wise and skip-wise motion), set up and resolve tension, have a tonal center, employ repetition, have a distinct form, stay within a reasonable range, and be unique.
- Longer melodies are built from simple motifs and short melodic phrases.

Exercises

Exercise 5-1

Listen to a variety of songs and compositions, paying particular attention to the main melodies. Analyze the melodies in question and determine what qualities they have in common. Listen for step-wise and skip-wise motion, melodic range, motifs, the building of short and long melodic phrases, and other techniques discussed in this chapter. Determine how these techniques combine to give each melody its unique nature.

Chapter 6

Using Scales and Modes

In This Chapter

◆ How to base a melody on the notes of different scales and modes

◆ Deciding which scale or mode to use

◆ Choosing specific scale tones for a melody

◆ Writing melodies with step-wise and skip-wise motion

There are many different ways to construct a melody. We examine several of them over the next few chapters, but all of these approaches have one thing in common: they utilize, in one way or another, the notes of the underlying scale. It might seem blatantly obvious, but in most forms of music, you want to base your melody on the notes of a specific scale. (There are exceptions, of course—specifically, when you're creating a chromatic or atonal composition—but we're not talking about those forms here.)

What's not so obvious is that you have a variety of choices for *which* scale you use in any given situation. There are the familiar major and minor scales, of course, but you can also utilize the pentatonic and blues scales, as well as any of the so-called church modes. And even after you choose a scale or mode, you still have to decide which notes from the scale to use.

Which tonality you choose is important because different scales and modes impart different musical feels and colors. In this chapter, we look at some of the most popular choices and show how to use those scales and modes to help you construct melodic themes.

Basing a Melody on the Notes of the Scale

Good melodies are often strengthened by having a harmonic center, a feel that centers on a specific tone and its relationship with other tones—in other words, a scale or key. In most cases, the notes of your melody will come from the notes within the composition's chosen key. If you write a piece in G major, you'll use the notes of the G major scale. If you write a piece in A minor, you'll use the notes of the A minor scale.

You can make several other harmonic choices, however, beyond the traditional major and minor scales—most of which you can employ without using a single chromatic note. Let's take a look at some of the options that are available.

Major Scale

When you're writing a major-key composition, the most common scale to use is the major scale. No surprise there. The major scale is a safe choice and a relatively easy scale to use. You don't have to worry about any chromatic notes, or stopping and starting on strange tones in the middle of the scale. If you're writing a piece in C major, use the C major scale. It's that easy.

Minor Scales

When you're writing in a minor key, the obvious scale of choice is a minor scale. Minor scales sound a little less "up" than major scales. This is partly because the third note of the minor scale is a minor interval, whereas the third note of the major scale is a major interval. That little half-step between a minor third and a major third makes all the difference in the world!

If you choose to employ a minor scale, this forces you to make a second decision: which minor scale should you use?

You see, unlike the singular major scale, there is more than one type of minor scale—three, in fact: natural, harmonic, and melodic minor.

The easiest minor scale to use is the *natural minor scale*. You can think of the natural minor in terms of its corresponding major scale. When you start and end a major scale on the sixth note instead of the tonic, you get a natural minor scale.

To construct a natural minor scale, then, simply think of the major scale as a minor third above, and use the notes of that scale. For example, if you want to use the A minor scale, think of the C major scale (C is a minor third above A), and use those notes—but starting on the A, of course. It looks like this:

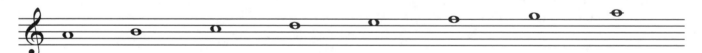

The A natural minor scale.

There are two other minor scales, although they're both less widely used than the natural minor scale. The *harmonic minor scale* is similar to the natural minor scale, except that the seventh note is raised a half step. The *melodic minor scale* raises both the sixth and seventh notes of the natural minor scale by a half-step each. (And, to make things even more confusing, some music theorists raise these notes only when ascending the scale; when descending, they use the same notes as the natural minor scale.) Not to worry, though; it's far easier (and far more common) to construct minor-key melodies by using the simpler natural minor scale.

The A harmonic minor scale.

The A melodic minor scale (ascending).

Pentatonic Scale

Not all scales have seven notes (or eight, if you count the octave). You can paint your compositions with a simpler harmonic palette when you employ the *pentatonic scale*. As the name implies, the pentatonic scale is a five-note scale (not counting the octave). Even though the pentatonic scale might appear to limit your melodic choices, that limitation sometimes makes it easier to create interesting melodies.

In relationship to a major scale, the scale degrees (not counting the octave) go 1-2-3-5-6. For example, the C pentatonic scale looks like this:

> **Note**
>
> Another good demonstration of a major pentatonic scale can be had by playing all the black notes on a piano (starting with G♭); this happens to be the G♭ major pentatonic scale.

The C pentatonic scale.

If you play the major pentatonic scale one note after another, the resulting sound is a trifle Oriental. However, if you alter the order of the notes, you get a very versatile tool chest with which to construct your melodies; it can be used in any number of musical situations. Chord-wise, you can harmonize pentatonic scales with major chords, minor chords, and dominant seventh chords, and they all sound good.

And here's something particularly interesting. Within any given major key, there are actually *three* pentatonic scales you can use. The first one, of course, is the one that starts on the tonic (1-2-3-5-6). The second one starts on the fourth of the scale (4-5-6-1-2). And the third one starts on the fifth of the scale (5-6-7-2-3). For example, in the key of C major, you can use C pentatonic (C-D-E-F-A), F pentatonic (F-G-A-C-D), or G pentatonic (G-A-B-D-E). Each of these pentatonic scales has a much different feel when played against the underlying key; try writing melodies based on each of the three pentatonic scales to hear the differences.

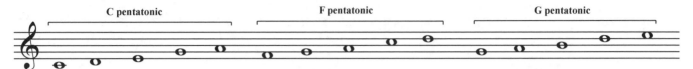

The three pentatonic scales within the C major scale.

Whole Tone Scale

We're just getting started with this scale business; there are quite a few non-standard scales that you can use for your melodies. The one we'll look at next is called the *whole tone scale*.

The whole tone scale is unusual, in that it has just seven notes (including the octave), each a whole step apart—hence the name. In relationship to a major scale, the scale degrees (not counting the octave) go 1-2-3-♭5-♭6-♭7. For example, the C whole tone scale looks like this:

The C whole tone scale.

The whole tone scale is surprisingly versatile, especially in the jazz idiom. You can harmonize it against various forms of the dominant seventh chord, particularly dominant seventh chords with a raised fifth.

Diminished Scale

Next, let's consider another unusual scale called the *diminished scale*. This scale is distinguished by alternating whole-step/half-step intervals. This results in a scale with nine notes (including the octave)—not the expected eight. In relationship to a major scale, the scale degrees (not counting the octave) go 1-2-♭3-4-♭5-♭6-6-7. For example, the C diminished scale looks like this:

The C diminished scale.

Note
The diminished scale is also known as the *octatonic scale*.

As unusual as it is, the diminished scale is quite popular in the jazz idiom and is relatively easy to harmonize. You can use the diminished scale with minor sixth, minor seventh, half-diminished seventh, and dominant seventh chords.

Blues Scale

If you're writing in the jazz or popular idioms, be prepared to utilize the *blues scale*. This is a seven-note scale (counting the octave) that is typically used with the blues chord progression you learned back in Chapter 3. The blues scale is unusual, in that it doesn't have a second or sixth degree, but it does throw in a flatted fifth in addition to the regular perfect fifth. In relationship to a major scale, the scale degrees (not counting the octave) go 1-♭3-4-♭5-5-♭7. For example, the C blues scale looks like this:

The C blues scale.

When you're writing a melody based on the blues scale, it's the flatted third, flatted fifth, and flatted seventh that define the scale's color. This scale is easily harmonized with dominant seventh chords—although playing one note after the other (in order) might sound a little odd. Because of this, most composers vary the intervals when creating blues-based melodies.

Bebop Scale

The *bebop scale* (sometimes referred to as the *bebop dominant scale*) is nothing more than the Mixolydian mode with a major seventh added. (We get to modes in just a few paragraphs.) That's right, this is a scale with *nine* notes (including the octave) instead of the normal eight.

In relation to a major scale, the scale degrees (not counting the octave) go 1-2-3-4-5-6-♭7-7. For example, the C bebop scale looks like this:

The C bebop scale.

As you might expect from its name, the bebop scale is used predominantly in jazz-flavored compositions.

Modes

Before there were scales, there were *modes*. Many think of these scalelike series of notes as coming from the medieval church (and Gregorian chants), but several modes actually date back to the ancient Greeks. In any case, a mode is just like a scale, except with different sequences of intervals—and you can employ any and all of these modes in the creation of your melodies.

There are seven essential modes, each of which can be thought of as starting on a different degree of the major scale. To play the mode, you use the same notes of the relative major scale; you just start on a different tone.

Note

The Ionian mode is identical to the major scale; the Aeolian mode is identical to the natural minor scale.

For example, the Dorian mode starts on the second degree of the major scale. In relation to the C major scale, the D Dorian mode starts on D and continues upward (D, E, F, G, A, B, C, D). The same holds true for the Phrygian mode, which starts on the third degree of the related major scale—in C major (E Phrygian): E, F, G, A, B, C, D, E. And so on for the other modes, as shown in the following table.

Modes

Mode	Starts on This Relative Major Scale Tone	Example (Based on the C Major Scale)
Ionian	1	C-D-E-F-G-A-B-C
Dorian	2	D-E-F-G-A-B-C-D
Phrygian	3	E-F-G-A-B-C-D-E
Lydian	4	F-G-A-B-C-D-E-F
Mixolydian	5	G-A-B-C-D-E-F-G
Aeolian	6	A-B-C-D-E-F-G-A
Locrian	7	B-C-D-E-F-G-A-B

C Ionian   D Dorian

E Phrygian   F Lydian

G Mixolydian   A Aeolian   B Locrian

The common modes, in relationship to C Major.

Note

Melodies based on specific modes are called *modal* melodies.

You might think that a melody based on a mode would sound the same as one based on the related major scale—they use the same notes, after all. But when you center that melody on the tonic of the mode (as opposed to the tonic of the scale), you change the entire color of the notes. That's because the notes you use are serving different functions within the mode. When you write in the F Lydian mode, for example, F serves as the tonal center; when you write in the related C major scale, F serves as the subdominant tone. They serve completely different functions, thus helping you to create totally different types of melodies.

Choosing the Right Scale or Mode

The key question, then, is, which scale should you use in your composition? There is no correct answer; it depends on the type of sound and mood you want to impart. That said, here are some suggestions:

◆ For traditional-sounding melodies, especially in the popular idiom, it's safe to stick with melodies based on the traditional major scale.

◆ For a slightly more sophisticated popular sound, use the pentatonic scale based on either the fourth or the fifth of the underlying major scale.

◆ If you're going for the more subdued minor-key sound, use the natural minor scale (AKA the Aeolian mode).

◆ For a Middle-Eastern sound, use the Dorian mode.

◆ For either a cowboys-and-Indians or Oriental sound, use the pentatonic scale based on the tonic of the major scale.

◆ For blues-based compositions, use the blues scale.

◆ For jazz compositions, consider using the diminished, harmonic minor, or bebop scales.

◆ For a more open, less tonally centered sound, use the whole tone scale.

These are just suggestions, of course. You should use those scale and modes with which you're most comfortable and that sound right to your ear. But don't ignore the less common scales; forcing yourself to compose in a less familiar scale or mode is a good way to expand your creative thinking.

Picking the Right Notes to Use

Basing a melody on a specific scale or mode is just a start; all this does is tell you notes you have at your disposal. You now have to use those notes—you have to choose which notes to employ and in what order.

Stable and Unstable Tones

Certain tones in the scale sound stronger or more stable than others. The strongest, most stable scale tone is, of course, the tonic. The weakest, least stable scale tone is the seventh—which is so unstable that it just begs to resolve up a half-step to the tonic. The other scale tones align themselves in a continuum between the tonic and the seventh, in this order:

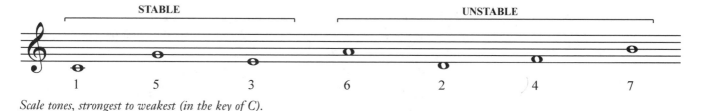

Scale tones, strongest to weakest (in the key of C).

Interestingly, the least stable tones (the fourth and the seventh) have half-step relationships to the most stable tones (the third and the tonic, respectively). Thus, one way to resolve the instability of these tones is to move a half-step to the closest stable tones—from the fourth to the third, or from the seventh to the tonic.

Other unstable tones tend to resolve downward to the next closest stable tone. The sixth resolves down (a whole step) to the fifth, and the second resolves down (a whole step) to the tonic. The resolution is always a diatonic step away, whether that's a whole step or a half-step.

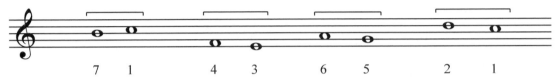

Resolving unstable scale tones.

In general, you want your melody to move from unstable to stable tones, especially at the end of a phrase. You probably don't want your melody to consist entirely of stable tones; that would be a little boring, with very little tension. (Instability creates tension.) So a melody might start unstable and move toward stability, or start stable, become unstable, and then regain stability. Unless you deliberately want to invoke unresolved tension, you want your melodic phrase to end on a stable note.

A short melody that starts unstable and becomes more stable.

Emphasizing Key Scale Tones

Beyond the concept of stable and unstable tones, it's important to note those scale tones that help to define the nature of the scale. Used properly, these tones can become target tones in your melody.

In a major scale, these are the three most important degrees:

◆ **Tonic.** You can't neglect the home tone of the scale. To emphasize the tonal center of a composition, start or (particularly) end your melody on the tonic note.

◆ **Third.** The third degree of the scale defines its harmonic nature—that is, whether the scale is major or minor. Emphasize the third to emphasize the color of the music.

◆ **Seventh.** The seventh degree of the scale is the leading tone; this note positions your melody for a return to the tonic. It also, along with the third, defines the major or minor (or dominant) nature of the scale. Emphasize the seventh to add tension to a melody.

The three key tones of the C major scale.

The important thing to remember is that not all notes of the scale are equally important. You need to choose a handful of notes to emphasize in your melody, and then use the other scale tones in subservience to these notes.

Implying Harmonies

Another factor to consider when choosing which notes of the scale to use is that of the underlying harmony, or chord progression. Even though we're not writing chords at this point, your note choices for the melody can help imply a given harmony.

The simplest way to see this is to base the main notes of your melody on the root notes of a given chord progression. This is particularly noticeable at the end of a phrase, where you might be leading into a perfect cadence (V-I chords). You can, for example, have the melody emphasize the fifth of the scale (to imply the V chord) and then resolve to the tonic of the scale (to imply the I chord). If this is a little heavy-handed for you, use the seventh of the scale instead of the fifth (this implies the third of the V chord), and then resolve this to the tonic (to imply the I chord). Another variation is to use the fourth of the scale (implying the seventh of the V7 chord) and resolve it to third of the scale (implying the third of the I chord). You get the picture.

A melody that implies a V-I perfect cadence (in the final two measures).

You don't have to limit this technique to the ends of phrases. The main notes of your melody can be chosen throughout to imply all the underlying chords. In fact, the best melodies imply distinct chord progressions—and make it easy for you to harmonize the melodies, when the time comes.

Using Step-Wise and Skip-Wise Motion

When you base your melody on the notes of a scale, you can move up or down the notes in any given order. Of course, if all the notes do is go up or down in strict consecutive order, then your melody sounds just like someone playing a scale exercise—because that's what you wrote!

Tip

Although writing diatonically is the easiest way to approach a composition, you don't have to limit yourself to the notes of the underlying scale. Learn more about using chromatic tones in Chapter 16.

This is why, in most cases, you want to avoid strict scalar movement in your melodies. A better approach is to vary the intervals between the notes of the melody. Some notes can move up or down to the next scale tone, but others should employ larger intervals, of a third or more. The upshot is that you need to employ a mixture of *step-wise* and *skip-wise* motion.

Step-wise motion is just as it sounds. You move from one note to the next note one step away in the scale. So, in the C major scale, step-wise motion moves from C to D to E and so on (or, going in the other direction, from C to B to A and so on). When you run the notes of a scale, you employ step-wise motion.

An example of a step-wise melody.

Skip-wise motion employs larger intervals. Instead of moving in smooth steps, you skip from one note to the next, in intervals of a third or more. For example, in the C major scale, a skip-wise melody might skip from C to E to G, or from C to F to A, or from C to G to B—up or down, or in some combination of direction.

An example of a skip-wise melody.

Step-wise melodies are smoother sounding than the alternative. Skip-wise melodies are more angular. To create the most interesting melodies, you should vary your lines between step-wise and skip-wise motion.

Tip

You don't have to limit your melodies to intervals of a third or less. Feel free to introduce larger leaps in your lines—fourths, fifths, even sixths or sevenths. It's even okay to include the occasional jump of an octave or more. Just remember, the larger the leap, the more distinctive it sounds—and the more attention it draws to itself. Large leaps are best used sparingly and for dramatic effect.

Remember the Structure

In Chapter 5, you were introduced to the concept of musical structure. You should definitely keep structure in mind when you're constructing your melodies. Most melodies are constructed of two- or four-measure phrases.

Longer melodies combine several shorter phrases into 8- or 16-measure phrases. Until you become more adept at your craft, you should avoid the construction of odd-measure phrases. It's not that you can't build three-, five-, or seven-measure phrases; it's that these types of asymmetrical phrases are slightly more difficult to work with. Make sure you know what you're doing before you extend a four-measure melody into a five-measure phrase.

The Least You Need to Know

◆ Most melodies are based on the notes of a specific scale or mode.

◆ Different scales and modes have different sounds; which you choose affects the sound and mood of your composition.

◆ You can create a melody with the notes of a scale by paying attention to stable and unstable tones, key scale tones (the tonic, the third, and the seventh), and tones that imply underlying harmonies.

◆ Create more interesting melodies by using a mixture of step-wise and skip-wise motion.

Exercises

Exercise 6-1

Write four- or eight-measure melodies based on the notes of the following scales and modes:

> a: F major
>
> b: E natural minor
>
> c: G pentatonic (in the key of C major)
>
> d: C whole tone
>
> e: G diminished
>
> f: D blues
>
> g: C bebop
>
> h: A Dorian
>
> i: F Lydian
>
> j: D Mixolydian

Exercise 6-2

Write an eight-measure melody in B♭ major that moves from stable to unstable to stable tones.

Exercise 6-3

Write a series of eight-measure melodies in F major that imply the following chord progressions:

a: I-IV-I-V7

b: I-vi-IV-V

c: I-vi-ii-V7

d: ii7-V7-I

e: IV-V-IV-I

Exercise 6-4

Write an eight-measure melody in G major that uses primarily step-wise motion.

Exercise 6-5

Write an eight-measure melody in E♭ major that uses primarily skip-wise motion.

Chapter 7

Working With a Melodic Outline

In This Chapter

- ◆ Building a melodic outline from structural tones
- ◆ Choosing structural tones from chord tones, key scale tones, and stable/unstable scale tones
- ◆ Approaching and connecting structural tones
- ◆ Embellishing structural tones with neighboring tones
- ◆ Working outside the major scale

Not all melodies spring to life fully formed. One approach to melody writing is to start with a *melodic outline*—the harmonic equivalent of a skeletal framework, using only the most important tones in the melody. Then you can put flesh on the bone, so to speak, by elaborating on this melodic outline, using approach notes, passing tones, neighboring tones, and the like. It's a good way to create the shape of your melodies in macro, before you add the important details.

Deconstructing a Melody

Most melodies consist of a mixture of notes, some more important than others. The most important notes define the shape of the melody and often its harmonic structure. If you strip all the less important notes from the melody, what you're left with is the skeleton of the piece—the melodic outline—that you can build on in any number of ways.

The notes of the melodic outline are called *structural tones* because they shape the overall structure of the melody. Determining a melody's structural tones is often as simple as listening for the primary pitch within each measure. This note is, more often than not, either the first note of or the longest note within the measure. This isn't a hard-and-fast rule, of course; some measures might have more than one structural tone, and some melodies might stretch structural tones over two or more measures. The important point is to listen for the base tone changes—not each individual note, mind you, but those essential tones that define the melody.

Let's look at a real-world example of a melodic outline, starting from the structural tones on up. Here's a simple melody that has been reduced to a single structural tone per measure:

The outline of a familiar melody.

Sound familiar? Maybe, maybe not; while the structural tones provide a flavor of the finished melody, the other (currently missing) notes also play an important part. So let's flesh out this melodic outline with a few subsidiary notes— let's call them "lesser" structural tones:

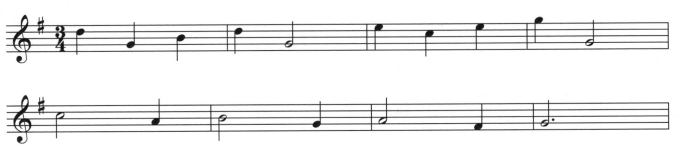

The same melodic outline, with some "lesser" structural tones added.

Still can't figure out the tune? Then let's put in all the connecting and embellishing notes:

The fully embellished melody—recognize it now?

That's right, all this time you've been listening to J. S. Bach's "Minuet in G," from its skeletal melodic outline to the fully formed final version. See how it works?

With the Bach melody, structural tones drove the melodic outline, although the final melody also contained numerous embellishing notes—in fact, it's the embellishing notes that gave this melody its distinctive signature. But some melodies are pretty much nothing but structural tones, as you can see from the next example. Recognize it?

The outline of a familiar operatic melody.

Add just a few embellishing notes, and you have the main melody from Richard Wagner's "Ride of the Valkyries." Pretty easy!

The full melody from "Ride of the Valkyries."

Composing a Melody—Structural Tones First

There are many benefits to composing from an initial melodic outline. Perhaps the most significant advantage is that the melodic outline lets you shape the melody (and the implied harmony) in general terms, without bogging you down in the details. Once you get the general form of the melody down in writing, you can sweat the details and "fill in the blanks" between the structural tones. And, as important as the structural tones are, it's the details that help to make a melody unique.

With that in mind, let's examine how you can build a melody using the melodic outline approach. The first step? Choosing the most important notes.

Chord Tones

In many, if not most, melodies, the structural tones are picked from the tones of the underlying chord structure. This makes sense; the chord structure defines the harmonic nature of a composition, and you want your melody to imply and reinforce those harmonies.

If you're pulling structural tones from a chord, you have three or more tones to work with. Each of these tones imparts a slightly different flavor to a melody:

◆ **Root.** Although you can use a root tone anywhere in the melody, it's most often used at either the very beginning or very end of a melodic phrase. The root is especially effective at the end of a phrase, when it's hard to beat the finality of a chord's root note. The root note plays an important role in the harmony throughout a song as well and is always good when you need to release any tension you build in a melodic line.

- **Third.** Just as the third of the chord defines its harmonic nature (major or minor), emphasizing the third in a melody helps to emphasize the composition's underlying harmony. The third is particularly powerful when moving from a major to a minor chord, or vice versa; using consecutive thirds in a melody reinforces the major-to-minor change.

- **Fifth.** Of all the available chord tones, the fifth is probably the least harmonically important. A melody totally centered on the fifth of the chords rings a bit hollow, without much of a harmonic center. For that reason, you probably want to avoid overuse of the fifth, especially at the ends of melodic phrases.

- **Extensions.** You can create a very sophisticated melody by emphasizing the extended notes of a chord, in particular sevenths and ninths. (Sixths and elevenths are also good, if you want to go there.) A melody based in these upper extremities of the harmony can sound light and airy; by deliberately not emphasizing the underlying harmony, extended-note melodies have a more contemporary sound, in any musical setting.

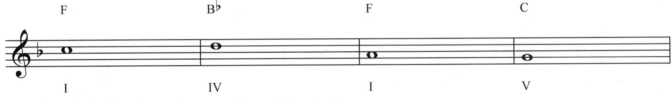

A melodic outline built on the primary notes of the underlying chords.

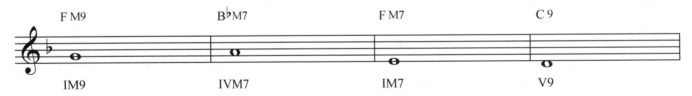

A melodic outline built on chord extensions.

Warning

You don't want to build a melodic outline that includes only the roots of the underlying chords. Although a single chord tone outline would definitely describe the chord progression, that's all it would do; there won't be much melodic interest beyond that. You want to avoid melodic outlines (and complete melodies) that do nothing more than follow a chord progression. A good melody is more than simple chord movement!

Key Scale Tones

An alternate approach to using chord tones for your melodic outline is to use the most important tones of the underlying scale. As you learned in Chapter 6, the most important tones in a major scale are the tonic, third, and seventh because they define the harmonic nature of the scale and (in the case of the seventh) function as a leading tone back to the tonic. Although you probably don't want to construct a melody that centers only on these three tones, you can use them in prominent places within your melody.

root   third   root   seventh

A melodic outline built on the tonic, third, and seventh of the scale.

Stable and Unstable Scale Tones

In Chapter 6, you also learned about stable and unstable tones, the theory being that stable tones are harmonically the strongest tones in the scale. The three most stable tones in a major scale are (in order) the tonic, fifth, and third. You should use these stable tones at key points in your melody, especially at beginnings and ends of major phrases.

You can use the less stable tones of the scale to introduce tension at the ends of subsidiary phrases or in the middle of phrases. When you introduce an unstable tone, make sure to resolve it (either immediately or over the course of a few measures) to the nearest stable tone. For example, if you introduce the seventh of the scale as a structural tone, the next structural tone should probably be the tonic of the scale—thus resolving the unstable seventh to the stable tonic.

stable   stable   unstable   stable

A short melodic framework built on the use of stable and unstable scale tones.

Tip

When you're creating a melodic outline, make sure that the structural tones themselves flow naturally from one to another in a melodic fashion. However you choose them, select those structural tones that sound best to your ears. Your melodic outline should be capable of functioning as a freestanding melody, before you add any embellishing notes. Let your ears be your guide; write a melodic outline with a pleasing shape and flow, one that makes harmonic sense. When your melodic outline is hummable, you have the basis for a truly memorable melody!

Working Toward—and Connecting—the Structural Tones

When you've used structural tones to construct a melodic outline, it's time to play "connect the dots." That is, you have to add the necessary subsidiary notes between these structural tones, to create a fully fleshed-out melodic line.

There are two primary approaches to adding subsidiary notes to your melodic outline. The first approach focuses on those notes leading up to or connecting the structural tones; the second approach emphasizes embellishment of the structural tones. We'll address the first approach first, with the use of approach notes and passing tones.

Approach Notes

You can write a structural tone as the very first note in a musical phrase, or you can lead up to that note gradually, using one or more subsidiary tones. The concept of leading up to a structural tone has appeal, in that it lets you approach the note gradually, kind of the way an approach ramp to an interstate highway lets a car get up to speed before entering traffic. Done correctly, it's a smooth and gentle way to introduce a structural tone.

> **Note**
>
> Approach notes are sometimes called *pickup notes*.

The notes that lead to a structural tone are called approach notes because they help you "approach" that note musically. Approach notes are typically a single scale step away from the structural tone and can approach from either above or below.

A melody consisting of single approach notes leading to the structural tones.

> **Note**
>
> Approach notes don't have to be part of the underlying scale; you can use chromatic approach notes that move in pure half-steps toward the main note. Learn more in the "Chromatic Neighbors" section, later in this chapter.

The approach doesn't have to be right next door to the structural tone, however. If the approach note is more than a step away from the structural tone—that is, if it's a *non-neighboring approach note*—the two notes should have some sort of strong harmonic relationship. That might mean any of the following:

♦ Any note from within the underlying major scale

♦ If you're working with an alternate scale, such as a pentatonic or blues scale, a note from within that scale

♦ A neighboring note from within the underlying chord

♦ A note that harmonically leads to the structural tone, such as the dominant note a fifth above (or a fourth below)

The same melody, with non-neighboring approach notes.

In addition to the traditional single approach note, you can also create multiple approach note runs. The approach note run must be strictly linear, using step-wise motion within the underlying scale. For example, to lead down to a note with four sixteenth-note approach notes, you start four steps above the structural tone and run down one scale step at a time, like this:

The previous melody, this time with approach note runs leading to the structural tones.

Passing Tones

Similar to approach notes are passing tones. Where approach notes lead into a structural tone, passing tones connect two structural tones. It's kind of a connect-the-dots methodology; instead of interval jumping between structural tones, you use passing tones to get from one note to the other more smoothly.

Tip

You can use as many passing tones between two structural tones as you need. That might mean a single passing tone or a multiple passing tone run. It's your choice.

If you're connecting two structural tones that have a small interval, you should try to smoothly bridge the gap between the two notes. For example, if the two notes are a third apart, use a single passing tone a diatonic second from each note. If the two main notes are a fourth apart, use the two passing tones that lie between them.

Using passing tones to bridge a small interval.

If you're connecting two structural tones that have a large interval, a single passing tone can be any of the scale notes between the two. If you want a smoother passage, use a multiple passing tone run in a scalar passage.

Moving up the scale with multiple passing tones to bridge a large interval.

Non-Neighboring Connecting Notes

When you're trying to connect two structural tones, you're not limited to using just the passing tones between the two notes. As with approach notes to a structural tone, you can also connect two structural tones with a non-neighboring connecting note.

The key here is to think of the connecting note as an approach note to the second structural tone. That means using a connecting note that has some sort of harmonic relationship to the second note. Of course, the connecting note must also follow naturally from the first structural tone. It's a bit of a challenge, but worth working at.

For example, you might want to use a connecting note that's dominant to the second structural tone—that is, either a fifth above or a fourth below. Let's say you're trying to connect two notes, the second of which is a third above the first. Instead of using the passing tone between the two notes, use a non-neighboring connecting note a fourth below the second structural tone. Because this note is just a single step below the first structural tone, it flows nicely, while still maintaining the dominant harmonic relationship to the second structural tone. It's a smooth transition.

Connecting structural tones with non-neighboring notes.

Embellishing Structural Tones

Obviously, not all melodies use structural tones that last an entire measure. When you lead up to a structural tone, you don't have to stay there; you can elaborate on that main note in a variety of ways.

Repeated Notes

Harmonically, the easiest way to embellish a structural tone is not to change it at all, and instead to write a rhythmic embellishment. This means repeating that structural tone, in some sort of interesting rhythm. (With this approach, you don't have to worry about clashing harmonies!)

Repeating a structural tone.

Neighboring Tones

A more interesting way to embellish a structural tone is to move the pitch around a little. The most common method is to use what is called a *neighboring tone* after the first instance of the structural tone.

You create a neighboring tone by starting on the main pitch, moving up or down by a step (diatonically or chromatically), and then returning to the original pitch; the neighboring tone is the one that "neighbors" the original note.

Creating a more elaborate melody with neighboring tones.

You can vary the effect of the neighboring tone by using different rhythmic patterns. A fast neighboring-tone pattern almost sounds like an affectation or slow trill or turn; a slower neighboring-tone pattern can actually mask the effect, sounding more like a "lesser" structural tone.

The same neighboring-tone approach, but with an extended rhythmic pattern.

Changing Tones

A *changing-tone* pattern is a two-note pattern that functions like a neighboring tone. This embellishing figure uses a combination of upper and lower neighboring tones to surround the structural tone, like this:

A melody embellished by a changing-tone pattern.

You can use changing tones both as elaborations of a structural tone and as leading notes to that tone. The leading note application places the changing tones before the structural tone instead of after it.

A changing-tone pattern placed before a structural tone.

Working Outside the Major Scale

Depending on the type of music you're writing, you may not want to limit yourself to using approach, passing, and neighboring tones from the underlying major or minor scale. You can create more interesting melodies by taking your neighboring notes from different types of scales.

Chromatic Neighbors

One somewhat common approach, especially when working with single approach notes or neighboring tones, is to employ the use of chromatic notes. In particular, this means using the neighboring note that's a half-step away from the structural tone, even if that note doesn't fall within the underlying scale.

For example, if you're in the key of C major and your structural tone is a G, you can lead up to that note with an F# approach note—not part of the C major scale. Similarly, you can add an A♭ as a neighboring tone—again, a note that isn't part of the C major scale. It's an interesting sound that may or may not fit within your composition's harmonic structure; let your ears be the judge.

Using chromatic approach notes and neighboring tones.

Neighbors from Different Scales

Another interesting approach is to work with approach notes and neighboring tones from a scale other than the expected major scale. For example, if you're writing a jazz or blues composition, you can use the notes from the underlying blues scale. Or, for a really unique sound, you can use only those notes from within the underlying pentatonic scale. By using approach notes and neighboring tones in this fashion, you work to reinforce the unique harmony of the chosen nontraditional scale.

Using approach notes and neighboring tones from the blues scale.

Using approach notes and neighboring tones from the pentatonic scale.

The Least You Need to Know

♦ The most important tones in a melody are called structural tones.

♦ You can build a melodic outline from structural tones and then fill in the detail with the necessary subsidiary notes.

♦ The structural tones of a melody can be based on chord tones, key scale tones, or stable scale tones.

♦ Subsidiary notes that lead up to a structural tone are called approach notes; subsidiary notes that connect two structural tones are called passing tones.

♦ You can embellish a structural tone with repeated notes, neighboring tones, or two-note changing tone patterns.

♦ Approach notes and neighboring tones don't have to be from the underlying major scale; they can also be chromatic (a half-step away) or from a nontraditional scale, such as the blues or pentatonic scales.

Exercises

Exercise 7-1

Identify the structural tones in the following melodies:

Exercise 7-2

Create melodic outlines based on the following chord progressions, using combinations of chord tones, key scale tones, and stable/unstable tones:

a:	A	F#m	Bm	D	E7		
b:	F	Gm	B♭	C			
c:	G	C	Am	D7			
e:	Dm	C	Dm	F	Dm	C	Dm G
f:	B♭	E♭M7	Adim	Dm7	Gm	Cm7	F7

Exercise 7-3

Add approach notes (in the form of quarter notes) to the following melodic outlines:

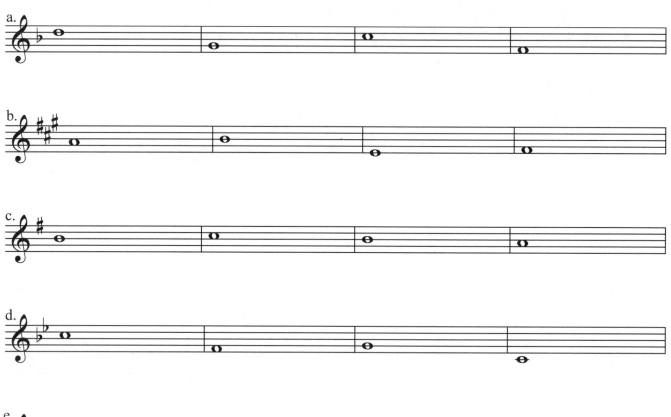

Exercise 7-4

Add passing notes and passing note runs between the notes in the following melodic outlines:

a.

b.
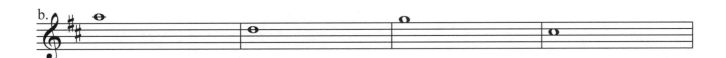

c.

d.

e.

Exercise 7-5

Embellish the following melodic outlines with repeated notes, neighboring tones, and changing-tone patterns:

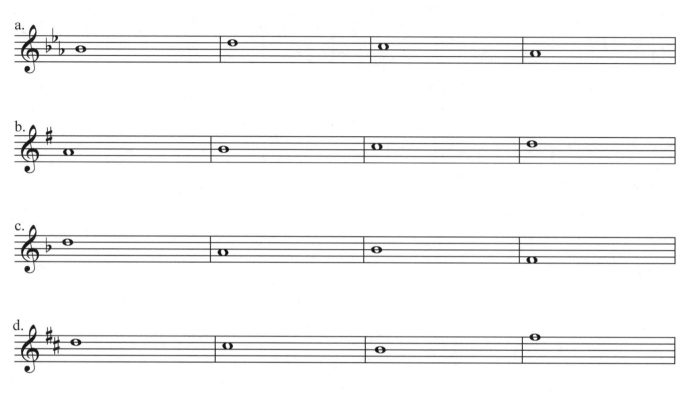

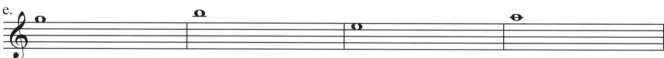

Chapter 8

Using Rhythm and Syncopation

In This Chapter

- Learn how to change the rhythmic pace of a melody
- Embellish a simple rhythmic pattern with repeated notes
- Add more rhythmic interest with syncopation
- Use back and front phrasing to move a melody frontward and backward in time
- Develop interesting rhythmic motifs

To this point, we've focused on the tonal aspects of a composition's melody. But a melody is more than just a series of pitches; those pitches exist in time and space, based on a particular rhythm. To that end, the rhythm of a melody is every bit as important as its tones.

Although some melodies sound just fine with a series of simple, straight rhythms, other melodies are defined by their interesting rhythmic natures. Instead of flowing smoothly from one note to another, all of the same length, a melody might slow down and speed up, stop a bit and then start up at a different pace, or avoid putting a note on the downbeat and instead place a note or two where you least expect them. That's the nature of rhythm; it defines the pace of your composition.

Changing the Rhythmic Pace

One way to make a melody more rhythmically interesting is to simply change the length of the notes. More often than not, shorter notes are more rhythmically interesting than longer ones; in general, longer notes have a more flowing legato feel, while shorter notes sound a bit choppier.

> **Note**
>
> When talking about rhythms, I assume you have a working familiarity with rhythmic notation—not only the various note and rest values, but also dotted notes, ties, and all the other building blocks of complex rhythms and syncopations. If you don't, then read up on rhythm in my companion book, *The Complete Idiot's Guide to Music Theory.*

As an example, let's look at the following excerpt from a simple melody. It's nothing more than a structural tone embellished with a neighboring tone.

A rhythmically simple phrase.

Now, there are many ways to vary the rhythmic pace of this phrase. If we want to keep a slower pace but move away from the straight quarter-note pacing, we can substitute a dotted-quarter-note pattern, like this:

The same melody, with a dotted-quarter-note feel.

For a slightly more syncopated effect (and we'll get to syncopation in a moment), we can put the neighboring tone on the upbeat of 1 instead and lengthen it. This is actually the rhythmically inverse of the previous example, as you can see:

The same melody, with the neighboring tone off the beat.

To speed up the rhythmic pace, all we have to do is turn the first two notes into eighth notes and move the concluding structural tone to the second beat as a dotted half note, like this:

Speeding up the rhythmic pace.

As you can see, you can make numerous variations without altering a single tone in the melody. All the changes come in the rhythm, and each variation creates a distinctive melodic line.

Let's take another example, this one of four straight quarter notes followed by a whole note—a nice legato phrase, but definitely rhythmically uninteresting.

Another rhythmically simple phrase, all quarter notes.

We can alter the rhythm of this phrase in a number of ways. In order, we can (a) speed up the pace by using eighth notes instead of quarter notes; (b) speed up the first part of the phrase only; (c) speed up the second part of the phrase only; (d) speed up the middle of the phrase only; (e) back-load the notes in the phrase, turning them into approach notes to the final note; and (f) put all the quarter notes on the offbeat, giving a very syncopated feel. There are more possible variations, of course, but this gives you an idea of what's possible and how the rhythmic changes dramatically alter the flavor the melody.

Six rhythmic variations on the previous melody.

Smooth or Choppy?

The length of the notes in your melody are also important. Two notes can both fall on the same beat, but if one is a half note and one is an eighth note, they'll sound different. (Or they should, if played properly.)

To that end, it's important to determine whether you want your melody to sound smooth or choppy. To create a smooth melody, use longer notes so that there isn't much (if any) free space between notes. To create a choppy melody, use shorter notes and insert rests between the notes.

Tip

You can also make a smoother melody by using legato markings across a phrase, or make a choppier melody by applying staccato markings to individual notes.

Here's an example of a melody that can be either smooth or choppy. The first instance is the smooth one, with nice long notes at the end of each rhythmic phrase. The second instance sounds choppier because the final note of each phrase is made shorter.

A melody with few notes written smoothly.

The same melody with the same basic notes, broken into choppier phrases.

Embellishing the Rhythm

Another way to vary the rhythm of the melody is to add notes to the basic rhythm, in the form of either repeated notes or embellishing notes.

Adding Repeated Notes

The simplest way to make a series of long notes more interesting is to chop the longer notes into shorter ones. This means adding a series of repeated notes to the phrase—notes that stay on the same pitch but fill up additional rhythmic space.

This technique is really easy to apply. Let's start with a melody that consists of several long notes—half notes and whole notes. As is, it's a very slow-paced melody:

A slow-paced melody with lots of long notes.

Now, in place of that long whole note in the third measure, let's substitute four staccato quarter notes, on the same pitch. This approach makes a static melody more dynamic, adding movement where there wasn't much.

The same melody, but with shorter notes replacing one of the long notes.

Want to spice it up even more? Then replace the straight quarter notes with a series of repeated notes in a more interesting rhythm, like this:

Our original melody, but with the repeated notes in an interesting rhythmic pattern.

You can use this technique with any longish note. You can substitute halves and quarters for whole notes, quarters for half notes, eighths for quarter notes, and even sixteenth notes for quarters or eighth notes.

Adding Embellishing Notes

To avoid having too many repeating notes in a melodic phrase, consider using extra melodic notes in a new rhythmic pattern. That's right, we're talking about the use of approach notes, passing notes, and neighboring tones, as first discussed in Chapter 7. These melodic embellishments allow you to add both rhythmic and melodic interest to an otherwise static melody.

Warning

Overuse of repeated notes tends to make for a tonally uninteresting line. Even as you're adding rhythmic interest, you're still stuck with the original slow-paced tonal pattern.

For example, let's start with this extremely boring little melody:

A slow-paced, melodically uninteresting melody.

Although we could improve this melody with a few repeated notes, let's instead introduce some new melodic interest by adding approach notes and approach-note phrases in front of some of the longish notes—but in an interesting rhythm:

The original melody embellished by approach notes, passing tones, and new rhythmic patterns.

Another strategy uses neighboring tones instead of approach notes, again in an interesting rhythm:

Another variation, this time with neighboring tones and new rhythmic patterns.

As you can see, both of these variations sound completely different from the original melody—both rhythmically and tonally.

Employing Syncopation

A more dramatic approach to rhythmic variation involves the use of syncopation. If you remember your music theory, syncopation is the art of playing a note where it's not expected, or of not playing a note where it *is* expected. The use of syncopation enables you to take a "smooth" melody and make it more angular, by turning straight quarters and eighths into syncopated rhythms.

How do you syncopate a rhythm? Simple—by taking a quarter note that's on a beat and placing it on the off-beat, or by taking straight eighths and placing them on the "e" and the "ah" of the beat.

Let's look at a few examples. Our first melody, as you can see, is all quarter notes. Nice and smooth, but more than a bit boring.

A melody composed of smooth quarter notes.

We can make this melody more rhythmically interesting by displacing several of the quarter notes—putting them on the "and" of the beat instead of on the downbeat, as shown here:

The same melody, syncopated.

Here's another melody, this one with a lot of straight eighth notes. Syncopate the eighth notes, and you get a more interesting and contemporary-sounding rhythmic pattern:

A straight eighth-note melody.

Use syncopation to create a contemporary-sounding rhythm.

> **Warning**
>
> The use of complex syncopation can make a piece harder to play. For some reason, many musicians (percussionists excepted) have more trouble reading rhythms than they do reading pitches. Keep this in mind when you employ more sophisticated rhythmic patterns in your compositions.

Moving the Melody Forward and Backward in Time

A more extreme form of syncopation literally displaces the entire melodic line—often across bar lines. When you start a melody after its natural starting point, the technique is called *back phrasing*; when you start a melody before you expect to hear it, it's called *front phrasing*.

Back Phrasing

To back-phrase a melodic phrase, you write the melody notes as starting later than expected. This creates a dramatic tension because the listener is waiting for the melody, but you hold it back—and then release the tension when the melody finally starts, a beat or so later than expected.

For example, let's assume that the first note of the melody sounds like it should begin on beat 1 of the first measure. This is a good assumption because many melodies start on beat 1, like this:

> **Note**
>
> Back and front phrasing are techniques employed by many jazz improvisers. You can find out what other improvisation techniques apply to composition in my companion book, *The Complete Idiot's Guide to Solos and Improvisation* (Alpha Books, 2004), available wherever fine books are sold.

The original melody, starting on beat 1 of the first measure.

To back-phrase this portion of the melody, you might insert a rest on the first beat of the measure and then start the melody on the second beat. You would then adjust the rhythm of the melody to end the musical phrase in the correct place.

The previous melody, with back phrasing.

Tip

The more you back-phrase, the shorter those notes of the melody that you held back. You also have the option of dropping some notes out of the held-back melody; this is more common with heavy back phrasing, where you might not have enough space to throw in all the embellishing notes of the melody.

Front Phrasing

The opposite of back phrasing is front phrasing. In front phrasing, you start a melodic line before where it might normally occur. In essence, front phrasing leads or anticipates the normal flow of the melody. Instead of starting the melody on beat 1, for example, a front-phrased melody might start on beat 4 of the previous measure. You then have to stretch a note or two to get the melody back on its normal track.

The previous melody, front-phrased to start one beat early.

Tip

For a more syncopated effect, you can start the melody on the upbeat before the expected first note—the "and" of 4 in the previous measure. If you continue this front-phrase syncopation throughout the rest of the phrase, the melody will anticipate the normal flow of the notes by half a beat throughout.

Developing Rhythmic Themes and Variations

Another use of rhythm in a composition is to create short rhythmic motifs. These are similar to melodic motifs but are dependant solely on rhythm, not on tones. By assigning different tones to different instances of a rhythmic motif, you help to unify various sections of a melodic phrase or composition.

We talk more about themes and variations of all sorts in Chapter 13, but let's take a quick look at how a rhythmic motif might work. First, your rhythmic motif has to have a distinctive and interesting rhythm; a group of four half notes is probably not distinctive or interesting enough to qualify. The motif doesn't have to be syncopated (think of the four-note rhythmic motif in Beethoven's Symphony no. 5—it's syncopation-free), but it does have to be memorable.

Beethoven's "fate" motif from the Fifth Symphony—a great example of a simple rhythmic motif.

For our example, we'll use this simple four-note phrase:

A simple four-note rhythmic motif.

Now look at how this rhythmic motif is used over the course of a longer musical phrase. Even though the tones of the melody change, the rhythm stays the same—thus lending a sense of unity to the piece.

Our rhythmic motif, used throughout a melodic phrase.

The key point to remember is that you have more than just structural tones at your disposal. Rhythm is equally important to tonality and harmony; the use of rhythm is one of the most important compositional tools available.

The Least You Need to Know

- The use of rhythm is essential to developing unique melodic lines and compositions.
- The rhythmic pace of a melody is determined by the length and rhythm of the notes chosen.
- Simple rhythms can be embellished with repeated notes and rhythmic patterns that use approach and neighboring notes.
- You can add even more rhythmic interest by employing the technique of syncopation—playing melodic notes where they're not expected.
- To displace the entire melodic line, play it a beat or two earlier (front phrasing) or later (back phrasing) than expected.
- To unify tonally different parts of a melodic line or composition, create a rhythmic motif that repeats throughout.

Exercises

Exercise 8-1

Using a variety of different note pacings, create five rhythmic variations of the following melodic phrase:

Exercise 8-2

Using repeated notes and embellishing phrases, create five rhythmic variations of the following melodic phrase:

Exercise 8-3

Using the technique of syncopation, create five rhythmic variations of the following melodic phrase:

Exercise 8-4

Back-phrase and front-phrase the following melodic phrase:

Exercise 8-5

Use the following rhythmic motif to create an eight-measure melody, in the key of F major.

Chapter 9

Shaping a Melody

In This Chapter

◆ Examining the overall shape of a melody

◆ Using various types of melodic contours

◆ Combining shapes for a longer melody

◆ Working toward a melodic climax

◆ Creating both smooth and disjunct melodies

A good melody has a distinct shape. As it moves from start to finish, it goes in a particular direction—up or down, or maybe up *and* down, in an arch or inverted arch. And it moves in that direction either smoothly or in ragged steps—its movement is either smooth or disjunct.

When constructing a melody, it's important to plan an appropriate combination of contour and movement. A melody with the wrong contour won't convey the correct impression; for example, if you want an uplifting melody, you shouldn't utilize a descending contour. Similarly, you want the movement of your melody to reflect the overall tone of your composition; you wouldn't compose a lyrical ballad with lots of disjunct movement. This is why melodic shape is important.

Examining Melodic Shape

Before we start shaping our own melodies, let's take a quick look at how contour and movement works in the real world. As you'll soon see, most melodies can be distinguished by their unique contours and movements.

To examine melodic shape, we'll create a graph of the individual notes of a melody. The graph essentially describes pitch over time.

The first melody we'll examine is Bach's "Minuet in G," which we first looked at in Chapter 7. As you can see, the melody has a contour that looks a little like an arch—it rises from its initial point to peak about a third of the way through, then it descends from there. Movement-wise, the first half of the melody is a little ragged, with a mixture of scalar steps and some large interval leaps, but the second half is much smoother, moving mainly in step-wise motion.

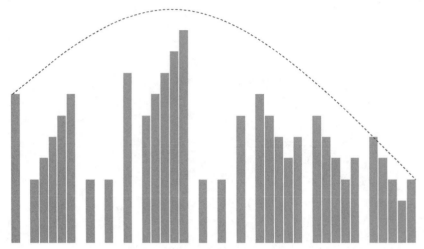

A shape analysis of Bach's "Minuet in G"—an arch contour.

Now let's look at the other melody we discussed in Chapter 7, Wagner's "Ride of the Valkyries." Like the Bach melody, this one also has an arch contour, with a peak a little past the midway point. The melodic movement is less smooth than with the Bach melody, with the movement somewhat ragged throughout.

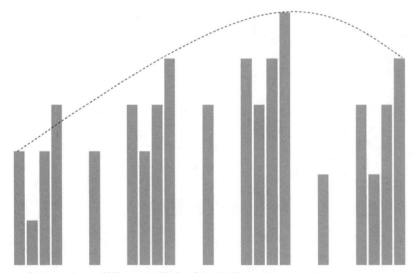

A shape analysis of Wagner's "Ride of the Valkyries"—an arch contour.

This type of analysis can be applied to any type of melody, in any genre. As an example, let's move to the popular song and look at the shape of Jerome Kern's "The Way You Look Tonight." Notice anything familiar? That's right, it's the same old arch shape, this one peaking about two thirds of the way through. The melodic movement is fairly smooth, with only a single large leap (an octave!) just after the climax.

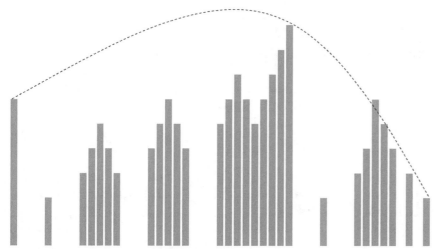

A shape analysis of Jerome Kern's "The Way You Look Tonight"—an arch contour.

Not all melodies have the same contour, of course. Some melodies have either a descending or an ascending melodic line. For example, the verse of Van Morrison's "Moondance" ends a minor third lower than it starts (after the pickup notes). Although there's step-wise movement in between, the general contour is a simple descending line; it doesn't rise and fall, as a melody with an arch contour would.

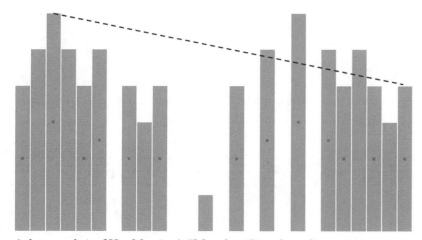

A shape analysis of Van Morrison's "Moondance"—a descending contour.

What does this kind of shape analysis tell us? First and foremost, it points out how important it is for a melody to have a direction—whatever direction that might be. And it's also important to take an interesting route in getting to where the melody eventually goes. Melodies with little or no movement, whatever the contour, are often quite boring.

Choosing a Melodic Contour

There are many different types of melodic contours, but we'll focus our attention on five of the most common shapes—arch, inverted arch, ascending, descending, and stationary. Which shape you use depends on the type of melody you're writing and the way it's employed within your composition.

Arch

The first melodic contour is the one we've already examined, the arch. In an arch-shape melody, the highest notes come somewhere near the midway point—typically just a little afterward.

A melody with an arch contour.

Note that the arch doesn't have to be symmetrical. The starting and ending notes can be different pitches, and the peak of the arch doesn't have to be exactly halfway through the phrase. What's important is the general shape, moving up and then back down; the exact points of the arch are less defined.

Inverted Arch

The mirror image of the arch contour is the inverted arch. This is a melody that starts high, descends to a low point, and then rises again toward the end. This type of melody has an interesting feel, and the climax can come either at the bottom of the descent or at the very end of the line.

A melody with an inverted-arch contour.

Ascending

A melody with an ascending contour starts low and ends high. It's like an arch contour with no descent after the climax. It's an effective substitute for an arch shape, with a little more punch at the end.

A melody with an ascending contour.

Descending

Reverse the ascending contour, and you have a descending contour, which gives your melody a bit of a depressed or resigned feel. It's easy to construct: just start on your highest note and descend from there.

A melody with a descending contour.

Warning

The descending contour doesn't build to a climax as readily as the other shapes we've looked at.

Stationary

A melody with a stationary contour really doesn't go anywhere. The starting and ending notes are basically the same (they don't have to be exactly the same note, just close), and the notes in the middle aren't much higher or lower. As you might expect, this type of static melody typically has a lot of repeated notes.

A melody with a stationary contour.

Tip

When a stationary contour doesn't give your melody direction, there may be times when a hovering sensation is what you're looking for.

Combining Contours to Shape a Longer Melody

Each individual melodic phrase within a longer melody or composition can have its own distinct contour and movement. In fact, you probably want each phrase to be shaped slightly differently from surrounding phrases. That's because too many phrases with a similar shape can get monotonous.

For example, if a long melody contains four individual phrases that all move downward, the effect is one of perpetual resignation. Similarly, four phrases that all move upward sound as if you're shouting from the rooftops. Even four

Note

Learn more about planning longer structures in Chapter 12.

arch-shaped phrases in a row sound a little same-old, same-old. What you want is a sequence where the different shapes set each other off to their mutual advantage.

The other thing you have to keep in mind is the overall shape of the longer melody—that is, the shape formed from the combination of phrases. The contours of individual phrases combine to form the larger contour of the entire composition and thus have to be considered holistically.

Building Toward a Climax

The arch contour's popularity comes from its ability to generate a climax at its peak and then provide some moments of relaxation afterward. Before adding in dynamics, phrasing, orchestration, and so on, a line's climax is frequently the top of the contour, although this is by no means always the case. For example, many melodies drive all the way to the end of the line, even if this is at or near the bottom of a contour.

In most instances, however, the climax occurs about two thirds to three quarters of the way through the line. In general, you don't want to climax too soon, or everything following will be anticlimatic. It's musically satisfying to leave a little space for the melody to relax after it peaks.

Tip

For the reasons noted here, the large-scale arch contour has been money in the bank for Western composers for hundreds and hundreds of years. All composers should have it in their toolbox to use when appropriate.

When you're talking about using the arch controur for a longer melody—one composed of two or more shorter phrases—you want the contour to apply to the overall melody, not necessarily to each component phrase. For example, you may construct a long melody from four shorter phrases. Each phrase can (and should) have its own distinct contour, which may or may not be the arch shape. But when you analyze the entire melody, all four phrases worth, then you should see the arch contour take shape over the entire four-phrase melodic line.

So if you can plan it, you can get a lot of mileage out of the same general arch shape that Bach, Wagner, Kern, and numerous other composers have used. Start low, move gradually upward until you reach the peak, and then let it settle back down. It's a great way of letting your melodies breathe.

Planning a convincing climax will help intensify the listening experience and make your music more memorable. But you're not limited to just one large-scale climax in a piece. The build-up to (and coming down from) a large climax can be locally accented by small climaxes that keep the listener interested.

In planning climaxes both large and small, it's always key not to peak too soon or too late; somewhere toward the end but not at the very end is a good place to start. Ultimately, you'll want to listen over and over again until you yourself are musically convinced. Don't rest until it's right!

Establishing Melodic Movement

Beyond the overall contour of a melodic line, you also have to consider the smoothness of the melodic movement. In general, smooth movement results from the use of small intervals in step-wise motion; disjunct movement comes from the use of larger intervals in skip-wise motion.

Smooth Movement

A smooth melodic line is one that moves evenly from one point to another, typically in a scalar pattern without a lot of large leaps. Smooth melodies tend to sound more soothing and relaxing than a more disjuncted skip-wise melody.

As an example, let's look no further than Beethoven's main theme from his Symphony no. 9 ("Ode to Joy"), which is as smooth a melody as you're likely to find:

Beethoven's "Ode to Joy" theme from the Ninth Symphony.

Perform a shape analysis on this theme, and you see the smooth step-wise movement. (You also see a rather unusual descending contour for the larger melody, although each individual four-measure phrase uses the standard arch contour—and there are further mini arches every two measures!)

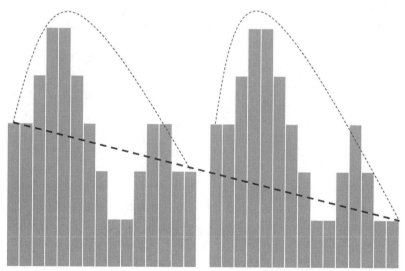

A shape analysis of the "Ode to Joy" theme.

> **Note**
>
> As lyrical as Beethoven's melody is, it has a range of only a perfect fifth—and contains several repeated notes. It shows what a master composer can do with just five notes!

As exemplified in the "Ode to Joy" theme, most smooth melodies use a lot of scalar patterns to get from one note to the next. This is easy enough if the melodic outline is fairly step-wise, but you can also create smooth movement from a disjunct melodic outline. When the structural tones are a fourth or more apart, you have to insert scalar passing tone patterns to get from one main tone to the next. The passing tones are used to smooth out the disjunct melodic outline.

A disjunct melodic outline, with structural tones separated by large intervals.

A melody based on this ragged melodic outline, fleshed out with scalar passing tone patterns to create a smoother melodic line.

Of course, you can also create a smooth melody by using structural tones that flow in a step-wise motion. When the structural tones are separated by a third or less, you don't have to insert too many passing tones to keep the smooth flow.

A melodic outline with structural tones separated by small intervals—a naturally smooth melody.

> **Note**
>
> The use of structural tones was first discussed in Chapter 7.

Disjunct Movement

Not all melodies are smooth, nor should they be. Many memorable melodies contain lots of skip-wise motion and relatively large leaps—often of a fifth or more. Listen to Burt Bacharach's "Alfie," for example, with its signature leap of a fifth on the title lyric—and even larger leaps afterward. This is not a smooth melody, as you can see by looking at the shape analysis.

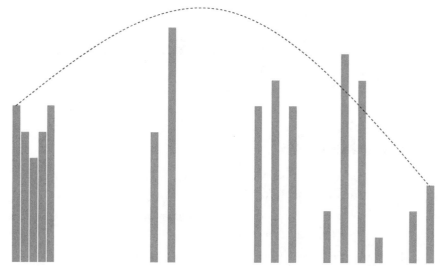

A shape analysis of Burt Bacharach's "Alfie."

A disjunct melody, especially one that covers a wide melodic range, takes skill to write well—although it can make up for what it lacks in simple lyricism by an added intensity. Large intervals provide a distinctive sound to any melody; it's often the large intervals that define a tune. Try it for yourself by composing a melody that consists only of intervals of a third or more—and emphasizing several larger leaps.

Mixed Movement

Of course, a melody doesn't have to be exclusively smooth or ragged; many notable melodies mix different step-wise and skip-wise movement to create maximum interest. Reflect back to Bach's "Minuet in G," for example, with its fourths, fifths, sixths, and octave leaps alongside its scalar runs. The mixture of large leaps and step-wise runs give the melody its unique flavor.

I keep returning to the quote from songwriter Jimmy Webb back in Chapter 5, where he said that a good melody is, effectively, both pleasant and unexpected. The pleasant part comes from smooth step-wise movement; the unexpected part comes from the large-interval leaps of skip-wise movement.

The craft of composition is full of these kinds of balancing acts. A melody can be primarily smooth and still contain some unexpected leaps. Likewise, you can create jagged melodies that employ some smoother step-wise motion. Use the occasional leap to add interest to a scalar melody; use the occasional scalar run to take the edge off a jittery skip-wise melody. A healthy mixture of rolling, scalar steps and dramatic leaps is a well-practiced way to achieve a satisfyingly singable yet stimulatingly surprising melody.

Note
Some musicians feel that the term "disjunct" is too pejorative, preferring the term *intervallic*, instead.

CAUTION Warning
Depending on the intervals used, a melody with lots of skip-wise motion can sometimes be difficult to sing or play, especially for less-skilled performers.

Disjointed:

Smooth:

A melody that mixes smooth and disjunct movement.

The Least You Need to Know

◆ Melodies have contours of specific shapes, including the arch, inverted arch, ascending, descending, and stationary contours.

◆ The arch shape is most common, often reaching a climax about two thirds or three quarters of the way through.

◆ Melodic movement can be either smooth (with lots of step-wise motion) or disjunct (with skip-wise motion).

◆ Many interesting melodies have some sort of mixed movement, with both smooth and disjunct elements.

◆ When shaping a longer melody, care should be taken to avoid repetitive shapes and motion; your music will often benefit from creating a larger climax for the entire piece.

Exercises

Exercise 9-1

Label the contours for the following melodies as either arch, inverted arch, ascending, descending, or stationary:

Exercise 9-2

Create melodies with the following contours:

      a: Arch

      b: Inverted arch

      c: Ascending

      d: Descending

      e: Stationary

Exercise 9-3

Label the melodic movement of the following melodies as either smooth, disjunct, or mixed:

Exercise 9-4

Create melodies that incorporate the following melodic movements:

    a: Smooth

    b: Disjunct

    c: Mixed (primarily disjunct with smooth elements)

    d: Mixed (primarily smooth with disjunct elements)

    e: Mixed (equally between smooth and disjunct)

Exercise 9-5

Create a 16-measure melody in the key of F major, composed of four individual 4-measure phrases. Make the first phrase smooth and arch-shaped, the second phrase smooth and descending, the third phrase disjunct and ascending, and the fourth phrase mixed and arch-shaped.

Building Tension and Release

In This Chapter

- ◆ Discover why tension is valuable in a composition
- ◆ Learn how to introduce tension via unstable tones and chords
- ◆ Find out which chords in a progression introduce the most tension, and why
- ◆ Discover how to introduce tension via suspended notes and chords
- ◆ Learn even more ways to introduce tension into a piece

Tension is a critical component of musical drama. It generates energy, interest, surprise, and suspense. Music without tension is like a life without any stress; relaxing, perhaps, but more than a little boring.

Of course, once you introduce an element of tension, you can't just leave things up in the air—you then have to decide how the tension will be resolved. (Or, sometimes, not resolved.) This concept of tension and release is extremely important to the art of composition, and that's what we'll examine in this chapter.

Why Tension Is Important

As I've noted before, a good melody or composition is like a good story—and good stories very often center around some sort of tension or conflict. If I were to tell you the story of how Little Red Riding Hood walked uneventfully to her grandmother's house and had a pleasant little picnic lunch, that wouldn't be much of a story. It's when you add in the tension and conflict resulting from the Big Bad Wolf that the story comes to life. The tension makes the story interesting.

In a way, tension in a story lends character and importance to the protagonist. By resolving the conflict, the protagonist earns our respect—and often changes for the better because of the struggle. Tension can define characters—and make them stronger.

It's the same thing with music. Tension can define the dramatic outline of a musical experience—make it more vivid and impactful. Music often needs to work its way through some sort of tension or conflict in order to prove its worth; the tension makes the music stronger. When a composition works through a period of tension, it becomes more powerful. The contrast between stability and tension makes for more interesting music.

How, then, does one introduce tension into a composition? There are many ways, as you'll soon discover—techniques that you can apply to an individual melody or to the structure of a larger composition.

Introducing Tension via Unstable Tones

Within a melody, one way to introduce tension is via the use of unstable tones. As you learned in Chapter 6, certain notes in the scale are less stable than others. Where the tonic and the dominant (fifth) are the most stable tones in the major scale, the fourth and the seventh are the least stable. Their instability lies, in part, in the fact that they're each a half-step away from a very stable tone—the fourth is a half-step away from the third of the scale, and the seventh is a half-step away from the tonic.

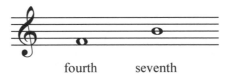

fourth   seventh

The two least stable tones in the C major scale—the fourth and the seventh.

When you use the fourth or seventh as a structural tone in a melody, you make the melody unstable—which creates tension. The listener wants the instability resolved; one's ears long for stability. So a tension exists until the unstable tones resolve to more stable tones.

One way to set up this tension is to end a short phrase on one of the unstable tones. When you start the next phrase with the nearest stable tone, the tension is resolved.

Introducing tension in a melody via an unstable tone.

You can also use unstable tones in the middle of melodic phrases. Just introduce the unstable tone at a natural pause, and then resolve to the nearest stable tone to release the tension.

Introducing Tension in a Chord Progression

Moving away from pure melody for a moment, another way to introduce tension is via the use of specific chords in a composition's harmony. There are two ways to do this.

The first is to pick up on the concept of stability/instability by using chords based on unstable scale tones—in particular, the IV and the vii° chords. Both chords are somewhat unstable in the underlying harmonic structure and want to resolve to more stable chords. The IV wants to resolve to either a V or I chord, and the vii° wants to resolve up a half-step to the I.

Introducing tension via an unstable IV chord.

Another, even more dramatic, approach is to use the dominant chord in the scale (the V chord). Even though it's built on a stable scale tone, the V chord introduces tremendous tension into any composition because it so strongly wants to lead to the tonic chord (I). Leave a phrase hanging on a V (or, even better, a V7), and listeners stay on the edge of their seats, waiting for the anticipated tonic.

Introducing tension via an unresolved dominant chord.

Introducing Tension via Dominant Seventh and Diminished Chords

While we're on the topic of dominant chords, any time you include a dominant seventh chord in a progression, that chord wants to resolve to whichever major chord is a perfect fifth below. This is obviously the case with the V7 (which wants to resolve to the I), but just sticking that minor seventh on top of any major chord makes it function as a temporary dominant chord.

> **Note**
>
> To refresh your memory, a dominant seventh chord is a major chord with a minor (or flatted) seventh, like this: 1-3-5-♭7.

For example, if you turn a standard IV chord into a IV7, that chord now wants to resolve to the major chord a perfect fifth below—which happens to be the nonscale ♭VII chord. If you turn a I chord into a I7, it wants to resolve down a perfect fifth to the IV chord. If you turn a ii chord into a II7 (by adding the diatonic seventh and raising the third), it wants to resolve down a perfect fifth to the V chord—and so on.

Resolving various dominant seventh chords, in the key of C.

Introducing tension via dominant seventh chords.

Another related phenomenon concerns diminished chords—a minor chord with a flatted fifth. Diminished chords, wherever they lie, want to resolve up a half-step to a major chord. You've already seen this with the vii° chord, which wants to resolve up a half-step to the I chord. Well, if you lower the fifth of any minor chord, you create a tension-filled diminished chord that wants to resolve up a half-step to whatever major chord you can build. So a iii° chord wants to resolve up a half-step to the IV chord, a ii° chord wants to resolve up a half-step to the nonscale ♭III chord, and a vi° chord wants to resolve up a half-step to the even stranger ♭VII chord. This is a very interesting way to both introduce tension into a line and change the harmonic nature of the composition.

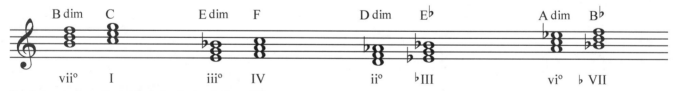

Resolving various diminished chords, in the key of C.

Introducing tension via a diminished chord.

Introducing Tension via Suspended Notes and Chords

Now let's look at how the melodic line and the underlying chords can combine to introduce tension into a piece. This is most often done via the use of suspended chords and by using the suspended note as a structural tone in the melody.

First, some theory about suspensions. A suspended chord temporarily shifts a note in the triad by a scalar step, typically upward. The most common type of suspension in Western music moves the normal major third of a major chord up a half-step to a perfect fourth. (That is, the fourth replaces the third.) We're so used to hearing a chord as a 1-3-5 triad that any change to this arrangement creates a powerful expectation for resolution. Resolving the fourth down to the third is very satisfying, but it's the delay of this gratification that is often the more memorable pleasure.

> **Note**
>
> When it's the fourth that's suspended, a suspended chord is sometimes called a suspended fourth chord, notated *sus4*.

For example, a C suspended chord that includes the notes C-F-G, instead of the expected C major triad of C-E-G, sets up a tension that is released when the F moves down to the E—which creates the normal C major triad.

A C suspended chord, resolving to a C major triad—the suspended note is the F (the fourth).

When you place that suspended note in the melody, you introduce a level of tension that is very powerful. Your ears want that fourth to resolve down a half-step to the third of the chord, and you sit on edge until that happens. The resolution is harmonically satisfying and lets your listeners breathe a little after the tension-filled passage. For maximum effect, make sure that you introduce the suspended note as a structural tone, not a passing or neighboring tone, (where it wouldn't have near the impact).

Introducing a suspension into the melody—and then resolving it.

A typical place to introduce—and resolve—this kind of tension is at the end of a melodic phrase. You can use the suspended chord to set up the desired end-of-phrase tension, and then get an end-of-phrase release by resolving the suspended chord to the normal major chord.

Other Ways to Introduce Tension into a Melody

There are several other ways to introduce tension into a melody. All of these methods are more subtle than the harmonic methods we've just discussed and, thus, won't have quite the dramatic impact.

Larger Intervals

Smoother melodies can sometimes reduce tension, which implies that more disjunct melodies can sometimes increase tension. When you introduce larger intervals (a fourth or more) into a melody—particularly one that has been primarily scalar to this point—you subtly increase the tension in a melody. To resolve the tension, simply return to a more step-wise melodic pattern.

Introducing tension via larger intervals in the melody.

Higher Pitches

Another subtle way to increase tension is to raise the overall pitch of the melody. This means writing higher and higher notes, with the most tension falling on the highest note in the melodic line. Resolve the tension by lowering the following notes.

Introducing tension via a rising melodic line.

Faster Rhythms

Tension isn't always associated with pitch; it can also be introduced via rhythmic techniques. One particularly effective technique is to increase the pace of the rhythms—that is, to use shorter notes, and more of them. As the melody becomes more rapid-fire, it exudes more tension. The tension is then resolved when you move back to a slower-paced rhythm, with longer notes.

Introducing tension via faster rhythms.

Increased Syncopation

Because listeners expect to hear rhythms on the beat, tension can also be introduced via the use of syncopation. The more syncopated a melody is—that is, the more the melody occurs on the upbeat, or between the beats—the more tension begins to build. You can resolve the tension by moving the melody back to the downbeat.

Introducing tension via syncopation.

Increased Volume

Volume also affects tension. Just as when someone raises their voice in excitement or anger, an increase in volume can drive musical tension. The climax comes at the loudest point of the crescendo; tension is resolved by bringing down the volume.

Introducing tension via volume.

Reduced Repetition

> **Note**
>
> Yet another way to introduce tension into a melody or composition is to use chromatic notes and chords. Learn more in Chapter 16.

The more restless a melody, the more tension-filled it becomes. This restlessness is created by making the melody less predictable, typically by reducing the repetition of familiar motifs and figures. As the piece progresses, the listener hears less and less of what he knows, thus increasing the tension. To resolve this tension, simply reintroduce the main theme or a familiar motif; in this instance, repetition breeds relief.

Introducing tension via a restless melodic line.

The Least You Need to Know

◆ Harnessing tension is a powerful way to give a melody or composition dramatic interest.

◆ Tension can be introduced into a melody via the use of unstable tones and chords.

◆ Within a chord progression, the V chord introduces the most tension because it strives to be resolved to the I.

◆ Dominant seventh and diminished chords also introduce tension wherever they're applied within a composition.

◆ Tension always results from the use of suspended chords, especially when the suspended note is a structural tone in the melody.

◆ Tension can also be built by using larger intervals, higher pitches, faster rhythms, increased syncopation, increased volume, and reduced repetition.

Exercises

Exercise 10-1

Write a melody in the key of F major that introduces and resolves tension via the use of unstable tones (fourth and seventh).

Exercise 10-2

Write a chord progression in the key of G major that introduces and resolves tension via the use of the IV and vii° chords.

Exercise 10-3

Write a chord progression in the key of B♭ major that introduces and resolves tension via the use of the dominant chord.

Exercise 10-4

Write a chord progression in the key of D major that introduces and resolves tension via the use of nonscale dominant seventh and diminished chords.

Exercise 10-5

Write a melody (with chord progression) in the key of E♭ major that introduces and resolves tension via the use of suspended chords and notes.

Harmonizing (and Reharmonizing) a Melody

In This Chapter

◆ Discover how to use the melodic outline to determine a chord progression

◆ Learn how to look for chord tones in the melody

◆ Find out how to determine the harmonic rhythm of your melody

◆ Learn various techniques for reharmonizing an existing chord progression

So far in this book we've worked through two different compositional methods: writing the chords first, and writing the melody first. If you've written the chords first, you can then fit a melody to those chords, using the techniques we've discussed over the past several chapters. If you've written the melodic line first, you can then harmonize that melody—that is, compose a series of chords that fit with and enhance the melodic line.

The relationship between chords and melody is complex—and works a little like the proverbial chicken and the egg, in that each one implies the other. A given melodic line will most likely suggest a specific chord progression, just as a chord progression can suggest one or a number of melodies.

In this chapter, we assume that you've already written a melodic line and that it's time to flesh out the composition harmonically. Let's figure out which chords fit best!

Fitting Chords to a Melody

The first thing to note when harmonizing a melody is that there is no one correct chord progression that will work. Almost all melodies can be harmonized in a number of ways; which chords you choose are just another part of your personal compositional process.

That said, often some obvious chord choices come to mind when one hears a melody. That's because many melodies actually outline or imply a certain harmonic structure. It's your job to decipher the clues and find those chords that work best. To do that, you can employ one of a number of techniques, which we now discuss.

Try the Obvious

One quick way to determine a harmonic structure is to simply try to fit one or more common chord progressions to your melody. Examine the popular chord progressions presented back in Chapter 3 and see if any of those progressions fit the melody you've written. You'd be surprised how many melodies fit with the I-IV-V progression.

For example, you can see how the downward progression of the following melody fits easily within the I-vi-IV-V7 progression. You can try other progressions (such as I-vi-ii-V7), but when you find a good fit, you're home free.

A melody made to order for the I-vi-IV-V7 chord progression.

Use the Melodic Outline

Instead of just guessing at the chords, you can use a more analytical approach to deconstruct your melody, looking for clues to an implied harmony. What you want to do, in essence, is strip out all the embellishing tones and create a melodic outline. The structural tones of the melodic outline will quite often suggest the underlying chords.

> **Note**
>
> We first discussed melodic outlines and structural tones in Chapter 7.

In most cases, each structural tone will be one of the notes of the underlying chord triad. You can try fitting chords around each structural tone, having that tone function as either the root, the third, or the fifth of the three possible chords.

For example, let's say you're in the key of C major and one of the structural tones in your melody is a C. Working diatonically, you can fit that C into either a C major chord (as the root), an A minor chord (as the third), or an F major chord (as the fifth). So for any structural tone in your melodic outline, you have three possible diatonic chords that could fit. Play each of the three chords in the context of the melody, and see which one fits best.

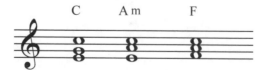

Fitting three possible chords to a single structural tone.

Let's work through an example, starting with a full melody. When we reduce the melody to its structural tones, you can see that they create a framework for the underlying harmony. Through a process of trial and error, we choose those chords that (1) sound best and (2) make the most harmonic sense within the framework of the composition.

Start with your complete melody ...

... then extract the embellishing tones to create a melodic outline ...

... and fit the proper chords to each of the structural tones.

For example, once you get to the final measure, you have to determine which chord to fit with the C note. You could choose F (the IV chord), Am (the vi chord), or C (the I chord). The question you have to ask is whether it's more likely that the preceding V chord (against the D) would lead to the IV, the vi, or the I. If you remember your chord theory, you can be pretty sure that a V-I progression (the good old perfect cadence) makes more sense than any of the alternatives, so you harmonize that C with a C (I) chord. There's some guess-work involved, of course, but the theory should provide at least one possible way to proceed. You can test your harmonization by playing the chords against the entire melody; if it sounds good, you made the right choices. (If not, try again!)

Your chord choices, fit against the original melody.

Look for Chord Tones in the Melody

You can also get clues to the correct harmony by looking at the other, nonstructural tones in the melody. In many cases, the subsidiary notes in the melody are taken from the underlying chord structure—and often outline the chord.

Take the following melody, for example. You can see that the notes in the first measure distinctly outline a G chord, the notes in the second measure outline a D chord, and the notes in the third measure outline an E minor chord. It doesn't take a Mozart to figure out which chords you need to apply in each measure.

Looking for chord tones in the melody.

Work Backward

Here's another trick for easier harmonization: work backward.

That's right, you can often figure out the proper chord progression by working backward from the final chord in a phrase, using rudimentary chord-leading theory. Remember that most traditional melodic phrases end on the tonic harmony. This means that the final chord in your melodic phrase, more often than not, will be a I chord. You then can figure out the cadence leading to the I (probably a V chord) and work backward from there using the chord-leading rules you learned in Chapter 3. With this approach, you can have half the harmony decoded fairly quickly.

For example, if you assume that this melody ends on the I chord, then the penultimate chord should be a V or V7. What chords best lead to a V7 chord? Try the ii (the dominant of the V7), and you'll see that it works. Which chords lead to the ii chord? There are a few, but again try the dominant of the ii—the vi chord. This also works. And how do you get to the vi chord? There's nothing like a I to lead to a vi, and because that I would sit on the very first beat of the phrase, you know that's the best (if not the only) choice. By working backward, you've fit a I-vi-ii-V7-I progression to your melody.

Start at the end (with a V7-I cadence) and use chord-leading theory to work backward from there.

Start Simple

Here's something else to keep in mind when working out the harmony of a piece. Don't make things more complicated than they have to be. In context, this means starting with simple triads rather than complex extended chords. You can always add extensions later (see the "Reharmonizing a Melodic Line" section, later in this chapter), but working with simple three-note chords puts a limit on the available chords, which means you have to work through fewer options.

To illustrate why it might be best to keep things simple, let's say you have a structural tone on the note F, in the key of C major. If you're working with triads, only three chords can include that F (B diminished, Dm, and F). If, on the other hand, you open up your harmonic options to include extended chords, that F could also be part of a G7, Em9, CM11, or Am13 chord—and that's not even considering the use in a Csus4 chord. Do you really want to consider all these options when harmonizing each single note? Although you certainly can (and might want to once you start writing more sophisticated compositions), when you're first starting out, it might be best to ignore some of the more elaborate possibilities. Bottom line: if your melody is somewhat traditional, you're probably safe working with the triad (or, at most, seventh-chord) options.

Tip

The advice to start simple is mitigated only slightly by the prevalence of the dominant seventh chord, especially when that chord is built on the dominant scale tone. This is why you'll have to break the "simple triad" rule to consider V7 chords when harmonizing your melody.

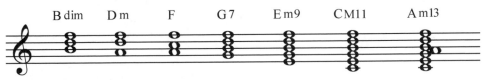

Even more chords that can fit with a given structural tone (the F).

Determine the Harmonic Rhythm

Another factor to consider is the harmonic rhythm of your chord progression—that is, when and how often you change chords. Do the chords change once a measure or more (or less) frequently? Do all the chord changes take place on major beats (the first or third beat of each measure), or are some fitted in on weaker beats—or even off-beats? Does the composition keep the same harmonic rhythm throughout (changing chords on the first beat of every measure, for example), or does the harmonic rhythm vary (with some measures having a single chord, some having two chords, and so on)?

In most cases, the composition's melodic outline will suggest a harmonic rhythm (one chord per structural tone), but you can't always depend on this. Although a melodic outline with one structural note per measure implies a harmonic rhythm of one chord per measure, it's also possible that a single chord might stretch over two measures (two structural tones), or that you might fit two chords within the space of a single structural tone. It's a choice you have to make.

Remember, though, there's no such thing as a single perfect harmonic rhythm. A given melody can be fitted to harmonic rhythms of various speeds. It's yet another personal compositional choice that you have to make.

Tip

In general, the slower the tempo of a composition, the more frequent the chord changes. In addition, chord changes generally fit within the traditional measure and metric structure, which means you're likely to see new chords introduced on either the first or third beats of a measure.

Creating a one chord-per-measure harmonic rhythm.

The same melody, this time with a faster-paced harmonic rhythm (two chords per measure).

Don't Assume the Obvious

Don't assume that a stationary melody has to be accompanied by a slow-paced chord progression, or that a melody with lots of movement needs to have a lot of chord changes. Sometimes the chord progression assumes the same pace as the melody; in other cases you might want somewhat of a contrast between the pace of the chords and the melody.

For example, a static melodic line can be made more interesting by the use of a faster-paced, dynamic chord progression. By changing chords several times over the course of a single melodic tone, that melody note appears to change, relative to the underlying harmony; that note takes on a different harmonic role with each different chord.

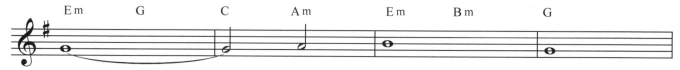

A slow-paced melody harmonized with a fast-paced chord progression.

Similarly, a fast-moving melodic line sometimes needs the stabilizing influence of a slow-paced chord progression. Let the melody accept the brunt of the workload, and keep things centered with a well-rooted chord or two.

A fast-paced melody harmonized with a slow-paced chord progression.

Reharmonizing a Melodic Line

Once you've established the basic harmony for a given melodic line, you don't have to stop there. As I noted earlier, there's no one set chord progression that's exactly perfect for any given melody. Any melody can be harmonized with a number of different chord progressions; depending on the chords you choose, the melody can take on a dramatically different feel.

Make Different Choices

One way to reharmonize a melodic line is simply to go through the initial harmonization process a second time, making different choices this time around. If you could harmonize a given note with either a ii, IV, or vi chord and you chose the IV, this time around, choose the ii or vi and see where that leads you. Sometimes changing just one chord will make a significant difference.

A melody with its original chord progression.

The same melody, reharmonized with different chord choices.

Use Chord Substitutions

Along the same lines, you can use chord substitution theory to replace one or more chords in your original progression. You first learned about chord substitutions in Chapter 4; the rules presented there apply for when you want to reharmonize a given melody.

For example, chord substitution theory says that you can replace a minor chord with a diminished chord with the same root, and a V chord with a iim7/V chord. Try these (and other) substitutions and see how they sound.

Our original melody, with several chord substitutions.

Add Extensions

Another approach is not to change the harmony itself, but rather to extend it—that is, to switch from simple triads to more sophisticated extended chords. Add some sevenths, ninths, and elevenths, and see how they sound; in most cases, the harmony you create will have a fuller and more contemporary sound.

Our original melody, reharmonized with extended chords.

Beyond Harmonization

Once you've fit chords to your melody, you might think you're done—but you're not. The harmony you create has to be applied within the context of your final composition; if it's a solor line, you may need somebody to play or sing those chords behind your melody. That could be a simple piano or guitar accompaniment, a second instrument playing in counterpoint, or a fully arranged orchestra or choir. The voicings and orchestrations you create are as much a part of the compositional process as your choice of melody and chords.

You can learn more about applying your harmonization in Chapters 14 and 15. Until then, read straight on to Chapter 12, where you'll learn how to develop your melody into more formal musical structures.

The Least You Need to Know

- When you want to fit chords to a melody, start by trying some common chord progressions.
- When you reduce a melody to its melodic outline, the structural tones often imply available chord progressions.
- Many melodies are constructed from chord tones; look for these tones to determine the underlying harmony.
- Another way to create a chord progression is to work backward from the ending tonic chord, using chord-leading rules.
- When you fit chords to a melody, you also have to determine the harmonic rhythm—the pacing and placing of the chords themselves.
- You can reharmonize a melodic line by making different chord choices, using chord substitutions, and adding chord extensions.

Exercises

Exercise 11-1

Harmonize the following melody three different ways:

Exercise 11-2

Harmonize the following melody three different ways:

Exercise 11-3

Harmonize the following melody three different ways:

Exercise 11-4

Harmonize the following melody three different ways:

Exercise 11-5

Harmonize the following melody three different ways:

Part 4

Developing the Composition

A professional composition is more than just a melody and a chord progression. You need to expand that melody into a full-length work, using repetition and variation and other techniques, and build it up for multiple instruments and voices. It's a lot of work, but it's quite logical—assuming you know the right tricks!

12

Creating Longer Compositions

In This Chapter

- ◆ Why musical structure is important
- ◆ Creating form from motifs and themes
- ◆ Writing in musical phrases
- ◆ Learning key compositional forms
- ◆ Constructing multiple-section compositions
- ◆ Building toward a climax

To this point, we've focused our attentions on two of the primary components of composition—melody and harmony (chords). For most types of compositions, however, you need to incorporate the chords and melody within a larger framework. That is what we'll examine in this chapter—how to build on your basic melody and harmony to create a longer composition.

The Importance of Structure in Composition

Structure and form are important in any musical composition. Without some sort of organized structure, a composition is nothing more than a meandering series of notes. A structural framework helps to define the composition by providing a roadmap that guides the composition from point A to point B. The musical boundaries implied by even the most subtle structure help to highlight the individual components of the piece—introduction, melody, climax, conclusion, and so forth. Structure organizes the music.

One key function of musical structure is to "create the feeling of formal balance," as composer Aaron Copland noted in his classic book *What to Listen For in Music.* Because music by nature is ephemeral, the use of repetition is perhaps the most critical aspect of musical structure. Or, more to the point, it is the balance and relationship between the familiar and the unfamiliar that plays such an important role in the experience of musical form, even if that "balance" is actually asymmetrical in nature.

We'll talk more about specific musical forms later in this chapter. For now, know that the longer your composition is, the more important it is for you to have a solid structural plan—whatever type of structure you adopt.

Working With Motifs and Themes

In Chapter 5, we first addressed the building blocks of melodic form. Two of the most important building blocks are motifs and themes—the primary identifying parts of any composition.

Building Melodies with Motifs

The melodic motif is a short group of notes that serves as the "calling card" for a longer melody. The motif—typically between two and eight notes long—is repeated throughout the melody to establish its identity; the repetition can either be exact or have variations, such as transposing the motif up a particular interval, playing it backward, or writing the same notes but with an altered rhythm (or vice versa). The point is to let the motif define the melody, and then use that motif to expand the melody.

You can also use a motif beyond the initial melodic line. By repeating the motif (and its variations) throughout the longer composition, it constantly reminds the listener of the initial melody. In addition, the motif provides useful material for an enterprising composer; the motif can be used to develop additional melodies or to extend sections of the piece through repetition and variation. The key is to treat the motif as a seed, which you then nurture throughout a composition.

One of the most recognized motifs in music history is Beethoven's "fate" motif from his Fifth Symphony, which we first discussed in Chapter 8. This four-note motif is both a rhythmic motif (the four-note rhythm) and a melodic motif, and all you have to do is listen to the symphony to hear how Beethoven exploits that motif throughout the piece. While a single motif need not serve as the sole musical inspiration throughout a composition, the repetition of a motif can help to unify different sections of a piece.

The introductory section of Beethoven's Symphony no. 5 in C Minor, and the use of the "fate" motif.

Establishing a Musical Theme

Whereas a motif is a very short musical phrase—no more than a half-dozen or so notes within a longer phrase—a musical *theme* is a complete melodic phrase, albeit the main phrase in the entire piece, anywhere from two to eight measures long. You might think of the theme as the main musical idea of your composition; it's often what listeners will remember when the performance is over.

You use a musical theme much the same way you use a motif—to define the composition, to reinforce the composition (via repetition), and to serve as the basis for musical expansion and elaboration (via variation). The theme repeats whenever you want to remind the listener of your main idea. It's your main melody.

> **Note**
>
> Learn more about the technique of theme and variation in Chapter 13.

A four-measure melodic theme.

> **CAUTION** **Warning**
>
> While there is no set limit to the number of themes or motifs you might use, it's important to make sure that you're not just moving on to a new theme because you're not sure how to develop an old one. It might seem easier to generate new themes, but in the long run juggling lots of material can be just as (if not more) difficult as thoroughly developing a single idea.

Some types of compositions might employ multiple themes. For instance, an opera or a film score might include themes for each of the work's main characters. This type of theme, called a *leitmotif,* is played whenever the character appears on stage or on screen. A good example is the dark theme that plays whenever Darth Vader appears in *Star Wars*—a marvelous leitmotif written by composer John Williams.

In addition, a multiple-section composition will typically have different themes for each section. A four-movement symphony, for example, will generally have four themes—one in each movement. The theme is how listeners identify each individual section.

Writing in Phrases

It's a good idea to start with melodies that are constructed in phrases—individual segments within a longer section. Phrases are created when you connect related notes or motifs into a single coherent musical thought.

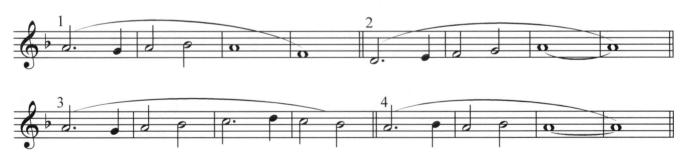

Four separate melodic phrases, based on the initial theme.

Think of a musical phrase as an in-and-out breath. The phrase begins when you breathe in; the phrase ends when you let out the final breath. (In fact, most wind instruments structure their breathing around musical phrases.) Even better, think of a phrase as a sentence, composed of individual words (motifs) and letters (notes). When you arrange one phrase (sentence) after another, you create a longer phrase (the musical equivalent of a paragraph). Thus, phrases give your music structure.

That said, you can't just connect a bunch of random phrases and expect to create a musical whole, just as you can't connect a bunch of random sentences and create a coherent paragraph. One musical phrase has to logically lead to the next; they not only have to be well connected, but they also have to have some sort of musical relationship to each other. You have to think of the longer phrase as a whole, not as just a collection of unrelated shorter phrases.

Symmetry and Asymmetry

Although you can combine any number of individual musical phrases into a longer phrase, the way you combine them affects the overall feel of the section. When the phrases combine in a symmetrical fashion, your music feels balanced; when the phrases are asymmetrical, the feel is somewhat unbalanced.

A symmetrical phrase contains an even number of shorter phrases of the same length. Or, thought of another way, the longer phrase is symmetrical when you can cut it in two and have an equal number of shorter phrases in each part. For example, if you combine four two-measure phrases, you create a balanced phrase.

A symmetrical phrase containing four two-measure phrases.

An asymmetrical phrase contains an odd number of shorter phrases of the same length, or any number of phrases whose lengths vary. In other words, it's not easily divisible by two; break it in half, and the halves aren't even. For example, five two-measure phrases creates an unbalanced phrase, as do three two-measure phrases plus a fourth three-measure phrase.

An asymmetrical phrase containing five two-measure phrases.

Which is better, symmetry or asymmetry? There's no right answer to this question. While a symmetrical section might feel more balanced and stable, it may also seem generic and predictable—which is a good argument for varying the types of phrases you use. Over the course of a longer composition, you may want to include a mix of symmetrical and asymmetrical sections to make the piece more interesting.

Matched and Unmatched Phrases

> **Note**
>
> Matched phrases are sometimes called *parallel phrases*; unmatched phrases are sometimes called *contrasting phrases*.

When you combine several shorter phrases into a longer phrase, the individual phrases either can relate closely to each other or can look and feel completely different. When two shorter phrases are similar in rhythmic form, they're said to be matched; when the phrases are dissimilar to each other, they're said to be unmatched.

Two matched phrases; notice the rhythmic similarity.

Two unmatched phrases; notice how different they are rhythmically.

> **Note**
>
> When the rhythms of two phrases are similar but not identical, they're called *inexact matches*. They function more or less like matched phrases.

A matched phrase often has a feeling of familiarity and finality to it, whereas an unmatched phrase keeps the music moving. As with symmetrical and asymmetrical phrases, you probably want to use a mixture of matched and unmatched phrases throughout your composition.

Creating Multiple-Section Compositions

As your compositions get longer, their structures become more complex. All of a sudden, you're not talking about just shorter and longer phrases; you're looking at the need to break your composition into two or more distinct sections.

When a composition is long enough to warrant multiple sections, you now have to work with each section as if it is a discrete composition. Yes, the individual sections have to relate to each other musically (and in service of the larger musical whole), but they also need to have their own individual structure and form. That may mean composing separate themes for each section, or employing separate keys, time signatures, and so on.

How long should each section be? It depends on the type of composition you're writing. If it's a short- or medium-length composition (or a popular song), you might be looking at sections anywhere from 16 to 64 measures long. If it's a longer composition, section length might be measured in minutes rather than measures.

As you build a longer composition, keep in mind how many sections your piece should have and what function each section should serve. In a typical sectional composition, you can work with any or all of the following components:

- ◆ Introduction
- ◆ A section
- ◆ B section
- ◆ C section
- ◆ Interlude(s)
- ◆ Coda

> **Note**
>
> Learn how section construction applies to popular song structure in Chapter 18.

We discuss each of these sections separately, and they can be combined in any number of ways, as you can see here:

Section A	Section B	Section A

A simple A-B-A composition.

Section A	Interlude	Section B	Interlude	Section A

An A-B-A composition with interludes between the major sections.

Introduction	Section A	Interlude	Section B	Section A	Interlude	Section A	Coda

An A-B-A composition with interludes, an introduction, and a coda.

The Introduction

Not all compositions feature an introduction; many compositions go straight into the A section and the main theme. If you want to include an introduction, you need to make sure that those first few seconds of music engage listeners (so they want to hear the rest of the piece) and set up all of what follows. This might mean pre-stating a portion of the main theme or creating a harmonic "question" that is "answered" by the main theme in section A. The goal is to provoke interest, no matter how you go about it.

Many composers use the introduction to open up into the main section of the composition. One way to do this is to start at a low volume and then crescendo louder; similarly you can start with a limited tonal range and open up the music as it leads into the main theme. Another approach involves writing a rising line so that the introduction starts on a low pitch and rises until it hits the starting pitch of the main theme.

If you want the introduction to ask a "question" or introduce a tension that is then resolved in the main theme, employ some form of unresolved harmony—unstable tones, suspended chords, or a dominant chord. Don't resolve the tension in the introduction; use the tension to lead into the first section.

Another way to use the introduction is in contrast to the first section. That might mean writing the introduction in a different key, at a different tempo, or with different orchestration. Know that the introduction doesn't have to be thematically related to the following section.

That said, many composers use the introduction as an exposition—that is, to introduce the listeners to the themes they'll hear in the following section(s). In this manner, the introduction becomes more like an overture and serves to reinforce the balance of the piece.

The Main Sections

Once you're past the introduction, it's time to move into the first main section of the piece. As discussed previously, a sectional composition can be built from one, two, three, or more separate sections. Make sure that you fully develop each section as if it were an individual composition, with its own overall contour and climax.

Of course, there needs to be some sort of logical flow between sections. That might mean establishing a harmonic relationship between sections (section B might be dominant to section A's tonic, for example), or employing a variation of section A's main theme in each subsequent section.

That said, many pieces have a noticeable contrast between their individual sections. If section A is fast and dynamic, section B might be slow and mournful. You might use different keys in each section, or write section B in the natural minor related to the major key used in section A. Just don't forget that you can employ common themes and motifs to help tie together any two disparate sections, however subtly.

The Interlude

Many longer compositions separate or transition between the various A and B (and sometimes C) sections with short *interludes*. An interlude is a short piece of music that serves to connect two major sections, often blending themes contained in both sections. Sometimes the interlude doesn't have anything to do with either surrounding section, instead serving to cleanse the musical palette between courses, so to speak.

The Final Section

The final section of your composition (which might be a repeated A section, for instance) is often a good place to wrap up all the loose ends you've introduced so far and provide a firm resolution to the entire composition. Many pieces resolve rhythmic or harmonic tension in this section, and you might even think of this final section as a large-scale resolution to your entire piece.

Endings can be tricky, however. One typical way to go is with a decisive ending, where the final chord progression really sounds final. In this instance, the final cadence must be powerful and conclusive. That means resolving the chords, melody, *and* the rhythm in a fairly strong fashion. There must be no hint that there is more to come—because there won't be.

Of course, your composition doesn't have to end with a bang. Although a big, impressive climax is a tried and true way to go, another option is to end your piece by essentially fading away. In this instance, you diminish the rhythmic, harmonic, and melodic activity until the texture thins out to next to nothing. It's a "soft" ending, compared to the more traditional triumphant close.

Tip

It's not uncommon for the final section to restate the themes introduced throughout the entire piece.

The Coda

However you end your piece, know that the ending—like the beginning—will have a big impact on the listener's experience. Many compositions simply end at the end of the final main section. Others tack on a separate *coda*, a short section that reinforces the final resolution. You can do this by repeating the final cadence (one or more times), or by employing short melodic variations that quickly increase and then resolve the underlying tension, thus making the final resolution that much stronger.

The Importance of Contrast

The primary reason to utilize multiple sections within a piece—aside from making the whole thing longer, of course—is to provide contrast. Contrast is a great way to generate drama while freshening the ears.

For example, the second section of a composition traditionally represents some sort of contrast to the initial section. A contrasting section makes the initial section more distinct and highlights its important qualities. Think of it in terms of color; if the first section is white, a second section in black highlights the first section's whiteness. If the second section was also white (off-white, beige, or even tan), the two sections might well blend into each other; accentuating the contrast makes each section appear more distinct.

How do you introduce this type of contrast into a composition? There are many ways to do this, but the key thing is to think in terms of opposites. For example, if the first section is loud, make the second section soft. If the first section is rhythmically interesting, use a lot of nonsyncopated long notes in the second section. If the first section uses primarily major chords, use more minor chords in the second section. Make the second section whatever the first section is not.

Then when you repeat the first section (as is typical in an A-B-A form), the listener experiences a strong sense of return—not only to the original melody, but also to the original feel. Just as it feels good to hear something new, it also feels good to return to something familiar. The greater the contrast between the A and B sections, the more intense that return of the familiar A section will seem on the repeat.

Don't Forget the Climax

We first talked about the importance of the climax in Chapter 9. The concept of musical climax is important not only within a melody, but also within the larger composition. Whether your composition is 32 measures or 32 minutes long, having one point at which the music peaks, with everything coming together in a harmonic and melodic high point, can be an extraordinary moment that makes your piece.

Quite often, a composition's climax is quite literally its highest point, pitch-wise. The climax is also often the loudest point and, orchestration-wise, the busiest point. It's the part of your composition that you work toward and that you then recover from.

Tip

The thinking behind building a multiple-movement composition is no different from that of building a multiple-section composition—everything just takes place on an even larger scale.

If the high point of your composition comes too soon, the balance of the piece may appear long and drawn-out, an unwanted afterthought. Look for the high points in your composition, and make sure that they're placed appropriately— and if they're not, then do some rewriting! Having your climax near the end (a very common and logical position) gives the bulk of the piece something to drive toward. Having some room to wind down after a climax can be nice, too.

Creating Even Longer Compositions

To this point, we've discussed breaking a longer composition into distinct smaller sections. When you're creating even longer pieces, such as symphonies or concertos, the composition can include two or more separate *movements*. Each of these movements is like a separate composition, consisting of its own sections, interludes, codas, and the like. It's like building a structure out of Legos and then combining multiple structures into something even bigger.

The Least You Need to Know

- Musical structure helps to create a feeling of formal balance in a composition.
- Structure is built from short motifs and longer musical phrases.
- Shorter phrases combine to form longer phrases; these phrases can be symmetrical or asymmetrical, and matched or unmatched.

- You can build a multiple-section composition using any or all of the following components: introduction, A section, B section, C section, interlude, and coda.

- It's important to have significant contrasts between each section of your composition.

- Your entire composition should build toward a musical climax, late in the piece.

Exercises

Exercise 12-1

Build a complete melodic phrase using the following motif:

Exercise 12-2

Build a 16-measure phrase using the following theme:

Exercise 12-3

Add new phrases to the following phrase to create a longer symmetrical phrase:

Exercise 12-4

Add a new phrase to the following phrase to create a longer matched phrase:

Exercise 12-5

Compose a long piece of your choosing using the following structure:

Introduction (4 measures) - A (16 measures) - B (16 measures) - Interlude (8 measures) - A (16 measures) - Coda (4 measures)

Chapter 13

Employing Repetition and Variation

In This Chapter

- ◆ How to use the technique of theme and variation to create longer compositions
- ◆ Repeating the theme
- ◆ Learning various variation techniques

Some composers find a blank sheet of staff paper daunting; others are quite capable of starting out strong but then fade quickly. It's an intimidating task—where does your composition go after the first 20 seconds or so?

The challenge in creating a longer and more complex composition is how to make it interesting while still maintaining an internal logic. One approach to this challenge is to employ the technique of theme and variation, which enables your composition to develop organically, based on its original melodic theme.

Creating Longer Compositions with Theme and Variation

If you have the nugget of a musical idea, you can turn it into a full-length composition. All it takes is a knowledge of music theory, a fair amount of hard work, and mastery of the skill we call theme and variation.

The concept of theme and variation is a simple one. You start with a musical idea—short or long—and then rework that idea in a number of different ways. It's composition as deliberate intellectual construction, applying one variation after another to create a cohesive whole. Although it might sound less ideal than pure inspiration, it's how many of the masters work; besides, inspiration is only a part of the compositional equation.

Theme and variation is more accurately viewed as repetition and variation. That is, you start with a musical theme and then both repeat it and vary it. Repetition, of course, is exact; variation is repetition with some changes made. And you can employ these techniques with musical phrases of any lengths; repetition and variation work equally well with a one-measure motif as with an eight-measure phrase.

Repeating the Theme

Repetition is based on a simple concept: when you find something that sounds good, do it again!

There are several different ways to repeat a melody. If it's a short motif, you can repeat it immediately after the first presentation, even in the same measure. If it's a longer theme, you might want to leave some space between the first presentation and the repeat. And you don't have to repeat the phrase immediately—you can wait and drop in a restatement of the motif after you've played some additional phrases.

Repeating a short motif.

> **Note**
>
> Learn more about writing for more than one instrument or voice in Chapter 14.

The repetition can be in the same voice or (in a multiple-voice composition) in one of the other parts. Repetition employed in more than one voice is sometimes called *imitation* because the second voice imitates the first. For example, a motif might be introduced in the trumpet line, then repeated (imitated) in the clarinet line. The effect is to reinforce the melodic phrase by passing it around the ensemble.

Imitating a motif in a second voice.

Varying the Theme

The funhouse mirror image of repetition is variation. With variation, you use your original motif as the basis for related musical ideas. You don't even have to alter the entire motif; a variation can be as simple as changing a single note. Just make sure you retain enough of the original motif that listeners can tell where it came from—but then add enough variation so that you create a new but related melody.

That said, there are some established approaches to variation that bear learning. Employ any or all of these techniques to create your own unique variations on a theme.

Sequence

One of the most common forms of variation is called the *sequence*. In a sequence, you repeat the original motif or theme, starting on a different pitch. That is, you play each note of the variation a certain interval away from the original melody. Extended variations might have several sequences in a row, repeating the original melody at different intervals.

A sequence can be *exact*, in which case the exact intervals of the original motif are retained (even if it means employing chromatic notes), or *inexact*, in which the repeated intervals are diatonic. If you want to stay within the underlying harmony, use inexact sequencing—where a leap of a minor third could be turned into a major third, if that's what's required.

> **Warning**
>
> While just about any type of variation is fair game, if you vary the theme so much that it's no longer recognizable to your audience, they may simply hear it as a new, unrelated musical idea.

Our original motif.

Inexact variation of a motif, using diatonic intervals—the original minor third (E to G) becomes a major third (G to B).

Exact variation of the motif—the minor third (E to G) stays a minor third (G to B♭), requiring a chromatic note.

Side Slip

A particular form of sequence, known as the *side slip*, is commonly used in jazz composition and improvisation, especially in modal compositions. In side-slipping, the original motif is repeated either a half-step higher or a half-step lower. After the side slip, you then repeat the original pattern at the original pitch. This rapid return to the original motif reinforces the original, while still allowing for the half-step sequence.

Side-slipping a motif up a half-step, then back again.

Rhythmic Displacement

The technique of rhythmic displacement repeats the original phrase, but at a different place in the measure. For example, instead of starting a phrase on beat 1, you might start it on beat 2—and play it through in its entirety, a beat off. You can displace the rhythm by any note value; particularly jarring are eight-note displacements, which start the phrase on the offbeat.

Rhythmically displacing a motif.

Inversions

An inversion (sometimes called a *melodic inversion*) starts on the same pitch as the original melody but then moves in the opposite direction—but by the same diatonic intervals. So if the original melody moves up a third, the inversion moves down a third, and so on. The result is a rough melodic mirror image of the original melody, using the same rhythm as the original.

Melodically inverting a motif.

A *mirror inversion* is a specific type of inversion in which the inverted intervals are exact. That is, if the original melody moved up a major third, the mirror inversion moves down precisely a major third—even if that means using chromatic notes.

A mirror inversion of the original motif.

A *contour inversion* isn't nearly as precise. In this type of variation, all you need to do is invert the general contour of the original melody; if the original goes up a little, the contour inversion goes down a little. You don't have to stick to the precise intervals of the original, which means an upward movement of a third could be inverted into a downward movement of a fourth or so, for example.

A contour inversion of the original motif.

Retrograde Inversion

A retrograde inversion plays the pitches of the theme exactly backward. (The rhythms don't have to be played backward—although they can be.) This has the effect of playing a record backward, sort of. It's a very subversive effect.

Applying a retrograde inversion by reversing the pitch order only.

A retrograde inversion with retrograde rhythmic inversion.

Permutation

Permutation essentially rearranges the pitches of the original melody in a some-what random order. To permutate a melody, all you have to do is shuffle the original pitches around and then apply them to the original melody. There are no rules for permutation; the only requirement is that you change the order of the notes.

A permutation of the original motif's pitches.

Note
Permutation on a larger scale is called *interversion*. Instead of switching individual notes, you change the order of complete motifs within a longer phrase. The motifs are played exactly, but just switched in order.

Same Rhythm, Different Pitches

This form of variation retains the rhythm of the original motif but lets you vary the pitches in any manner that makes harmonic or melodic sense. The theme is retained strictly by the repetition of the rhythmic phrase, so this technique is best employed when the original phrase has an interesting rhythmic motif.

Repeating the rhythm while varying the pitches.

Same Pitches, Different Rhythm

In this type of variation, the pitches of the original phrase are retained, but the rhythm is allowed to change in whatever manner you deem necessary. This can be a very useful technique, enabling you to replay the original theme in a variety of different rhythms.

Repeating the pitches while varying the rhythm.

Augmentation

Augmentation is another form of rhythmic variation; the pitches stay the same, but the rhythm is lengthened by some degree. Instead of using quarter notes, for example, an augmented theme might be restated using half notes instead. While augmentation doesn't have to be mathematically precise, in so-called strict augmentation the length of each note is precisely doubled.

Stretching out a melody via augmentation—in this instance, doubling the length of each note via strict augmentation.

Tip

You can also augment different parts of the theme by different amounts, thus changing the pace of the melody completely.

Diminution

Diminution is the opposite of augmentation; you take the theme and shorten the note values, thus speeding it up. In the sub-form known as strict diminution, each note is shortened by precisely half—quarter notes become eighth notes, eighth notes become sixteenth notes, and so on. But, as with augmentation, diminution doesn't have to be strict.

Condensing a melody via diminution—in this instance, a strict diminution where each note is exactly half the length of the original.

Truncation

Truncation cuts the original phrase short. That is, it literally deletes one or more notes from either the beginning or the end of the phrase. In essence, you write only part of the motif, thus implying the full phrase through an abbreviated segment.

Truncating the end of a motif.

Expansion

Expansion adds to the original phrase. That is, you add new material to the original melody, typically (but not exclusively) at the end, thus lengthening the phrase.

Expanding a motif by adding notes at the end.

Modulation

Modulation repeats the theme or motif exactly, but in a different key. If you change keys in this fashion, you may want the second key to be somewhat closely related to the first. For example, you might modulate to a key a fourth or fifth away from the initial key. In this instance, if the initial theme is in the key of G major, you might modulate it to the key of D major (a perfect fifth away) or C major (a perfect fourth away). You can make the modulation by doing a full key change or just by using accidentals.

Modulating a motif to a different key.

Note
The technique of modal mixture is sometimes called *mutation*.

Modal Mixture

The technique of modal mixture is related to modulation in that you change keys from major to minor or vice versa. The easiest way to accomplish this is by mutating to the relative minor or major key, or by changing the current key from major to minor (or vice versa). For example, if the initial key is E minor, you could rewrite the theme in either G major (the relative major) or E major.

Using modal mixture to change a motif from E minor to E major.

Note
Reharmonization involves the use of chord substitution, which you learned back in Chapter 4.

Reharmonization

Reharmonization varies the harmony behind the melody, not the melody itself. The original theme is maintained, but put in a different light because of the different chords.

Repeating the theme with different harmonization.

Thinning

When you thin a melody, you remove less essential and embellishing notes, reducing it to a more pure state. It's kind of like reducing a melody to its structural tones, but not necessarily that extreme.

Thinning out the less critical notes of a melody.

Ornamentation

Our final variation technique is perhaps the easiest. The technique of ornamentation involves "decorating" a simple melody—that is, embellishing it with neighboring tones, changing tones, and the like.

Ornamenting a melody with additional notes.

Varying the Variations

Now let's take the whole concept of theme and variation a step further and note that you can build on your variations exponentially. That is, you can take a given variation and apply another variation to it. For example, you might start with the original motif, apply the sequence variation, and then apply a retrograde inversion to the sequenced variation. And you don't have to stop there; you could then apply modal mixture to the retrograde inversion, and truncation to that, and thinning to that, and then sequence that one again. You can even apply two variations at once—by expanding and sequencing at the same time, for example.

The further you go in the variations, the further you get from the original theme—to the point that you develop completely new motifs. How far can you go? Your imagination is the limit!

An extended set of variations, where each new variation is then used as the base for the next variation.

Using Repetition and Variation in Your Compositions

The technique of repetition and variation is extremely important for all composers. You can use these concepts to expand a single motif into a full melody, to extend a short melody into a longer one, and to turn a single melodic line into a full-length composition.

There are no rules for how many or what kinds of variations you can employ in your compositions. Use your own best judgment to determine how far away from the original phrase you want to stray. Just remember that recognizable connections between variations will make your piece more cohesive. To that end, you may want to throw a few instances of the original into the middle of your variations, just to remind the listener of where you started. And it's frequently a good strategy to make your way back to the original theme when you're done with the variations, to put a nice little bow on the whole package.

Because mastery of repetition and variation is so vital, you should spend some time practicing each of the techniques presented in this chapter. Create a variety of themes, of different types and lengths, and run through all the available variations. You'll quickly see how useful this approach can be—whether you're writing a simple song or a lengthy symphony.

The Least You Need to Know

- ◆ Repeating and varying a main melodic theme is an effective way to create longer compositions.

- ◆ A theme or motif can be repeated in the same voice or imitated in a different voice.

- ◆ There are many different types of variation, including sequence, side slip, rhythmic displacement, inversion, retrograde, permutation, interversion, augmentation, diminution, truncation, expansion, modulation, modal mixture, and reharmonization.

Exercises

Exercise 13-1

Apply these variation techniques to the following theme:

    a. Exact sequence (up a minor third)

    b. Melodic inversion

    c. Retrograde inversion

    d. Strict augmentation

    e. Modulation (to F# Major)

Exercise 13-2

Apply these variation techniques to the following theme:

    a. Rhythmic displacement (by a whole beat)

    b. Retrograde with rhythms retrograded, as well

    c. Permutation (several answers possible)

    d. Same pitches, different rhythms (several answers possible)

    e. Diminution

Exercise 13-3

Apply these variation techniques to the following theme:

   a. Modal mixture (from F major to F minor)

   b. Truncation

   c. Augmentation

   d. Contour inversion (several answers possible)

   e. Side slip

Exercise 13-4

Apply these variation techniques to the following theme:

   a. Same rhythm, different pitches (several answers possible)

   b. Strict diminution

   c. Inexact sequence (up a second)

   d. Mirror inversion

   e. Expansion (several answers possible)

Exercise 13-5

Take the following theme and, using a variety of repetition and variation techniques, create a full-length composition for a single voice.

14

Creating Multiple-Voice Compositions

In This Chapter

◆ How to create an accompaniment to a solo line

◆ Writing for two separate voices

◆ Learning the rules of counterpoint

◆ Creating multiple-part harmony with good voice leading

◆ Adding even more parts

Writing a solo melody line is one thing; turning that single line into a full composition takes a bit more work. You've already learned how to extend a melody line horizontally into a longer composition, but now it's time to examine various ways to expand your work vertically, by adding parts to the piece.

There are a number of different ways to approach a composition for more than one voice. You can write a simple accompaniment part, to be played on an instrument (such as piano or guitar). You can turn the solo line into a duet by writing two different lines. Or you can envision a piece for a larger ensemble, with lots of different independent parts. We cover how to write for each of these instruments in Chapter 15; in this chapter, we focus on expanding a single melodic line into a multiple-voice composition.

Accompanying a Solo Line

Relatively few types of music are written for a pure solo voice or instrument. Aside from keyboard and guitar solos, most so-called "solo" pieces are actually works for a solo instrument with accompaniment. For example, a violin solo might have a piano accompaniment, or a popular song might use a guitarist to accompany the vocalist.

Note

The reason we have so many piano and guitar solos without additional accompaniment is that both of these instruments are polyphonic (capable of playing more than one note at a time) and can thus provide their own accompaniment. A vocalist or trumpet player can sing or play only one note at a time and, thus, needs another instrument to provide harmonic backing.

As we examine how to turn a solo melody into a fully formed composition, our first stop is the world of accompanied solos. Writing an accompaniment part is good practice for creating more sophisticated orchestration.

Creating a Lead Sheet

The simplest form of accompaniment comes in the field of popular music, through the use of what is called a *lead sheet*. A lead sheet, commonly used in both recording studios and live performance, is a piece of sheet music that contains a single staff for the melody, with the accompanying chords written above the staff. Accompanying musicians—keyboardists, guitarists, bassists, and the like—read the chord symbols and create their own accompaniment parts on the fly. Typically, there is no formal accompaniment written out; it's up to the performers to provide the appropriate accompaniment.

A typical lead sheet, commonly used in popular music.

As you can imagine, writing a lead sheet is extremely easy—just write out the melody and add the chord symbols above. Remember to include any special chord notation (altered bass, compound chords, and so on), and feel free to sketch in any desired rhythmic or melodic motifs as necessary.

Composing an Accompaniment

A step beyond the lead sheet is the more traditional piano accompaniment part. A melody with accompaniment is how much music gets played, whether you're talking about popular songs on sheet music or "classical" vocal and instrumental solos. An accompaniment part can be written separately from the solo (on two separate pieces of music) or notated on a grand staff below the solo line (on a single piece of music).

Creating a piano accompaniment sounds simple. But if you don't play the piano, how do you figure out what to write—especially if you can't begin to play it yourself?

Let's start out with the simplest form of piano accompaniment: block chords. You know the chord structure of your composition, so create a piano part with block-chord versions of the harmony. Try not to write all the chords in simple root inversion; use different inversions to make the chords easier to play and to provide some aural variety. Enhance the right-hand chords with a simple bass line in the left hand.

A simple block-chord piano accompaniment.

If you want to get fancier, try an arpeggiated accompaniment. Instead of block chords, simply break up the chords in the right hand, using some sort of simple rhythm.

An arpeggiated piano accompaniment.

Tip

Once you gain some experience writing piano accompaniments, you can try to create more interesting piano parts. A good accompaniment is interesting on its own, without getting in the way of or overshadowing the solo line. Use more complex piano figures to fill in the gaps in the solo line, to echo the solo line (in a "call and response" nature), and to provide musical interludes.

Employing Two-Part Counterpoint

Let's move beyond the solo-with-accompaniment genre into a type of piece written for two main instruments. A *duet* requires the construction of two primary melody lines that interact with each other over the course of a piece. It's like writing two separate compositions and then trying to fit them together.

When you write two or more notes together "vertically," you create harmony. When you create two or more melodic lines together "horizontally," you create *counterpoint*. This is what you get when you create two (or more) separate melody lines in two (or more) instruments or voices, and play those lines together. Put another way, counterpoint is the art of combining two or more simultaneous musical lines. Unlike the art of harmony, in which the harmony parts are subsidiary to the main melody, both melodic parts in counterpoint have equal weight.

Note

A duet can be written either with or without a separate piano accompaniment.

Counterpoint is two or more horizontal lines played simultaneously. (Example courtesy J.S. Bach.)

Counterpoint and harmony are related, of course; most compositions combine contrapuntal and chordal elements into a type of mixed texture. For example, you might have a piece in which two voices provide counterpoint, while additional voices provide harmonic, or chordal, support.

The two voices in traditional counterpoint must not only sound melodic when played separately; they must also fit together harmonically to suggest the chord structure of the song. That means if you play the underlying chords against the counterpoint, the melodic lines must still work; it also means you should be able to deduce the underlying chord structure from the melodic lines alone.

Note

Despite all of the changes in musical style over the years, the concept of counterpoint is still very relevant to composers in all genres. One will often have to write two (or more) lines together, and the art of counterpoint provides necessary guidance for doing just that. Although you needn't always follow the counterpoint guidelines or employ them slavishly, they can provide useful direction for fitting together two or more voices.

The key to successful counterpoint is the interaction of the different voices. (And when I say "voices," I mean melodic lines; counterpoint can be used in both vocal and instrumental music.) The two lines have to work together, not fight with each other. The second line has to be the melodic equal of the first, and neither line should dominate. It's important that both of the melodies in counterpoint be more than just a combination of notes to fit the chords; each part must be melodic, it must have its own internal musical logic, and it must fit with the other melody.

Tip

It's okay for the two melodies in a counterpoint to have their own rhythmic patterns. In fact, some forms of counterpoint demand that the two lines be somewhat different rhythmically.

The two contrapuntal melodies should also not duplicate each other; if you have two identical melodies, you're writing in unison, not in counterpoint. That means each melody should have its own motion—which should complement but not interfere with the motion of the other melody. Similarly, the pitches should compliment one another—dissonance often requires special attention, so give these intervals especially close attention.

Types of Contrapuntal Movement

When writing counterpoint, one of the things to pay attention to is the voice movement—that is, the way the two different parts move in relation to each other. You can employ four types of voice movement in your counterpoint, including these:

Tip

It's a good rule of thumb to mix up the various forms of contrapuntal motion—although you can focus on one type for a specific musical effect.

- ◆ **Parallel motion.** Both parts move in the same direction by the same diatonic or chromatic interval.
- ◆ **Similar motion.** Both parts move in the same direction, but by different intervals.
- ◆ **Oblique motion.** One part remains on the same tone, while the other part moves up or down.
- ◆ **Contrary motion.** The two parts move in opposite directions.

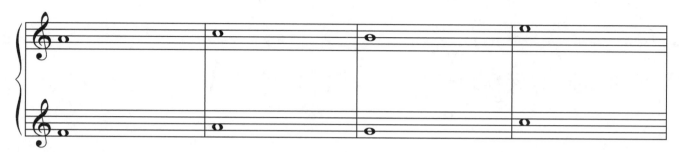

Parallel contrapuntal motion.

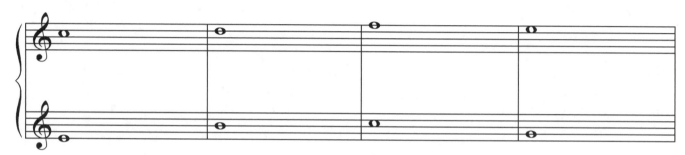

Similar contrapuntal motion.

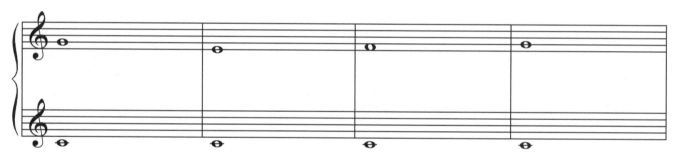

Oblique contrapuntal motion.

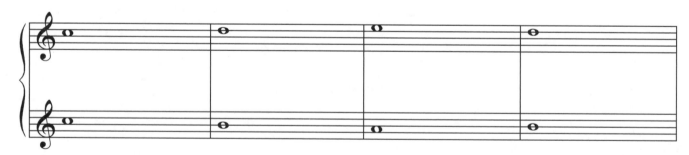

Contrary contrapuntal motion.

Note that using contrary motion and similar motion create more independence between the two lines. Parallel motion tends to sound more like traditional harmony than counterpoint, especially when the two voices move in close intervals (like a third).

General Rules for Good Counterpoint

In Bach's time, there were rather formal rules for writing counterpoint. Those rules have pretty much gone by the wayside today, although they still provide good guidelines for creating harmonious-sounding counterpoint. The following principles of counterpoint are now "suggestions" (and thus made to be broken), but adhering to these parameters can help you avoid some common mistakes.

Here are the parameters:

◆ Dissonant intervals are resolved by step-wise motion (usually downward, excepting the leading tone, which resolves upward).

◆ The lower part ultimately ends on the tonic of the key. (You typically begin on the tonic, as well—although this isn't hard-and-fast.)

◆ The upper part should begin and end on a consonant note in the harmony.

◆ Between the melodies, rely heavily on intervals of thirds and sixths. Avoid octaves and unisons (especially on downbeats), except for the first note or the final note.

◆ Try to move voices by the shortest distance possible.

◆ When you use a leap, the most common strategy is to make the next move in the opposite direction, especially by step.

The simplest counterpoint has a 1:1 rhythmic ratio—that is, both melodies use the same rhythmic patterns. As you become more skilled at writing counterpoint, you can write the second line with different rhythms than the first line, thus creating even more complexity in the composition. You can even experiment with advanced contrapuntal forms, such as the fugue, where you repeat the same or similar melody in different parts—as in the Bach example, previous.

> **CAUTION**
>
> **Warning**
>
> When writing counterpoint, you should avoid having the two parts sound the same note—either in unison or at the octave—especially over successive notes. The notable exception is the final note in a piece, where the unison or octave makes for a satisfying final sound.

Writing for Two Voices—Without Counterpoint

Not every two-part composition has to employ strict rules of counterpoint. Traditional contrapuntal forms sound so specific that many contemporary composers choose to abandon the rules of counterpoint in favor of other types of melodic invention.

If the second voice in a two-voice composition isn't contrapuntal, then what is it? The answer is that a second melody simply needs to be another melody—and to fit well with the first melody. While the greater part of good two-part writing pays some homage to contrapuntal guidelines, most composers today pick and choose which of counterpoint's valuable ideas they employ. Counterpoint is, after all, about successful interaction. The challenge is to fit together two melodic lines into a cohesive whole. Although trial and error sometimes works, you might prefer to try several more formalized approaches—which we examine next.

Countersubject

One very common approach to two-voice writing is to compose a completely different melodic theme for the second voice. Known as a *countersubject* or *countertheme*, this is a secondary theme heard against the main melodic subject. Although this countersubject should be relatively independent from the main theme, it shouldn't be so independent that it clashes extensively with the main theme. That means you need to examine where the two themes meet vertically, to avoid unresolved dissonances. (It's okay for a note or two to clash, as long as the dissonance is quickly resolved by moving one or the other voice to a more pleasing interval.)

The countersubject can be rhythmically similar to the original theme, can be rhythmically contrasting to the original theme (short when the first theme is long, and vice versa), or can just follow its own path. However you approach this secondary theme, you'll get the most mileage if it can stand on its own as if the first theme wasn't there.

A countersubject (on the second line) written to complement a primary theme (on the upper line).

Call and Response

This next approach uses the second voice to echo the melody as initially presented by the first voice. The first part plays a motif or phrase, and then that same motif or phrase is echoed in the second part—either exactly or displaced by a specific interval. For example, the second voice might echo the first voice's motif, but a diatonic third lower. This technique provides a lot of action and interplay between the parts, and also serves to reinforce the initial melodic line, via its constant repetition in the second voice.

Writing two voices in a call-and-response pattern.

Variations

Note that when you echo the line exactly in the second voice, you're employing the technique of imitation, as discussed in Chapter 13. You can also repeat the line with all manner of variations, as also discussed in Chapter 13. For example, the second line can be an inversion of the first—going up where the first line goes down, and so on. With so many variations available, this approach is particularly versatile.

Echoing the first voice with variations—in this instance, an inversion.

Contrasting Lines

One of the key aspects of call-and-response writing is that the second voice essentially fills in the gaps present in the first voice. Another way to do this is simply to write the second voice in a contrasting fashion to the initial voice. That is, if the first voice is playing a fast rhythmic pattern, write the second voice with unobtrusive half and whole notes. When the first voice calms down, then pick up the activity in the second voice. With this technique, the second voice doesn't have to mirror the melodic or rhythmic content of the first voice, only comment on it.

Writing two contrasting lines.

Parallel Lines (Melodic Coupling)

As you recall, counterpoint embraced four different types of movement between the lines—parallel, similar, oblique, and contrary. Nothing limits these types of movement to the contrapuntal form, which brings us to this next technique, in which the second voice is written to parallel the first voice rhythmically, but at a distance.

Writing in parallel is called *melodic coupling,* and it essentially treats the second voice as a harmony line to the main melody. Here's how it works. You choose a distinct and constant interval—say, a third—and always place the second voice that interval distant from the main voice. This interval will often be treated diatonically so that it's not always a major third distant, let's say; depending on the notes of the underlying scale, the second voice might vary between either a minor third or a major third distant.

Two voices written in parallel.

> **Tip**
>
> When you're writing parallel lines, thirds and sixths are the most consonant intervals to use. Writing in parallel fourths or fifths creates a droning effect, while parallel seconds and sevenths are entirely dissonant. (Traditional counterpoint emphasizes consonance and largely avoids parallel seconds, fifths, and sevenths—although today's composer has all of these options available.)

Similar Lines

A related approach is to write the second line using similar motion to the first line. That is, when the first line goes up, the second line goes up; when the first line goes down, the second line goes down, too. The difference between similar and parallel lines is that, with the similar approach, you don't keep the same interval between the lines. By varying the interval between the lines, you're free to place the second line on one of the notes of the underlying chord.

Two voices written with similar motion.

Contrary Lines

Following on the study of line movement, you can write the second voice so that its movement contrasts that of the main melody. That is, when the main line goes up, the second line goes down, and vice versa. (But not always by the exact interval, of course.) As you remember from your counterpoint, this is called contrary motion.

Two voices enjoying contrary movement.

Oblique Lines

The final movement-related approach is that of oblique lines. This technique is very simple to employ: all you have to do is write the second voice on a constant note. The main voice can move all it wants, but the second voice stays put on a single pitch—ideally, a pitch from the underlying chord. In practice, you can change pitches from measure to measure, but the oblique line should stay on the same pitch for several changes of the first melodic line.

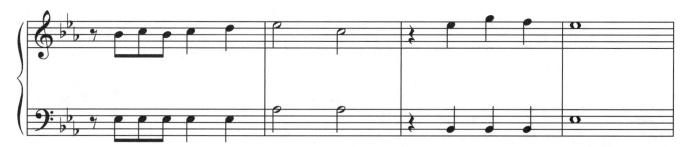

Two-voice writing employing oblique movement.

Doubling

This technique is best used sparingly because it really isn't a two-voice writing—both parts play the exact same line, either in unison or at the octave. You can employ voice doubling in a defined segment of a phrase or composition to provide an added emphasis to the current melodic line; it's very powerful when used judiciously.

Two voices written an octave apart.

Harmonization

This last approach uses the second voice not so much as a melodic line but as a harmonic accompaniment. The second voice follows the chord progression, playing long notes that imply the full underlying harmony. Naturally, the second line should be written as melodically as possible, employing smallish steps—even though its function is not melodic in nature.

The second voice functioning as a harmonic accompaniment.

Writing Multiple-Part Harmony

Tip

Harmony parts *can* mirror the rhythm of the melody, of course; in these instances, the harmony resembles counterpoint. Harmony can also be used to punctuate the melody, fill in breaks in the melody, and function as a kind of call-and-response mechanism.

Our last noncontrapuntal technique used the second voice in a harmonic fashion. This technique can also be employed when writing for larger ensembles. When you write "vertically" like this, you stack multiple parts on top of each other to create harmony.

Within a composition, harmony is the equivalent of playing a chord-based accompaniment behind a melody, but using a variety of instruments or voices. We add harmony parts to our compositions because harmony lends richness to a melody.

Multiple-part harmony provides several necessary functions in the construction of a composition. The harmony not only helps to "fill out" the piece, but it also provides atmosphere and completes the essence of the music. Used properly, the individual parts can impart the underlying harmonic structure and provide some sort of a rhythmic pulse. Adding harmony parts makes your music sound bigger.

You create harmony parts by using notes from the underlying chord progression. Unlike counterpoint, harmony parts are typically less rhythmically complex than the main melody. That is, they don't follow the same rhythmic pattern of the melody. It's not uncommon to find harmony parts consisting of whole notes or half notes while the melody maintains a more complex rhythm.

You can create harmony with just a single accompanying voice or with all the voices available in a full orchestra or choir. The more voices you have, the more challenging it is to create distinct harmony parts without doubling or duplicating other parts. (Not that there's anything wrong with doubling parts; it's an important technique to use when writing harmony parts.) Of course, writing a single harmony part is also challenging, but in a different way; that single part has to include just the right notes, suggesting the underlying chord without distracting from the main melody.

Harmony in a quartet setting; the first voice carries the melody, while the other parts provide harmony.

Writing multiple-part harmony can be as simple as assigning different chord tones to various instruments. That won't necessarily create the most interesting harmony, however. You can apply some specific techniques to create better-sounding harmony, which we examine next.

Choosing the Notes

When you want a group of instruments or voices to essentially play chord tones behind the lead melody, how do you choose *which* chord tones to use? It's not a problem if you have three instruments playing triads, but what if you have more or fewer than three voices—or if you're using extended chords?

First, know that you don't have to spell out all the notes of a chord in your harmony. It's okay to simply imply the full harmony by sketching in some subset of the total notes available. For example, if you want to express a four-note dominant seventh chord with just three voices, you might want to write just the root, third, and seventh, leaving out the fifth; this works because the third and the seventh express the chord's nature (major or minor in either case), and the root defines the scale tone. The fifth is the least necessary tone to express.

Sketching in a seventh chord using just three voices—the fifth is most often dropped.

Along the same lines, it's also okay to place a single tone from the underlying chord in more than one voice. Although it's typically the root that's doubled, you can double any of the tones, as necessary. Let's face it; if you're writing a simple three-note C major chord for an entire orchestra to play, you're going to have to write some of the same notes twice—or three, four, or five times! Be careful when voice-doubling, however, because the more instruments are playing a given note, the weightier that tone becomes. You probably don't want more instruments playing the seventh than the root, for example, because the seventh is almost never the most important tone. Take the chord tone that's most important at that point in your composition, and double that note in multiple voices. (When all else fails, just double the root—that's most often the right way to go.)

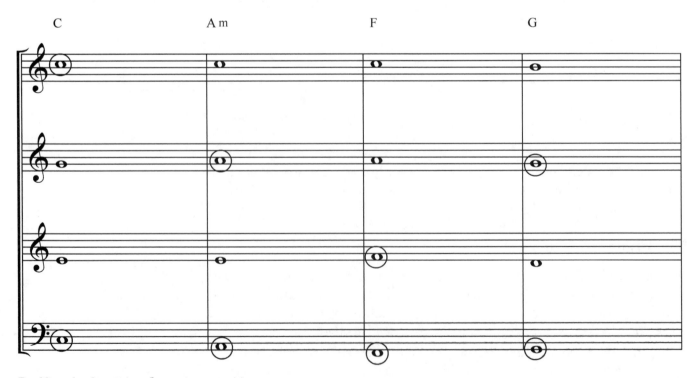

Doubling chord tones in a four-voice composition.

Varying the Voicings

The order of the chord tones is also important; the note that's placed on top of the chord (the one played by the highest instrument or voice) is probably going to be heard more clearly. For this and other reasons, using the instrumental equivalent of root-inversion block chords is not only lazy writing, but it also sounds somewhat boring. It's important to consider which notes of the chord are placed where and played by what instruments. This note order is referred to as chord *voicing*, and it's directly related to the concept of inversion that you learned in Chapter 4.

Voicing is important when you're writing harmony parts because you have to employ different voicings to avoid parallel motion between parts and to create different harmonic textures. If each instrument always plays the same voice in a chord, all the harmony notes will move in parallel to each other as you change chords. Too much parallel movement is frowned upon because it's boring. A better approach is to vary the voicings of the chords so that the harmony parts don't have to move in parallel.

For example, the first passage presented here uses static voicings across the entire chord progression, complete with the accompanying parallel movement—lazy writing that produces a somewhat boring sound. But if you change the voicings from chord to chord so that the same instrument isn't always playing the fifth of the chord, as an example, it helps to create more interesting lines for each instrument.

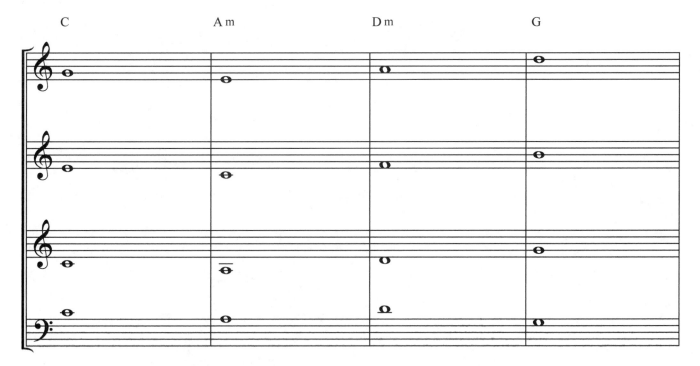

A passage with static voicings and parallel movement.

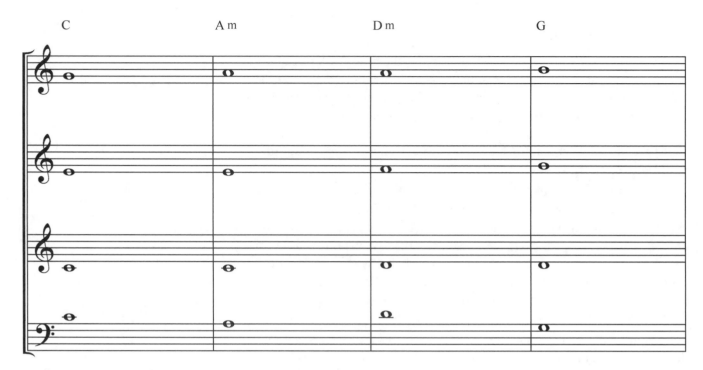

The same passage, rewritten with different voicings and nonparallel movement.

Tip

Voicings are also important when creating the "color" of a piece. Open voicings (in which similar instruments are spaced a fourth or more apart) create a more open sound, whereas closed voicings (with similar instruments spaced a second or third apart) impart a tighter and often more dissonant sound—especially with extended chords. Closed voicings also tend to create more tension, and, as you well remember, tension is good.

Tip

A good tip when you're creating either vocal or instrumental harmony is to physically sing each part yourself. If the part is boring or hard to sing, consider different inversions or swapping notes between parts. It's a fact; the best harmony parts sound great on their own.

Creating Melodic Harmony with Strong Voice Leading

Back to the issue of the individual harmonic lines. Even though you're writing the instruments "vertically," each instrumental line still has to be played "horizontally." To that end, it's important to examine the melodic line you create for each individual instrument. While the lines are functioning harmonically, you should strive to make each line as melodic as you can, given the circumstances. If a line is particularly unmelodic or difficult to sing or play (especially the case if you use awkward skips within the line), that line will tend to stick out. If listeners can follow each instrumental line separately and have each line hold together melodically, your piece will sound much more cohesive.

One way to create a more melodic harmony line is to follow general voice-leading principles. Voice leading is what you get when you follow one harmony part from start to finish; the different intervals between the notes follow a set of conventions and act to create a pseudomelody out of the harmony line. You have to make sure that one note properly leads to the next, to avoid having the harmony line sound like a bunch of totally unconnected tones.

This is one instance in which the rules don't get in the way of the process. In fact, there are only a few guidelines to keep in mind, as discussed next.

Move Smoothly

Tip

The lowest (bass) voice can accept larger leaps that move along with the chord progression.

Most often, voices should move the shortest distance possible and retain common tones between successive chords in the same voice. How big of a leap is too much? In traditional harmonic writing, you rarely see inner voices leaping more than an octave. Mostly they move in step-wise motion, or by leaps of a third or fourth.

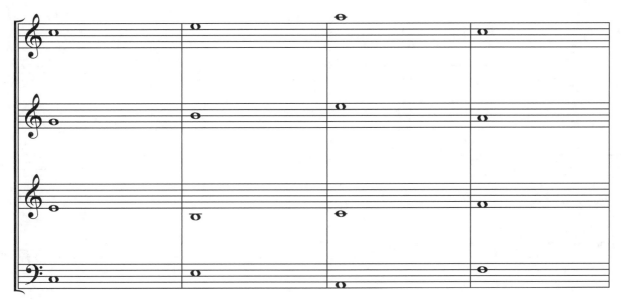

Voice leading with too much skip-wise motion—to be avoided.

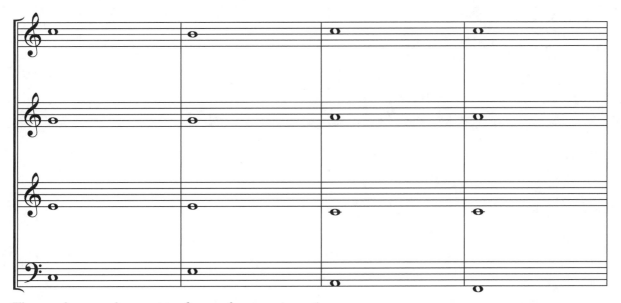

The same harmony, but rewritten for smoother step-wise motion.

Move in Different Directions

You should avoid moving all the voices in the same direction. If some of the voices move up over the course of a line, at least one voice should move down.

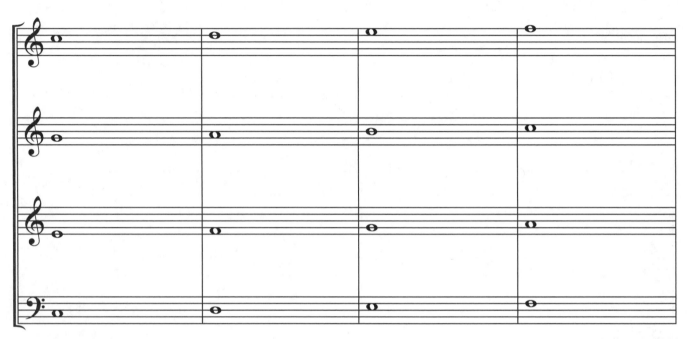

An excerpt with all the voices moving in the same direction—to be avoided.

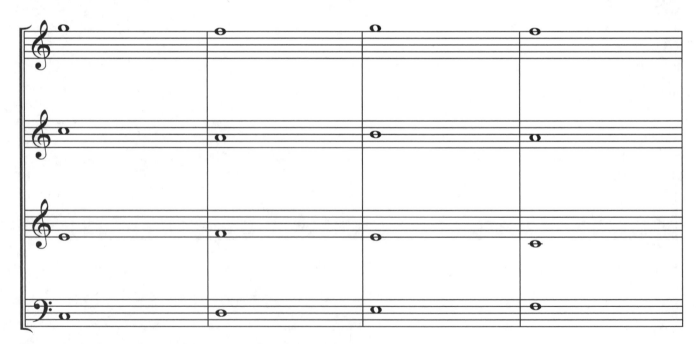

Better voice leading, with some of the voices moving in opposite directions.

Avoid Parallel Perfect Movement

Avoid moving two or more voices in parallel "perfect" intervals—fourths, fifths, or octaves. Voices *can* move in parallel thirds and sixths. The exception to this are the parallel octaves that result from voice doubling, especially in the upper voices, which are perfectly allowable.

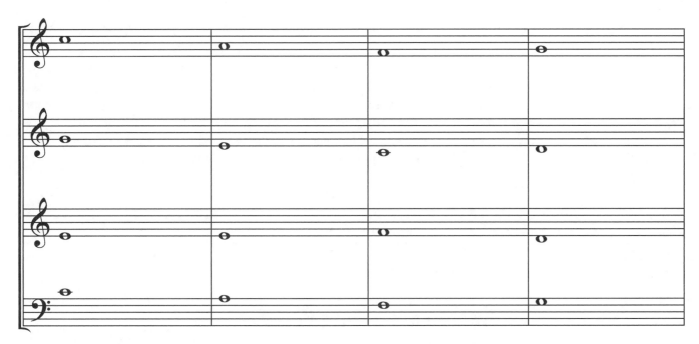

The first two voices move in parallel fourths—to be avoided.

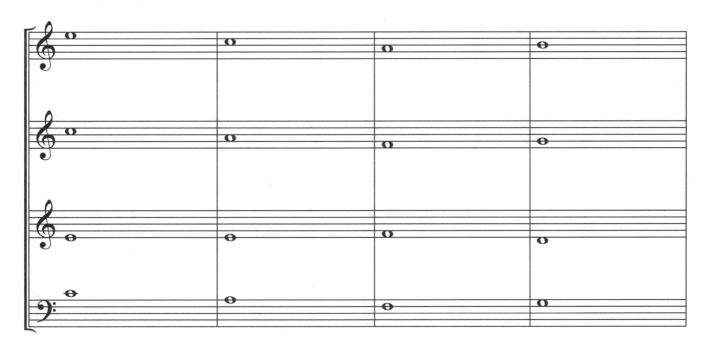

The same harmony rewritten with parallel thirds and sixths—perfectly acceptable.

Tip

To make life a little easier, you can often ignore this last guideline—especially in popular music and some contemporary forms. Although "classical" music adhered to the "no parallel intervals" rule, today that rule is honored more in the breech than in the observance.

Using Common Tones

Another popular technique is to identify those notes that are the same from one chord to another—what we call *common tones*. By emphasizing the common tones between chords, you can better connect one chord to the next within a given part. When a given voice holds the same note across two (or more) chords), it creates a powerful bridge between the two chords.

A harmony line using (mostly) common notes between chords.

Adding Even More Parts

Working with multiple instrumental or vocal parts is challenging, to say the least. The more parts you add, the more options you have—and the more challenging it is to make everything fit together. You can employ contrapuntal techniques, pure harmonic techniques, or anything else that sounds good to your ears.

Here are some of the techniques you can use:

◆ **Double the melody.** The melody doesn't have to reside in only a single line. When you're working with large ensembles, there's nothing wrong with doubling (or tripling) the melody in more than one part—even if that means playing the melody in octaves rather than in unison. The more parts are playing the melody, the more powerful it becomes. (And pay attention to how different instruments sound together; combining the right instruments in a single line can create some very interesting musical colors.)

◆ **Introduce secondary motifs and themes.** Additional voices in a composition offer the opportunity for you to include additional melodic lines beyond the main melody. These secondary motifs and themes can be employed in new sections of the piece (such as interludes) or in the background behind the main melody.

Warning

Like all tools, secondary motifs can be used to great effect or can be overused. Unless you listen carefully to what you're writing, your music can get much more dense than you realize. You don't want to be afraid of density, just in control of it.

♦ **Provide a rhythmic pulse.** Instrumental harmony doesn't have to be all half and whole notes. You can use the additional voices to impart a specific rhythmic pulse to your piece, simply by writing the parts with an interesting rhythm. Even straight quarter notes can prove interesting because this rhythm will help to propel the piece forward. Try a variety of rhythms; employing syncopation can really pick up the pace.

♦ **Provide an interesting bass line.** It's only natural to pay attention to the parts at the top of the pile—and to place the melody on top of all the other parts. But the parts on the bottom are equally important and can often provide an interesting counterpoint to the top lines. To this end, pay particular attention to your piece's bass line; it doesn't have to simply follow your chord progression. A rhythmically and melodically interesting bass line can be the difference between an average and an exceptional composition.

♦ **Don't forget the percussion!** While you're slumming with the basses, pay some attention to the nonmelodic instruments of the orchestra. The percussion section can supply a necessary rhythmic pulse, of course, but can also provide interesting colors to any composition. Consider all the percussion instruments at your compositional disposal, including timpani, snare drum, bass drum, cymbals, marimba, chimes, tambourines, and all manner of ethnic instruments. It's a world of different sounds and colors available for your use!

The Least You Need to Know

♦ Writing a piano accompaniment can be as simple as playing block chords or arpeggios—or as complex as creating subsidiary melodic sections.

♦ Writing a duet often involves the use of counterpoint—the fitting together of two separate melodic lines in a horizontal fashion.

♦ Two-voice writing doesn't have to be contrapuntal in nature, however; you can write two melodic lines that fit together in any number of ways.

♦ A good harmony part is also melodic and follows set voice-leading guidelines.

♦ The more instruments you have to work with, the more texture you can add to your composition—including secondary themes, rhythmic pulses, and "call and response" sections.

Exercises

Exercise 14-1

Create a simple piano accompaniment for the following solo line:

Exercise 14-2

Using the following line as the main voice, compose two different duets, one using the general rules of counterpoint, the other using a noncontrapuntal approach.

Exercise 14-3

Using the following melodic line as a starting point, use "vertical" harmonies to create a longer four-voice piece.

Exercise 14-4

Using the various voice-leading principles, reharmonize the following parts to create more melodic harmonic lines.

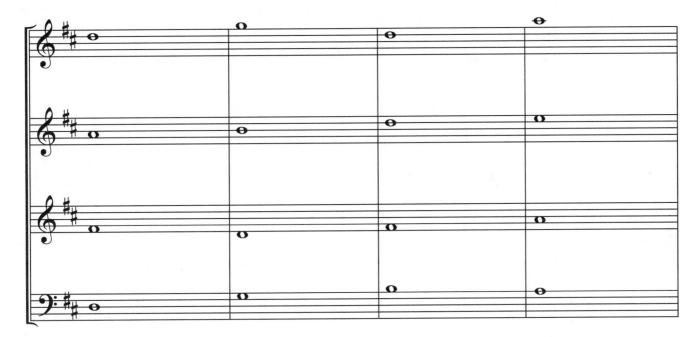

Exercise 14-5

Using the guidelines suggested in this chapter, compose a short piece (in concert key) for two trumpets, trombone, and tuba, employing a theme of your own design.

Part 5

Advanced Techniques

Want to compose for different instruments? Then you need to learn orchestration and arranging. Want to create contemporary concert music? Then you need to learn about atonalism, serialism, minimalism, and the like. Want to write popular songs? Then you need to learn basic songwriting techniques—all of which are covered in this part.

15

Orchestration and Arranging

In This Chapter

◆ Transposing from concert key

◆ Selecting the right key

◆ Learning the ranges and tonal characteristics of each instrument

◆ Choosing instruments for a composition

◆ Writing for common instrumental ensembles

◆ Following music scoring guidelines

Outside of popular songwriting (which we'll discuss in Chapter 18), composition seldom consists of just melody and chords. When you compose a piece, you're composing for a specific combination of instruments or voices. The management of these instrumental parts is every bit as important as the composition of the melodies and harmonies.

Of course, when you start writing for a variety of instruments, it helps to know a little bit about the instruments for which you're composing. You need to know the range of the instrument, how it sounds in various parts of its range, whether it sounds concert pitch or needs to be transposed, and how it sounds when played in conjunction with other instruments. All of this is part and parcel of what we call *orchestration*—or, in some genres, *arranging*.

As you might imagine, the topic of orchestration is one that can take years to learn. We're talking about learning the ins and outs of every instrument of the orchestra, how they sound, play, and fit together. I certainly can't teach you everything there is to know about orchestration in this single chapter—you'd need an entire book to cover the topic adequately. That said, it's important to know a little about orchestration as you begin to compose—which is where this chapter comes in.

Transposing from Concert Key

Before we get into the characteristics of individual instruments, let's pause for a moment and examine the concept of *transposition*. As you may know, many instruments read one note and play another, compared to what we call concert pitch (the actual notes as played on a piano). For example, when a trumpet reads a C on paper, the note that sounds is a B♭, a full step (major second) below the written note. These so-called *transposing instruments* need to have their music transposed to a different key to play in the same concert key as all the other instruments.

Let's take the trumpet again. Because the trumpet always sounds a major second lower than written, you need to write the trumpet part a major second *higher* than the pitch you actually want to hear. So if you want the trumpet to play a concert C, you have to write a D; the trumpet reads D, plays C, and everything is right with the world.

Most transposing instruments fall into three groups and are named according to how they relate to C:

- ♦ B♭ instruments, such as the trumpet, sound a major second below concert pitch. So if they read a C, they sound a B♭.

- ♦ E♭ instruments, such as the alto sax, sound a major sixth below (or a minor third above) concert pitch. So if they read a C, they sound an E♭.

- ♦ F instruments, such as the French horn, sound a perfect fifth below concert pitch. So if they read a C, they sound an F.

The following table details which instruments fall into which group:

Transposing Instruments

Transposition Range	Sounds	Instruments
B♭ instruments	Major second lower	Bass clarinet (actually a major ninth lower) Bass saxophone Clarinet (B♭) Cornet Flugelhorn Soprano saxophone Tenor saxophone (actually a minor ninth lower) Trumpet
E♭ instruments	Major sixth lower	Alto clarinet Alto saxophone Baritone saxophone (actually a major thirteenth lower) E♭ clarinet (actually a minor third higher)
F instrument	Perfect fifth lower	English horn French horn

With a few exceptions, instruments not listed here are nontransposing—that is, what they play sounds exactly as written, in concert pitch. The best example of a nontransposing instrument is the piano; you read middle C, you play middle C, the piano sounds middle C—no transposing necessary.

When you write a part for a transposing instrument, you do all the transposing up front by changing the key of the piece for that instrument's part. That is, you don't necessarily transpose each and every note individually; the transposition is done by shifting the key signature for the transposing instrument. For example, if a composition is in the concert key of C major, you would write the trumpet part in D major.

A passage in the concert key of C major, transposed to D major for the trumpet part.

Fortunately, today's music-notation programs automatically perform this transposition for you, saving you the trouble of transposing all the instruments manually. With a program like Finale or Sibelius, you can write the entire piece in concert pitch and then have the program output individual parts in the instruments' transposed pitch.

Notation programs aside, transposition is still a valuable skill to have. You never know when you'll need to make changes to individual parts on the fly, requiring real-time transposition. If you can transpose, you'll also be able to communicate better with individual musicians; when the trumpet player asks you if a given note on his part is supposed to be a D, you'll know he's talking about concert C and can respond accordingly.

 Warning

Music notation programs aren't perfect, especially when it comes to transposing. Two common mistakes are awkward choices of spelling (A# vs. B♭, for example) and the occasional missing accidental. It pays to double-check the program's notation!

Learning Ranges and Tonal Characteristics

Now that you're up on how different instruments transpose, let's examine how all the different instruments sound. In particular, it's important to know the range of each instrument so that you don't write anything that isn't technically playable. You should also learn a little about how each instrument works so you can avoid problematic passages, as well as the tonal characteristics of each instrument.

To get you started, the following sections present basic information about each of the most popular instruments and voices. Read on to learn more.

Strings (Bowed)

From the Baroque era onward, some of the most popular instruments for composers have been those of the string family—specifically, the bowed instruments, such as the violin, viola, and cello. These are exceptionally versatile instruments, equally capable of both solo and ensemble work; especially useful is the fact that their tone color stays constant over the entire range of the instrument.

These bowed instruments are typically played with a bow, of course, although they can also be plucked for staccato notes. In addition, double, triple, and quadruple stops are possible, by playing on more than one string at a time. (But you can't write more than one note on each string!)

The highest voice in the string section is the violin, followed (in descending order) by the viola, cello, and double bass. The violin is written with the treble clef, cello and double bass use the bass clef, and the viola—the oddball of the group—uses the alto clef. (Remember, the pointy part of the alto clef points at C.)

The following table describes the ranges and characteristics of these traditional stringed instruments.

> **Warning**
>
> In many cases, the upper limit of an instrument's range depends greatly upon the player and the situation. The upper ranges listed here should be considered reasonably safe, though somewhat challenging for inexperienced players.

Bowed String Instrument Ranges and Characteristics

Instrument	Range (concert pitch)	Transposition	Characteristics
Violin		Sounds as written	The soprano voice of the string section. Typically used as the lead voice in ensemble passages. Also extremely versatile as a solo instrument.
Viola		Sounds as written	The alto voice of the string section. Sounds considerably darker than a violin, and slightly lower in pitch. Equally versatile in terms of range and effects.

Instrument	Range (concert pitch)	Transposition	Characteristics
Cello (violincello)		Sounds as written	The tenor voice of the string section. Very warm and lyrical sound. especially in the middle and higher registers; the lowest octaves produce a rich, sonorous bass.
Double bass (string bass)		Write one octave above concert pitch	The bass voice of the string section. Can be bowed or plucked; more often plucked than other string instruments.

If you plan to write a lot for strings, it behooves you to learn more about how the instruments work, in particular the various types of performance techniques. There's not enough space to go into all that detail here; suffice it to say that taking an introductory violin course, or just spending some time with a string player, will offer tremendous benefits.

Strings (Nonbowed)

Violins and violas aren't the only stringed instruments out there. The guitar (along with the mandolin, ukulele, and banjo) is technically part of the string family, although most folks differentiate it from the violin-type instruments because the guitar is not bowed; it's plucked or strummed. The guitar also has six strings, compared to the four strings of the violin instruments. Guitar parts can be noted with notes on staves or, if you just want a strummed rhythm, by using chord notation.

The other oddball string instrument is the harp. The harp is kind of like a piano, but more vertical, although its strings are plucked (like a guitar) rather than struck.

The following table describes the ranges and characteristics of these nontraditional stringed instruments.

> **Note**
>
> In all of these tables, the notation *8va* means to play the note an octave higher than what is written. The notation *8vb* means to play the note an octave lower than what is written.

Nonbowed String Instruments Ranges and Characteristics

Instrument	Range (concert pitch)	Transposition	Characteristics
Guitar		Write one octave above concert pitch	There are many types of guitars, both acoustic and electric, 6- and 12-string. Can play single lines or full chords.
Banjo		Sounds as written (except for tenor banjo, which is written one octave above concert pitch)	Has five strings and produces a distinctive percussive sound.

continues

Nonbowed String Instruments Ranges and Characteristics (continued)

Instrument	Range (concert pitch)	Transposition	Characteristics
Mandolin		Sounds as written	Has eight strings, tuned in pairs. Best used for solo lines.
Electric bass		Write one octave above concert pitch	Similar in sound to the traditional double bass, but more widely usedin jazz and popular music. Exclusively plucked; seldom, if ever, bowed.
Harp		Sounds as written	Darkly colored in the lower two octaves, lightening progressively up the range. The middle two octaves are very rich and warm; the upper octaves are light and clear, but without much of a dynamic range or sustaining power. Ideal for playing single lines, octaves, arpeggios, and glissandos. With all open strings (all pedals up), the harp is tuned to C♭ major. All strings for a given note are controlled by a single pedal; when the C♭ pedal is depressed one notch, for example, the entire series of C♭ strings becomes a C-natural series. Therefore, you can't play natural notes in one octave and chromatics in another.

Woodwinds

Some woodwind instruments are made of brass; some are made of wood. But all (except the flute) use a vibrating wooden reed to produce their sound. (The flute produces sound when you blow across an open hole, kind of like blowing across a soda bottle.)

There are many different woodwind instruments, including flutes and piccolos, at least four different types of saxophones, a variety of clarinets, the unique-sounding oboes and bassoons, and even the less-common English horn (which isn't a horn and isn't even English—it's actually an alto version of the oboe). Woodwind instruments primarily use the treble clef, although the bassoon and contrabassoon both use the bass clef.

The following table describes the ranges and characteristics of these woodwind instruments.

Woodwind Family Ranges and Characteristics

Instrument	Range (concert pitch)	Transposition	Characteristics
Piccolo		Write one octave below concert pitch	A soprano version of the flute, extending the flute's range up an octave. Extremely piercing quality, especially in the top half of its range. Produces a whistling-type sound when multiples are played in unison.
Flute		Sounds as written	Mixes well with other woodwinds; good for ensemble work. Very agile instrument, also capable of great sensitivity. Beautiful warm tone in the lower octaves. Due to its soft volume, solo lines are best accompanied by sparse instrumentation.
Oboe		Sounds as written	Very lyrical instrument. Sounds particularly distinctive (and melodic) in its top octave. Tends to "honk" in the low part of its range; avoid notes below the D.
English horn		Write a perfect fifth above concert pitch	Produces a very deep and distinctive sound that gets thinner as it gets higher. Sounds most melodic in its top two octaves, although the lowest part of the range is particularly rich and expressive. Avoid notes below the G.
Clarinet (B♭)		Write a major second above concert pitch	Very flexible instrument with large range; color varies quite a bit across the range. Is easier to play in lower ranges than comparable saxophones. Good for both solo and ensemble passages.
Clarinet (E♭)		Write a minor third below concert pitch	A kind of "piccolo" clarinet. More difficult to play than the B♭ clarinet; requires frequent rest periods. Best in the upper register; lower range is quite thin.
Bass clarinet		Write a major ninth above concert pitch (using the treble clef)	Lowest register is the most distinctive, with the warmest tone. Can sound "pinched" in higher registers.
Bassoon		Sounds as written	The bass voice of the woodwind section. Produces a somewhat comical sound, especially in its lower registers. Blends well with other woodwinds. Expressively melodic in its middle and medium-high range.

continues

Woodwind Family Ranges and Characteristics (continued)

Instrument	Range (concert pitch)	Transposition	Characteristics
Contrabassoon		Write an octave above concert pitch	The lowest of the woodwinds, plays an octave below the bassoon. Less articulate than its smaller brother. Very low sustained tones have a "buzz" because of their slow vibrations.
Soprano saxophone		Write a major second above concert pitch	High, piercing, sound; can be quite lyrical in its middle range. Sometimes used instead of the clarinet in jazz settings.
Alto saxophone		Write a major sixth above concert pitch (on treble clef)	Sweet, sentimental sound. Blends well with other saxes, especially tenors.
Tenor saxophone		Write a major ninth above concert pitch (on treble clef)	Can be played sweetly or with a rougher edge. Blends well with other saxes, especially altos.
Baritone saxophone		Write an octave and a major sixth above concert pitch (on treble clef)	Very sharp, "honking" type sound when played staccato. Can also be used for low-bass sustain. Avoid the very lowest notes of the range (below F).

Brass

Brass instruments are wind instruments, typically made of brass, that utilize a mouthpiece (instead of a reed) and three or four valves to create different tones. The trumpet is the brash and annoying younger brother of the brass family, the trombone is the more stable older brother, and the tuba is the not-always-serious uncle. Also hanging around is the weird foreign relation, the French horn, and a few other unusual relatives, such as the baritone. Brass instruments use either the treble or bass clefs, depending on their predominant pitch.

The following table describes the ranges and characteristics of the brass family.

Brass Family Ranges and Characteristics

Instrument	Range (concert pitch)	Transposition	Characteristics
French horn		Write a perfect fifth above concert pitch (on treble clef)	Produces a naturally cool sound, good for long, sustained passages. Requires talented performers; it's a difficult instrument to play well.
Piccolo trumpet (B♭)		Write a minor seventh below concert pitch	Produces a clear and piercing sound. Very agile, but best used sparingly.
Trumpet (B♭)		Write a major second above concert pitch	The most flexible voice in the brass family. Produces a very powerful sound, especially in multiples. (Octaves are particularly powerful.) A very agile instrument, capable of playing very fast passages. Interesting colors can be produced with various types of mutes.
Cornet		Write a major second above concert pitch	Similar to the trumpet, but with a slightly more mellow tone.
Flugelhorn		Write a major second above concert pitch	A trumpetlike instrument that produces a mellow, lush sound, something like a French horn.
Trombone		Sounds as written	Surprisingly lyrical in the upper registers. Can also play "bleating" bass notes in the lower octaves. Learn slide positions, as to avoid difficult notes and transitions.
Bass trombone		Sounds as written	Used for very low bass passages. Beware of physical difficulty of playing notes in specific positions, particularly low E and B. (Moving from seventh-position B to first-position B♭ is particularly problematic.)
Baritone horn		Sounds as written	Very agile instrument. Blends well with other brass and woodwind instruments.
Tuba		Sounds as written	The bass voice of the brass family. A surprisingly versatile instrument, not just for the lowest of the low notes. Can be used as a solo voice in the upper registers, where it can be quite agile with a smooth tone.

Keyboards

Depending on whom you ask, keyboard instruments are either string instruments (because they have internal strings) or percussion instruments (because the strings are struck rather than plucked or bowed). In reality, they're a little of both and justify their own category.

There are many different types of keyboards, and they all have fairly wide ranges. The piano, of course, is the most-used keyboard instrument, but you can't forget about organs, or harpsichords, or any number of electronic synthesizers. A full piano has 88 keys; some smaller instruments can have smaller keyboards. Without exception, all modern keyboard instruments sound in concert pitch.

And let's not forget the newest category of keyboards, those electronic instruments known as synthesizers. Synthesizers can be either analog (creating new sounds via oscillators and other electronics) or digital (typically sampling and then reproducing the real-world sounds of other instruments). Digital synthesizers can be programmed to resemble other instruments or to create wholly new sounds of a virtually unlimited nature.

The following table describes the ranges and characteristics of various keyboard instruments.

Keyboard Family Ranges and Characteristics

Instrument	Range (concert pitch)	Transposition	Characteristics
Harpsichord		Sounds as written	Actually a plucked string instrument; instead of being hit by hammers, the strings are plucked by crow quills or leather tabs. Produces a delicate tone that is easily overwhelmed by other instruments.
Organ		Sounds as written	Can be either acoustic (pipe) or electric. Large pipe organs have the largest range of any instrument. A very powerful instrument; can sustain pitches almost indefinitely.
Piano (pianoforte)		Sounds as written	The workhorse of any instrumental ensemble, ideal for both solo and ensemble passages. Capable of incredible dynamic range; can be played lyrically or percussively. Has the widest pitch range of any instrument in the orchestra.

Percussion

When you talk percussion, you're talking about a lot of different instruments. Percussion instruments make noise when you hit or shake them, so the family includes everything from snare drums and cymbals to marimbas and timpani. Most percussion instruments are of indefinite pitch—that is, although they make a noise when you hit (or shake them), that noise isn't associated with a particular pitch. Other percussion instruments, such as timpani and the mallet family, do produce a definite pitch (or pitches).

When you're writing for an indefinite-pitch instrument, you don't have to follow standard staff notation. For example, when you write for drum set, you assign different parts of the staff to different drums and cymbals in the set. In the following example, the bass drum is the bottom space on the staff; the snare drum is the third space up. Cymbals are at the top, noted by X-shape note heads.

Writing for drum set.

Tip

When writing jazz or pop music, you don't have to compose a detailed drum part. You can notate how many measures there are in each section of the piece (as well as any specific rhythms you want played), and let the drummer make up his (or her) own part.

The following table describes the ranges and characteristics of those pitched percussion instruments.

Pitched Percussion Instruments Ranges and Characteristics

Instrument	Range (concert pitch)	Transposition	Characteristics
Chimes (tubular bells)		Sounds as written	Produces a loud, ringing tone when struck with a wooden mallet. Not very agile; best for longer sustained notes. Has a similar "out of tune" quality as a church bell.

continues

Pitched Percussion Instruments Ranges and Characteristics (continued)

Instrument	Range (concert pitch)	Transposition	Characteristics
Glockenspiel (bells)		Write two octaves below concert pitch	Metal bars hit with metal or hard rubber mallets produce a piercing, high-pitched sound. Notes ring for some time after being hit, unless damped.
Xylophone		Write one octave below concert pitch	The "piccolo" of the percussion section, with small wooden bars. Produces a very sharp, high-pitched biting sound, good for staccato figures. Typically played with only two mallets. Sustain is accomplished via a two-handed "roll."
Marimba		Sounds as written	A lower-pitched instrument than the xylophone, with a rounder tone. Very effective in the lower registers. The top octave has a similar sound to the xylophone. Sustain is accomplished by "rolls" on one or more notes. Can be played with four mallets (two in each hand). Notation can be on either the treble or bass clefs, or on two staffs.
Vibraphone (vibes)		Sounds as written	Vibes differ from other mallet instruments, in that the bars are made of metal, and an electronic motor can create a pulsating type of vibrato. A vibraphone also has a sustain pedal, which the other mallet instruments lack, which enables the use of sustained notes (with or without the vibrato turned on) without rolling. Can be played with either two or four mallets.
Timpani		Sounds as written	Actually a set of four or five separate drums, with overlapping ranges. Each drum is tuned by foot pedal. Retuning a drum to a different note cannot be done instantaneously; although you can change notes in the middle of a composition, you should allow several measures' rest for the timpanist to do this. For beginners it might be best to set a group of four notes (one for each drum) at the beginning of a piece and not change them. Extended notes are accomplished via a two-handed "roll."

Voices

Compared to an instrumental ensemble, a vocal ensemble is fairly easy to write for because all the voices reproduce exactly what you write, with absolutely no transposition (except for the tenor, that is, which sounds a octave lower than written). When you're writing for a choir, you typically have two female voices and two male voices at your disposal, with an optional third male voice (baritone) available.

The following table describes the range and characteristics of each of these voices.

Vocal Ranges and Characteristics

Voice	Range (concert pitch)	Transposition	Characteristics
Soprano		Sounds as written	The highest female voice, typically assigned the lead part. The highest part of the range often sounds quite shrill, especially with younger or less-skilled singers. Will sound s trained at the bottom of the range.
Alto		Sounds as written	The lower female voice, with a deep and resonant tone. Will sound strained at the top of the range.
Tenor		Write one octave above concert pitch on the treble clef (unless sharing a staff with the basses)	The highest male voice; overlaps significantly with the range of the female alto.
Baritone		Sounds as written	An optional male part; most vocal works don't have separate baritone lines. The baritone falls between the tenor and the bass, with more of a basslike sound—but without the very low notes.
Bass		Sounds as written	The lowest male voice. At the low end of the bass range, the sound gets a tad rumbly.

Choosing Instruments for a Composition

Knowing how each instrument sounds (and is written) is just the first step in the study of orchestration. What's more important is using that information to create your own compositions and arrangements.

When composing a piece, one of the first things you need to do is determine for what instruments you're writing. A piece written for solo bassoon and piano accompaniment will sound quite different than one written for full symphonic orchestra. The characteristics and range of each instrument will influence the music you write. Conversely, the sounds you hear in your head will help determine the instruments you choose to write for.

This is why it's so very important to have fixed in your mind how each instrument sounds—both generally and across various parts of its range. If you have a particular sound in your head, you should be able to choose which instrument(s) can best produce that sound—or, in some instances, which combinations of instruments can do the job.

For example, you might know what a flute sounds like, and you might know what a flugelhorn sounds like, but do you know what they sound like when played together? It's actually a quite interesting sound, especially when they're played in unison. (They sound a little different when they're playing together in harmony, but still interesting.) Or how about paring a trombone in its high range with a cello? Or a baritone sax with a bassoon? Or a violin with a French horn? Or a piccolo with a xylophone?

You get the point. There's an entire world of musical colors out there for you to choose from, if only you know how to choose.

And after you've chosen your instruments, you need to know how to best use those instruments within your composition. There are various ways to voice a saxophone section, for example, which produce entirely different sounds. Voice the saxes in nice open thirds, and you have a nice lyrical quality that sounds good in ballads and slow passages. Voice them in tighter blocks, and you get a buoyant sound that's good for fast passages.

I can't teach you all the possible combinations of instruments or how to best use each combination—at least, not in this book. For that, you have to embark on your own personal study of orchestration. It's definitely worth the effort.

Common Ensembles

Although you can compose for any combination of instruments and voices you like, there are certain established ensembles that you're likely to run into over the course of your musical career. When asked to compose a piece for orchestra or string quartet, it helps to know precisely what instruments are involved—and how they're used.

For that reason, we'll look at a half-dozen or so of the most popular instrumental and vocal ensembles. Read on to learn more.

Symphonic Orchestra

A full symphonic orchestra can include virtually every instrument available, including a complete complement of strings, woodwinds, brass, and percussion.

When you're composing the score, write for the following instruments (in top-to-bottom position):

* **Woodwinds.** Piccolo, flute (first and second), oboe (first and second), English horn, E♭ clarinet, B♭ clarinet (first and second), bass clarinet, bassoon (first and second), contrabassoon, French horn (first, second, third, and fourth)

* **Brass.** Trumpet (first, second, and third), trombone (first, second, and third), tuba

* **Percussion.** Timpani, percussion (including snare drum, bass drum, marimba, and so on)

* **Harp**

* **Piano**

* **Strings.** Violin (first and second), viola, cello, double bass

Tip

The symphonic orchestra is used for more than just symphonies. Many film and television soundtracks employ full orchestras; some rock bands even call in an orchestra to fill things out on occasion. Because of all the instruments available, the orchestra is perhaps the most versatile type of instrumental ensemble available and is worthy of your studies.

Chamber Orchestra

A *chamber orchestra* is a stripped-down version of the full orchestra, with widely varying instrumentation. The following is one of the most common chamber orchestra lineups, in top-to-bottom order:

* **Woodwinds.** Flute (first and second), oboe (first and second), B♭ clarinet (first and second), bassoon (first and second)

* **Brass.** French horn (first and second), trumpet (first and second)

* **Timpani**

* **Piano**

* **Strings.** Violin (first and second), viola, cello, double bass

Chamber orchestras typically have fewer musicians on each part. Instead of an entire section of violins, for example, there might be only a handful of string players on each part.

String Orchestra

A *string orchestra* is simply the five instruments of the string section (first violin, second violin, viola, cello, and double bass), sometimes accompanied by a piano (written below the strings on the score). There are no brass, woodwind, or percussion instruments in this ensemble.

String Quartet

Another common ensemble in both classical and contemporary music is the *string quartet*. As the name implies, this is a grouping of four string instruments (one each—no doubling per part), notated in the following top-to-bottom order: violin I, violin II, viola, and cello.

Note

The string quartet is just one of many different types of chamber music ensembles. Other chamber music ensembles include the brass quintet, woodwind quintet, piano trio, and so on.

Concert Band

A *concert band* includes virtually all the brass, woodwind, and percussion instruments from the larger orchestra, but without the strings. When you're writing a concert band score, you include the following groups of instruments, in top-to-bottom order:

- **Woodwinds.** Piccolo, flute, oboe, English horn, clarinet, alto clarinet, bass clarinet, bassoon, alto saxophone, tenor saxophone, baritone saxophone
- **Brass.** Cornet, trumpet, French horn, trombone, bass trombone, baritone horn, tuba
- **Percussion.** Timpani, percussion (with separate staves for snare drum, bass drum, and so on)

Jazz Band (Big Band)

Another popular ensemble, especially in the jazz idiom, is the so-called *jazz band* or *big band*. A typical jazz band includes some or all of the following instruments, listed from top to bottom on the score:

- **Woodwinds.** Flute (sometimes played by a sax player), soprano sax (sometimes played by an alto or tenor sax player), one to three alto saxes, one to three tenor saxes, one or two baritone saxes
- **Brass.** Three to five trumpets, three to five trombones
- **Rhythm section.** Guitar, piano, bass, drums, other percussion (such as congas or tambourine)

Choir

As noted previously, choral music normally has four parts (soprano, alto, tenor, and bass), and each part has to have its own line in the score. The parts are arranged with the highest voice (soprano) at the top, and the lowest voice (bass) at the bottom. The four vocal parts are grouped together with braces, and a piano accompaniment is included below the vocal parts. The top three parts use the treble clef; the bass line uses the bass clef. Lyrics are included below each staff.

Guidelines for Music Scoring

Whatever type of music you write, you should follow certain notation guidelines when creating the score. These rules include the following:

- The first instance of each staff for each instrument or voice must have its own clef sign, key signature, and time signature.
- Typically, the time signature is shown only in the very first measure and wherever a time change appears.

Note

A marching band has similar instrumentation to a concert band, minus the following instruments: oboe, English horn, bassoon, alto clarinet, cornet, bass trombone, and various concert percussion instruments.

Tip

Creating parts for the jazz band rhythm section is particularly interesting. In most cases, you can use slash notation and indicate the chord changes, but you don't have to create fully realized parts. The big exception to this is when you have important rhythms that you want the rhythm section to reinforce; you can note these rhythms using slash notes.

◆ Each instrument should be clearly marked at the beginning of each staff. (The first instance typically has the full instrument name, spelled out; subsequent staves can use abbreviations.)

◆ Group like instruments together (all the trumpets together, for example). If you want, you can combine all like instruments on a single staff.

◆ For instruments that use the grand staff (both bass and treble clef), group the two staves by using braces.

◆ Measure lines should be drawn through all the instruments belonging to the same section—but not through all the instruments in the score. (This is so you can visually group the sections together, at a glance.)

◆ If an instrument or voice will be resting for an extended period of time, you don't have to include the staff for that instrument or voice during the rest period (after the first page, that is).

◆ Use letter markings to notate individual sections of the music. (For ease of reading, letter markings are typically enclosed in a box or circle.)

◆ Number your measures—or at least the first measure of every line. (Alternately, you can insert a number mark every 5 or 10 measures.)

> **Note**
>
> Vocal scores are sometimes called *SATB* scores, for the soprano, alto, tenor, and bass parts.

These guidelines apply to the score you compose and that the conductor uses in rehearsal and performance. As for the music that the musicians themselves read, you have to create individual parts for each instrument. (This is not a requirement for vocal scores, which typically show all voices together.) So if you've written a piece for a big band, for example, you have to create a separate first trumpet part, and a separate second trumpet part, and a separate third trumpet part, and so on. When you write out the individual parts, include only that instrument's part—the conductor is the only person who gets to see all the parts together on the master score.

> **Note**
>
> The whole business of creating a proper score is made easier with computerized music-notation programs, such as Finale and Sibelius. Learn more in Chapter 2.

Learning More About Orchestration

If you're serious about composing, you have to be equally serious about orchestration. That means learning more about the topic than I can present in this chapter—and there are many ways to do this.

First, if you live near a college or university with a good music school, take advantage of all that is offered there. Ideally, that means taking a course or two in orchestration. Beyond that, you can ask to sit in on various instrument courses, or take the time to talk personally with various instrumentalists or teachers. If you get the opportunity to actually play (or try to play) a specific instrument, take it; there's nothing like hands-on experience to better inform your compositions.

If you don't have a music school nearby, you probably still have some venue for listening to live music. Don't limit yourself to just hanging out at the local tavern, although there's nothing wrong with that. No, I'm talking about a local concert hall, a place where you can listen to live performances in a variety of styles. Go to as many concerts as you can, and pay particular attention to the individual performers and their instruments—and how the composition uses those instruments.

Tip

You can also learn a little about orchestration from your computer and electronic instruments, as the digitized sounds in today's synthesizers and music software programs are certainly much better than the electronic sounds of the past. Know, however, that you can misuse these tools; they won't stop you from playing an instrument well outside of its range. So although this type of electronic experimentation might be useful, it doesn't replace listening to real, live instruments. Hearing a real violinist up close and personal beats listening to a digital sample any day.

I mentioned in the introduction to this chapter that the subject of orchestration was big enough to warrant an entire book. That's quite literally true, and there have been several important books written on the subject. As you progress with your studies, I suggest that you read one or more of the following books, all of which I heartily recommend:

- *Arranging and Composing for the Small Ensemble: Jazz, R&B, Jazz-Rock* (David Baker, Alfred Publishing, 1970—revised edition 1988). As the title implies, an excellent guide for arranging for jazz ensembles of various sizes, including trios, quartets, quintets, and the like.

- *Arranging Concepts Complete: The Ultimate Arranging Course for Today's Music* (Dick Grove, Alfred Publishing, 1972—second edition 1989). A comprehensive text for big band arrangers.

- *Principles of Orchestration* (Nikolay Rimsky-Korsakov, Dover Publications, 1964). The famed composer and orchestrator's classic presentation of orchestration fundamentals, complete with extensive original musical excerpts. This summary of late nineteenth century practices presents a good deal of information that's still useful today.

- *Sounds and Scores: A Practical Guide to Professional Orchestration* (Henry Mancini, Northridge Music Inc., 1973). An easy-to-read, extremely practical guide to jazz and popular music orchestration, from the master composer himself. Filled with dozens of examples from Mancini's own work.

- *The Study of Orchestration* (Samual Adler, W.W. Norton & Company, 3rd Edition 2002). An extremely comprehensive guide to classical and modern orchestration, one used by many college orchestration classes.

Which of these books are best for you depends on the type of composing and arranging you intend to do. If you're focusing on the jazz genre, go with the Baker or Grove books. If you're more classically oriented, go with the Rimsky-Korsakov text. If popular music or movies are of more interest, then definitely read Mancini's book. And whatever type of composing you intend to do, you can't go wrong with Adler's classic text. Whichever book you choose, I guarantee you'll come away with much important information.

The Least You Need to Know

- Orchestration is the art of composing or arranging for various instrumental and vocal groupings.

- Not all instruments play in concert pitch; these instruments require their parts to be transposed to a different key.

- It's important to learn the ranges and tonal characteristics of every available instrument so you can better choose which instruments to include in your compositions.

- The best way to learn about the instruments is to hear them played, live and in person.

- The most common ensembles are the symphonic orchestra, chamber orchestra, string orchestra, concert band, jazz band (big band), vocal choir, and various chamber ensembles (such as the string quartet).

Exercises

Exercise 15-1

Transpose the following concert-pitch passage for trumpet, B♭ clarinet, alto saxophone, tenor saxophone, and French horn, keeping all the instruments in their proper ranges.

Exercise 15-2

Transpose the following concert-pitch passage for flugelhorn, piccolo trumpet, E♭ clarinet, baritone saxophone, and English horn, keeping all the instruments in their proper ranges.

Exercise 15-3

Compose a short piece for string quartet (two violins, viola, and cello), with the viola part using the alto clef.

Exercise 15-4

Compose a short piece for jazz band, with transposing instruments in their transposed keys.

Exercise 15-5

Compose a short piece for full symphonic orchestra, with transposing instruments in their transposed keys.

Chapter 16

Working Outside the Basic Key

In This Chapter

- Learn how—and when—to change keys in a composition
- Discover how to use chromatic notes in your melodies
- Find out how to create nondiatonic chords and chord progressions
- Learn how to fit new melodies to nondiatonic chord progressions

Most of the melodies used as examples in this book have been fairly simple diatonic melodies. By *diatonic*, I mean that a given melody keeps to the notes of the underlying scale. If it's a major-key melody, it's built from the seven notes of the major scale; if it's a minor-key melody, it's built from the seven notes of the minor scale.

There are plenty of musical genres where it is perfectly normal to limit yourself to diatonic melodies that don't include any raised or lowered notes. But one of the great joys of composing today is that you need not limit your ear's imagination. You're not limited to using only the notes of a single major or minor scale in your compositions; you can use any of the 12 tones in the chromatic scale.

The more you alter the underlying scale, the more you obscure the tonal framework of a composition. That said, there is a large, expressive area between pure diatonic music and the type of chromaticism where the notion of a tonal center becomes unimportant.

Changing Keys

Probably the most common way to free a composition from a given harmonic framework is to effect a key change. When you modulate from one key to another, your composition changes color. Even if all you do is repeat the same melodies and chords in the new key, those melodies and chords sound different

in comparison to their original presentation. Not only do different keys have different sounds, but the very fact that a melody is now being played a half-step (or a whole step or a third, a fourth, or a fifth) higher triggers an emotional response from the listener. It's that comparison between the new key and the old one that makes the impact.

Changing keys is easy. Physically, all you have to do is insert a new key signature in that measure where you want the key to change. If the key change takes place at the start of a new staff, the old key signature should be cancelled out at the end of the previous staff. For example, if you move from the key of F (with one flat) to the key of G (with one sharp), you use a natural sign to cancel out the flat of the old key and a sharp to introduce the new key.

Changing key signatures—cancel out the old and introduce the new.

Harmonically, changing key signatures is a little more involved. Ideally, you want to modulate to a key that is somehow related to the previous key. You should familiarize yourself with several common types of modulation.

Modulating Up a Half-Step

This is a very simple modulation, moving your entire composition just a tad higher. This type of modulation is common in popular music and is effected simply by moving up a half-step to the new I chord—no connecting cadences necessary.

A half-step modulation—very uplifting.

Modulating Up a Whole Step

This is similar to the half-step modulation, but a little more dramatic. Again, there is no connecting cadence before the modulation; just step up to the new I chord.

A whole-step modulation—more of the same.

Modulating Down a Fifth (Up a Fourth)

Technically, this modulation is down a perfect fifth, although the melody is often transposed higher (up a fourth) rather than lower (down a fifth). This type of modulation sounds very natural because the old key functions as the dominant of the new key. For example, if you change from F to B♭, F is the dominant of B♭.

You typically make this modulation via a slight connecting cadence; all you have to do is turn the tonic chord (I) of the original key into a dominant seventh chord. This dominant seventh then cadences naturally to the tonic of the new key. For example, if you're modulating from C to F, turn the C chord into a C7 chord, and then lead from that into the F major chord—the I of the new key.

Modulating down a perfect fifth.

Modulating via Shared Chords

Another way to determine which key to move to is to move to a key that shares one or more chords in common with the original key. That shared chord can then serve as the pivot point for the modulation.

Let's look at an example, starting in the key of C major. The D minor (ii) chord also exists in several other keys, including the key of F major, where it serves as the vi chord. You can modulate from C to F by holding the D minor chord and then using it as the vi chord in the new key. From your chord-leading rules, you know that the vi chord easily leads to the IV chord, which, in the key of F, is a B♭ major chord. So you hold the D minor chord and then move to a B♭ major chord (and then to the next appropriate chord in the new key). Because B♭ major is definitely not a chord in the original key of C, the listener is immediately made aware of the modulation.

Modulating via a shared pivot chord.

Modulating Abruptly

There's no rule that says you have to follow these modulation guidelines; it's perfectly acceptable to change from any one key to any other key, with no warning or connecting cadence necessary. For example, you can modulate from the key of C to the key of A simply by moving from one tonic chord to the other. This is called an abrupt or direct modulation and has a very unsettling affect. It definitely calls a good deal of attention to itself.

An abrupt modulation.

Creating Melodies from Outside the Scale

Now let's turn our attention to melodies. For many types of compositions, you want to limit your melody to the notes of the designated scale. However, sometimes you want to throw in a surprise or two, which you can do by using notes that don't fit within the scale. These nonscale tones are called *chromatic* notes, and you can use them to add color to a piece of music. (That's where the term comes from, by the way; *chroma* means "color.")

For example, if a composition is in C major, listeners expect to hear the notes of the C major scale—C, D, E, F, G, A, and B. If instead your melody includes a G♭, you really get their attention. In fact, the more nonscale notes you include, the more outside the tonal center you get.

There are many different ways to create melodies that aren't strictly diatonic. We'll examine a few of these techniques next.

Chromatic Notes as Neighboring Tones

Inserting chromatic notes into a melody doesn't mean that you have to throw all tonality to the wind. If you want to retain the basic tonality but still add unexpected color to the melody, you can use chromatic notes as passing tones or approach notes. That is, the chromatic note isn't a structural tone, but rather a note you pass by on your way to the main tone. For example, if a structural tone (in the key of C) is a G, you might approach that note from below with a chromatic F#/G♭, or add an G#/A♭ neighboring tone. The structure of the melody doesn't change; it's only the embellishment that goes chromatic.

Using chromatic notes as neighboring tones.

Chromatic Substitution Tones

A more dramatic approach is to use a chromatic note as a structural tone. This is typically done via the technique of substitution. That is, you write a diatonic melody, and then take a main tone from that melody and either raise it or lower it a half-step—that is, you substitute a chromatic for a structural tone. For example, you might replace a G note in a melody with either a G# or G♭. This is totally unexpected and sounds very dramatic.

The original diatonic melody.

A structural tone in the melody replaced by a related chromatic note.

When you substitute a chromatic note for a diatonic one, you introduce significant tension into the melody. If you want to release that tension, one method is simply to return to the original (presubstitution) note. This might require inserting an additional note into the melody, but you'll have that release you're looking for.

Our new melody, updated to include a resolution of the chromatic tension.

Chromatic Motifs and Variations

Another approach is to develop a short pattern or motif based on a specific interval, and then create variations that displace that motif up or down chromatically. The first interval will, by nature, be diatonic, but as the motif goes through its variations, you move outside the scale via chromatic notes.

For example, you might create a two-note motif based on the interval of a major third (C-E). You then repeat that motif, raising it a half-step at a time. So your melody goes C-E, D♭-F, D-F#, E♭-G, and so on.

Tip

For a more dramatic impact, *don't* resolve the chromatic note. Leaving the melody hanging on a nondiatonic tone will have a potent effect on the listener.

A two-note pattern ascending chromatically.

One important aspect of this technique is that in many cases you'll eventually want to end your variations back in the original key. In this instance, you could continue the chromatic progression upward until you come to two notes that fit

Note

Learn more about motifs and variations in Chapter 13.

within the underlying major scale, or to two notes that define a new key (if you wanted to use the chromaticism as an opportunity to modulate).

Melodies Based on Nontraditional Scales

Some scale-based melodies can be naturally chromatic—if the scales themselves include chromatic notes. Back in Chapter 6, we discussed several nontraditional scales that include notes that fall outside the traditional major scale. For example, the blues scale includes three chromatic notes—a flatted third, flatted fifth, and flatted seventh. Create a melody based on the blues scale, and you'll automatically use these chromatic tones.

A chromatic melody based on the flatted notes of the blues scale.

Other scales that include chromatic notes (when compared to the related major scale) are the whole tone scale (flatted fifth, sixth, and seventh), the diminished scale (flatted third, fifth, and sixth), and the bebop scale (flatted seventh).

Creating Nondiatonic Harmony

It isn't just melody that can break free of diatonic constraints. The chords you use can also fall outside of the standard diatonic harmony, thus giving your composition a wider harmonic palette.

Any time you write a chord that includes a note not in the underlying major or minor scale, you're using chromatic or nondiatonic harmony. You don't want to flatten or sharpen chord notes willy-nilly, however, so let's examine some common techniques for altering your harmony in this way.

Nondiatonic Chord Substitutions

The first way to create nontraditional harmony is simply to substitute a nondiatonic chord for an existing chord in your composition. There are two classes of nondiatonic chords:

- ◆ **Chords containing altered chord tones.** This is a normal major or minor chord that you alter by raising or lowering one or more of the existing chord tones. For example, if you take a IV chord, such as F major (within the key of C), and flat the third, you turn it into a iv chord (F minor). It's typically the third that you alter, although you can also alter the fifth to create augmented or diminished chords.

- ◆ **Chords based on altered scale tones.** This is a chord based on a nondiatonic tone—that is, a tone that doesn't fall within the underlying scale. For example, you could base a chord on the flatted seventh of the scale (within the key of C, this would be a B♭); because this tone does not exist in the underlying scale, you've created a nondiatonic chord.

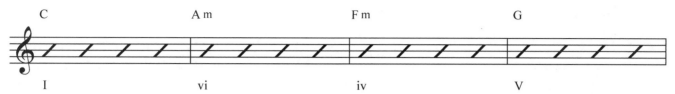

Altering a chord tone to create a nondiatonic chord (IV to iv).

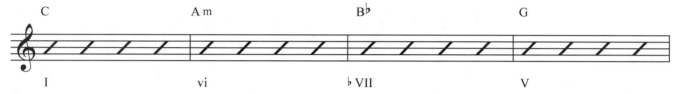

Creating a nondiatonic chord on a nonscale tone (♭VII).

Both of these approaches are widely used and equally effective. For example, if you take a standard I-vi-ii-V progression and change the ii chord from minor to major, the resulting progression (I-vi-II-V) feels significantly different from the original. Change the V chord from major to minor (creating a I-vi-II-v progression), and the feel changes even more; change the I from major to minor and the vi from minor to major, and you're miles away from what you started with—a i-VI-II-v progression.

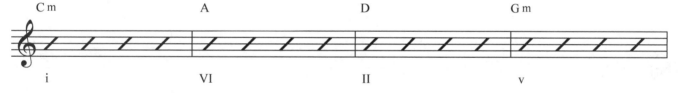

A chord progression completely altered by changing chords from major to minor—and vice versa.

The most dramatic effect comes from basing chords on nonscale tones. I particularly like using the flatted seventh of the scale as the basis for a major chord, but with the major seventh extension (♭VIIM7). Moving back and forth between the ♭VIIM7 and the IM7 chords creates an ambiguity when the listener isn't quite sure where the tonic really is.

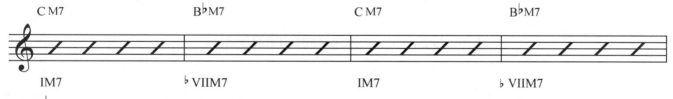

A IM7-♭VIIM7 progression—where's the tonic?

Here's something else to try. Take the standard I-vi-IV-V progression and alter each of the nontonic chords by a half-step; the resulting I-♭vi-♭IV-♭V progression doesn't sound anything like the original.

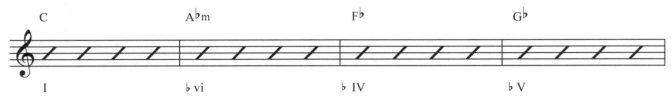

A progression in which all chords but the tonic are based on nonscale tones.

Nondiatonic Chord Leading (Circle of Fifths)

Here's another easy way to move beyond traditional tonality. All you have to do is base a chord progression strictly on the circle of fifths and let it lead you out of and then back into your original harmony.

Here's how it works. Start with the I chord, and then move to the V7. The V7, of course, is a dominant chord to the I, which is where it leads back to. But when you get to the I, alter it to play a I7 instead. This turns the tonic chord into a dominant chord for that chord a fifth below it—the IV chord. Instead of playing a straight IV chord, however, you alter it to play a IV7, which turns it into a dominant chord for the ♭VII chord. Again, alter this chord into ♭VII7, which then becomes the dominant chord for the ♭III chord. Keep this up, and you eventually get back to the original V7 and I chords.

Try this starting in the key of C. Your chord progression will go like this:

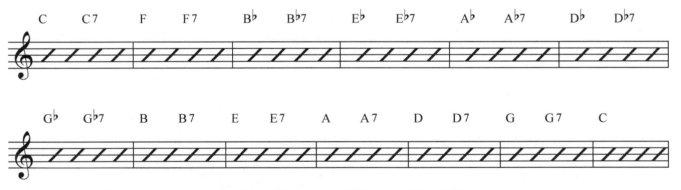

An increasingly nondiatonic (and then rediatonic) chord progression based on the circle of fifths.

See how it works?

Chords Based on Nontraditional Scales

Earlier in this chapter, we discussed melodies based on nontraditional scales. Well, some of these nontraditional scales will also lead to nontraditional chord construction and progressions. And the less traditional they are, the further you move away from diatonic harmony.

Let's take the whole tone scale as an example. As you recall from Chapter 6, the notes in the whole tone scale move upward a whole step at a time; in relation to the corresponding major scale, the notes look like this: 1-2-3-♭5-♭6-♭7. If you limit your chord construction to these six notes, you'll quickly discover that the only types of triads you can construct are augmented chords! No matter which degree of the whole tone scale you start on, any triad based on thirds always consists of a root, a major third, and an augmented fifth (that is, the fifth is always a major third above the third). So if you're using the C whole tone scale, you have just six triads at your disposal: C augmented, D augmented, E augmented, G♭ augmented, A♭ augmented, and B♭ augmented. Base your chord progression on these chords, and your composition will have a very interesting tonality, indeed.

A possible chord progression based on the C whole tone scale.

You run into a similar situation with the diminished scale, which contains the following notes: 1-2-♭3-4-♭5-♭6-6-7. Here, any three-note chord you construct is always a diminished chord—that is, a minor chord with a flatted fifth. Base a chord progression on this scale, and you create a very unique-sounding tonality.

A possible chord progression based on the C diminished scale.

Fitting Melodies to Nondiatonic Chords

When you create a harmonic structure based on nondiatonic chords, you're then faced with the challenge of fitting a melody to your new chord progression. Although this can be challenging, because of the nontraditional harmonies, it can also be somewhat liberating—the new and unusual chords can inspire you to create new and unusual melodies.

Probably the best way to approach this type of melody writing is to base your melody solely on the new chord tones, or on the new scale implied by each nondiatonic chord. Let's look at each approach separately.

Chord-Tone Melodies

In the first approach, you simply identify the tones of the nondiatonic chords and pick one (or more) of the tones to include in your melody. To make the nondiatonic chords sound more connected, pick a chord tone that is diatonic to the original scale; for a more dramatic approach, use a nonscale note instead.

As an example, we'll start with this little snippet of a melody as originally written—before we add the nondiatonic chords. This is an unassuming C-Am (I-vi) progression, with an equally unassuming melody.

Tip

If you do your composing chords-first and start with one of these nondiatonic chord progressions, you'll have to fit your melody within these unusual chords. This will force you to use chromatics in your melody, to match the chromatics in your chords. The further outside the scale your chord progressions are, the more chromatic your melody will be.

A chord progression and melody before alteration.

Now we'll alter this phrase by substituting an A♭ major chord for the Am chord, in essence creating a I-♭VI progression. To make this change sound less jarring, we'll identify the one tone of the A♭ chord included in the original C major scale, the C, and use that tone in the new melody.

The new chord progression and melody, using a diatonic chord tone in the melody.

If instead we wanted to emphasize the chord change, we'd change the new melody to include one of the chromatic tones in the A♭ chord—either the A♭ or the E♭. The resulting melody is more startling in its nature.

A second, more dramatic melodic approach, emphasizing the chromatic tone in the new chord.

Scale-Based Melodies

When you substitute a nondiatonic chord, you temporarily change the under-lying tonality of your composition. That is, the tonal center shifts to one that naturally includes the new chord. With this implied new tonality in mind, you can use any tone from the temporary tonality in your melody line—for the duration of that chord, that is.

Let's return to our example of the C-Am progression altered to a C-A♭ progres-sion. For the one measure of the new A♭ chord, the tonality is shifted from the C major scale to the A♭ major scale—which means that you can use any of the notes in the A♭ major scale in your melody over the course of this measure.

As you can see in the following example, this approach has an even more dra-matic impact than the simple chord-tone approach. Instead of changing a note or two, it changes everything; it's like being in an earthquake and having the ground shift underneath your feet. Everything seems shifted and just a trifle unsettled, at least until the introduction of the next diatonic chord and a return to the original tonality.

Using the new chord's tonality for the changed melody.

Moving Toward Atonalism

Each of the techniques discussed in this chapter starts with a diatonic tonal structure and then alters it to some extent. This means that, to some extent, you're still working with traditional tonality as the basis for your chromatic excursions.

A more extreme approach is to allow the chromatic twists to perpetually change the harmonic landscape—that is, to abandon traditional tonality from the start. When traditional tonality is totally obscured in this manner, the music is said to be freely chromatic or, more pejoratively, atonal—without tonality.

The freedom to be unabashedly chromatic dramatically altered both classical and jazz music during the twentieth century. Free chromatic or atonal techniques are so important—and so different from traditional harmonic techniques—that they deserve a whole chapter to themselves. So turn to Chapter 17 to learn more about these more contemporary approaches to composition.

The Least You Need to Know

- Chords and melodies do not have to be diatonic in nature; they can include notes and chords not found in the underlying major or minor key.

- The most common way to change tonality is to modulate to a different key in the middle of a composition.

- Melodies can be made more interesting by introducing chromatic notes, either as neighboring tones or as substitutes for structural tones.

- Another way to create a chromatic melody is to base it on a nontraditional scale, or such as the blues, whole tone, or diminished scales.

- Nondiatonic harmony can be created by altering the notes of an existing chord or by basing a chord on a nonscale tone.

- To fit a new melody to a nondiatonic chord progression, you can use either the primary notes of the changed chords or the scale tones from the new tonality implied by the chord.

Exercises

Exercise 16-1

Expand this passage to include a modulation to the key of G, using a dominant seventh cadence.

Exercise 16-2

Substitute (and then resolve) chromatic tones for one or more of the structural tones in this melody.

Exercise 16-3

Rewrite one or more chords in this passage to contain altered (chromatic) chord tones, and then compose a melody that fits the new chords.

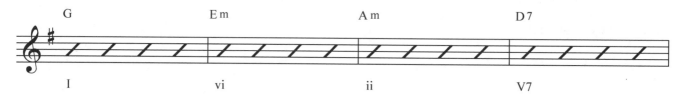

Exercise 16-4

Alter one or more chords in this passage so that the chords are based on altered scale tones, and then compose a melody that fits the new chords.

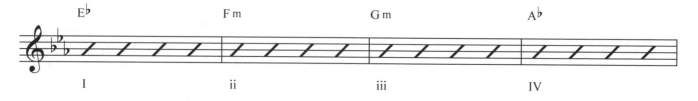

Exercise 16-5

Write a short piece (chords and melody) based on the G whole tone scale.

Chapter 17

Beyond Traditional Composition

In This Chapter

- ◆ Move from traditional tonality to chromaticism to atonality
- ◆ Discover how to create serial and twelve-tone music
- ◆ Examine alternate forms of tonality, including microtonality and polytonality
- ◆ Learn how minimalism arose in opposition to contemporary music's increasing complexity

All the compositional techniques we've discussed so far in this book have been based in traditional Western tonality. That is, all the approaches involve some sort of scale constructed from half-steps and whole steps, a home (or tonic) pitch, and harmony created from three-or-more note major and minor chords. This traditional tonality dates back hundreds of years and was developed throughout the Baroque, Classical, and Romantic musical periods—as well as in all of the popular music of the past few centuries.

At the dawn of the twentieth century, however, some composers pushed the boundaries of traditional musical forms and began to explore all manners of alternative music. Much of this exploration involved the use of sophisticated harmonies, nondiatonic (chromatic) scales, and nontraditional tonality. The result was a profusion of contemporary musical forms that redefined the very nature of composition.

Some of this music can be a little disorienting at first, especially for those listeners used to more traditional musical forms. Most listeners are accustomed to hearing the seven notes of the Western major scale, and having those notes used in a certain fashion. When a composition uses a different tonality, it can take a fair amount of time for people to develop a meaningful relationship to the music. That doesn't make contemporary music wrong, just as it doesn't make traditional music right; each of these approaches to composition is valid in its own way.

It's important to note that many modern composers don't limit themselves to just one school; they utilize both traditional and contemporary techniques in their work, either separately or in some blended fashion. These different approaches to tonality are just different tools that you can use—or not use, as you wish—to express the ideas inside your head.

Atonality

In Chapter 16, you were introduced to the concept of chromaticism—that is, music that includes tones from outside the underlying major or minor key. As music becomes more chromatic and less diatonic, it moves toward what is often called *atonality*—literally, music without a tonal center or underlying key.

Note
The term "atonality" has generated a good deal of misunderstanding. That's because most works that push chromaticism beyond the bounds of ordinary tonality still maintain pitch centers and even harmonic centers, and hence aren't totally without tonality. These focal points can assume all kinds of guises, but the craft of creating pitch and harmonic centers is remarkably similar to traditional tonal composing.

To me, one of the defining features of chromatic and atonal music is the focus on pitch intervals rather than on chords and harmony. To a large degree, atonality is about the lush quality of intervals. Chromatic and atonal composition often luxuriates in the rich sounds of seconds and sevenths—intervals that are highlighted less frequently in diatonic compositions.

A brief atonal passage.

You might think that by having no tonal center, atonal music would be extremely ugly or dissonant. Although atonal compositions can be dissonant, they don't have to be. It is possible to write chromatic melodies that are very smooth and lyrical, just as it is to write chromatic melodies that are ragged and dissonant. You may find—especially if you try experimenting with highly chromatic music yourself—that you start to hear lyrical, dramatic, and even poignant emotions coming through lines you once found jarring or simply dry.

While most atonal music has very few guidelines, letting the sound of sequential intervals be the primary guide, a particular form of atonalism dubbed *free atonalism* involves a more conscious attempt to avoid the patterns and tonalities of pre-atonal music. In free atonalism, composers are urged to avoid the use of traditional scales, major and minor triads, and any chord sequence that resembles a traditional cadence. This type of planned atonality isn't for everyone, but it does lead directly into the more rigidly defined serial music, which we'll discuss next.

> **Note**
>
> To experience the various forms of chromatic and atonal music, listen to the somewhat dissonant works of Arnold Schoenberg, Alban Berg, and Anton Webern—then compare those works to the more lyrical atonalism of Béla Bartók and Aaron Copland.

Twelve-Tone and Serial Music

In an attempt to more systematically distance this new music from more traditional forms, Schoenberg introduced a rigid system of composition that became known as the *twelve-tone method*. In this system, the twelve tones of the chromatic scale are used once each in a 12-note collection, called a *tone row*. This "melody"-like ordering can then be the basis for motifs, themes, and harmonies.

The tone row is repeated throughout the composition, either in the same order or in specific variations, such as retrograde (reverse) and inversion (with each interval moving in opposite directions). A strict application of the twelve-tone method to a composition demands that one full statement of the tone row must be heard before another can began. Adjacent notes in the row can be sounded at the same time, the notes can appear in any octave, and different rhythmic patterns can be applied to the notes, but the order of the notes in the tone row is maintained.

The 12 notes of a tone row.

A melody created from the previous tone row.

The twelve-tone method eventually evolved into another structured method called *serialism*. In this method, it's not just tones that are arranged in order; pitches, rhythms, and dynamics are all arranged in a predetermined fashion and then used (with accepted variations) to create the composition.

> **Note**
>
> Suggested listening includes the serial works of Karlheinz Stockhausen, Milton Babbitt, and Pierre Boulez.

Of course, it's all much more complicated than that because you can do a lot of things with serial sets within the whole of the composition—turn the sets upside down, play them backward, and so on. As you might suspect, there is not enough space here for a full discussion of serial technique; much further study is required to master the form.

Indeterminacy

Although serial music is highly programmed, composers such as John Cage and Earle Brown believed that some aspects of their music should be left to chance. This means reducing the role of the composer as the controller of the music by letting the performer choose which notes to play or basing some choices on the outcome of a random event (such as the rolling of dice). By employing the techniques of *indeterminacy*, a composition will never sound the same way twice.

There are five basic categories of musical indeterminacy:

- Composer determinacy of randomly ordered events
- Composer determinacy of randomly chosen events
- The use of graphic or other indeterminate notations, which allow the performer a degree of flexibility in interpretation
- Music notated traditionally but performed indeterminately
- Pure performer indeterminacy, which contains elements of improvisation

As you can see, the indeterminacy can be the province of either the composer (the first two categories) or the performer (the last three categories). With composer indeterminacy, the compositional process is made random in some fashion. With performer indeterminacy, the composer creates a framework to which the performer contributes with some degree of randomness or improvisation. The end result, in any case, is a composition that is created anew with each performance.

Polytonality

While some twentieth-century composers were working with highly programmatic serial compositions or highly random indeterminacy, both of which still used the 12 tones of the Western scale, other composers were looking for ways to expand the tonal alphabet. One such approach, known as *polytonality*, sought to use more than one tonality at the same time.

A polytonal composition is one that is written in two or more keys simultaneously. Although this sounds confusing, just imagine two separate ensembles, one playing in the key of F and the other playing in the key of G. The sound that results is polytonal.

There are two different ways to create a polytonal composition. One, as exemplified by the fanfare from Igor Stravinsky's ballet *Petrushka*, orchestrates a single melodic line as a duet between two different instruments, each playing the line in a different key (or, as notated here, a fixed nondiatonic interval distant). The second approach, often used by Charles Ives, involves the creation of two distinct compositions, in different keys, that are then played simultaneously. The end result is the same, a tonally unsettling experience for the listener.

A brief polytonal passage from the fanfare of Stravinsky's Petrushka.

Another polytonal approach, with two distinct compositions played simultaneously.

Polytonality can be more consonant or more dissonant, depending on the keys used. More consonant polytonality employs two or more keys that fit well together, such as C and G, which have a lot of notes in common. More dissonant polytonality uses two or more keys that don't fit well together—such as C and D♭, or C and A#—which have few, if any, notes in common.

Microtonality

The well-tempered system of tonality that we use today is by no means random, but neither is it absolute. Reproducing the twelve tones of the Western scale involves many small adjustments that are, in fact, out of tune with the natural harmonic series. Many other systems of intonation exist, though the exploration of them is fairly obscure in Western music. When playing such intonations on Western instruments, you end up using *microtones*—tones that fall in-between the well-tempered intervals, as represented by the keys on piano keyboard. By focusing on a stronger correlation to the harmonic series, such microtonal music can have a special kind of fresh radiance.

Another type of microtonality continues the evolution of tonality by dividing the octave into more and smaller harmonic intervals. So instead of having 12 chromatic notes in an octave, a microtonal scale might squeeze 24 pitches into the same space. The resulting sound is notably non-Western; some people might even think it sounds out of tune (at least, in relation to traditional Western tuning). Of course, a large quantity of world music would qualify as microtonal, at least to Western ears.

Warning

As you might expect, microtonal music is both difficult to play and difficult to notate.

Note

Western composers who pioneered the concept of microtonality include Charles Ives and Béla Bartók.

Minimalism

The style known as *minimalism* arose in response to the increasing complexity of both serious and popular music forms. Minimalism is hypnotic in its repetition, characterized by relatively simple melodies and rhythms employed with diatonic harmony and long pedal points.

A typical minimalist composition is based on a simple melodic motif, repeated numerous times with slowly evolving modifications in the form of melodic addition, reharmonization, or altered orchestration. Radical in the 1960s, minimalism has now become a completely normalized part of the compositional landscape. Consequently, it has evolved a much broader array of characteristics—and has achieved a great deal of popularity outside of classical music audiences, as well.

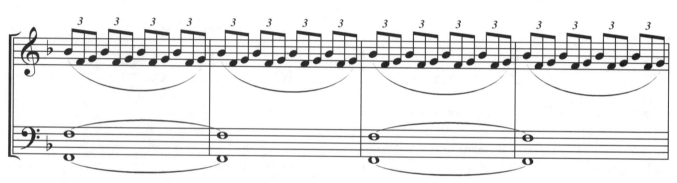

The start of a long minimalist piece, based on a simple three-note triplet motif.

Tip

Minimalism can also include long stretches of silence within a composition. After all, what is more minimal than silence?

Musique Concrète and Electronic Music

In 1948, the engineer and composer Pierre Schaeffer began to use the newly developed magnetic tape recorder to record various everyday sounds and then combine those sounds in various ways. The result was dubbed *musique concrète* (French for "concrete music") because it consisted of real-world sounds rather than the "artificial" sounds of musical instruments.

Musique concrète marked the beginning of what we now call *electronic music*. In this new and developing genre, electronic equipment—including but not limited to computers and synthesizers—is used to generate, modify, and combine all manner of sounds. This form has become more common in recent years, especially with the power of today's computers and digital musical instruments.

Other Experimental Forms

The musical forms presented in this chapter are merely some of the more popularly known approaches to contemporary composition. Other approaches forgo traditional notation to create *soundscapes* based on colors or shapes, which enable performers to interpret these symbols into pitches and rhythms; *pitch-class sets*, which apply mathematical constructs to the compositional process; and *biomusic*, in which sounds are created by animals or plants instead of human musicians. In these forms, the definition of music itself is being challenged; a piece can consist of any type of sound, not just traditional chords and melodies.

> **Note**
>
> If you're interested in experimental forms and other contemporary forms, I suggest that you listen to the works of the composers mentioned in this chapter and do some additional reading. In particular, I recommend David Cope's book, *Techniques of the Contemporary Composer* (Schirmer, 1997), a respected guide to these nontraditional musical forms.

The Least You Need to Know

- Atonality is a form of music that moves beyond the major and minor scales to use all the notes in the chromatic scale—without implying any traditional tonality.

- Serialism and the twelve-tone method arrange and repeat the 12 chromatic tones of the scale in a set order.

- Indeterminacy introduces the element of chance into composition and performance.

- Polytonality enables compositions that use more than one key at the same time; microtonality divides the scale into more than 12 tones.

- Minimalist compositions employ simple motifs repeated over and over in a hypnotic fashion.

- *Musique concrète* creates works using recordings of real-world sounds; electronic music uses synthesizers, computers, and other electronic instruments to generate, modify, and combine all types of sounds.

Exercises

Exercise 17-1

Use the guidelines of free atonalism to create a short composition for three voices.

Exercise 17-2

Create a brief twelve-tone composition using the following tone row:

Exercise 17-3

Create a short polytonal composition for two voices, with the first voice in the key of C and the second voice in the key of F.

Exercise 17-4

Use the following short motif and develop it into a longer composition, using minimalist techniques.

Exercise 17-5

Use a tape recorder, synthesizer, and other electronic effects to create a work containing both musical and real-world sounds.

Chapter 18

Songwriting

In This Chapter

- ◆ Putting words to music—or vice versa
- ◆ Employing proper song form
- ◆ Learning how to keep it simple

To many people, "writing music" really means "songwriting." In reality, songwriting is a particular subset of composition. Writing a popular song requires the same skills you need to create any other type of composition, and one more: the ability to fit words to music.

So while writing a song might, at first blush, appear to be simpler than writing a symphony, it's actually every bit as challenging. Granted, you probably won't be applying the twelve-tone method (or other modernist techniques) to a three-minute ballad, but everything else you've learned about composition should come into play.

Plus, of course, you have those words to worry about.

Putting Words to Music—or Vice Versa

Songwriting is the art of composing both music and words. Adding lyrics to the mix adds a whole other level of complexity; however, the words have to fit the melody, and vice versa, and (unless you have an ironic twist in mind) the whole thing—words and music—has to convey a uniform tone and mood.

Words and Music—Equally Important

Songwriters are often asked which comes first, the words or the music. This is kind of like the melody-or-chords question that all composers face, and the answer is the same: it all depends. Some songwriters start with a poem or a set of lyrics and then set the words to music; others start with a melody and then fit words to it; others start with words and a chord progression, and try to attempt to divine a melody that fits them both. There's no right approach, although, however you do it, I'll always campaign for keeping the focus on the melody.

Chanting lyrics over a chord progression doesn't often result in a great melody, although it's a fairly common formula—in my opinion, one much overused. For me, the melody needs to stand on its own, even (and especially) if the words are omitted.

In the classic era of the popular song, otherwise known as the Tin Pan Alley era, many songwriters worked in teams, with a dedicated lyricist working with a dedicated music composer; this practice continued into the Brill Building era of the 1960s, and allowed each member of the team to contribute in his or her area of strength. You've probably heard of some of these great songwriting teams, such as George Gershwin (music) and his brother, Ira (words); Richard Rodgers (music) and either Lorenz Hart or Oscar Hammerstein II (words, both of them); Burt Bacharach (music) and Hal David (words); Carole King (music) and Gerry Goffin (words); and Barry Mann (music) and Cynthia Weil (words).

Dedicating one person to words and another to music isn't the only way to do it, of course. With some songwriting teams, such as Paul McCartney and John Lennon, both partners wrote both words and music—and did so very well. And there have always been those single songwriters who are fluent in both words and music, such as Cole Porter, Jimmy Webb, and Paul Simon. But however you approach it, the marriage of words and music has to be well arranged.

Make the Rhythm Fit the Words

Whether you plan to write your own words or to work with a lyricist, your music needs to fit the words. In the simplest sense, this means arranging the rhythm of the melody so that it fits the natural rhythm of the lyrics. You don't want a singer to be forced into awkward phrasing to fit all the syllables into a given space. Most words and phrases have a natural pace and will suggest a rhythm to you. Make sure your music's rhythm fits this lyric rhythm—in particular, avoid putting an unaccented word or syllable on an accented part of the measure, like the downbeat.

The best way to do this is to simply say the phrase out loud. Note how some words are shorter and some are longer; note where you place the emphasis when you speak. Try to mirror this rhythmic pacing in the rhythm of your melody, making sure that emphasized words always land on an important beat—or, lacking that, are accented.

As an example, take the following phrase:

I went walking on a sunny afternoon

What natural rhythms do these words suggest? One possibility is the following:

Representing our sample lyrics with a natural rhythm.

You can see how someone could speak these words in a way that would mirror the rhythm we created. On the other hand, some rhythms would sound decidedly unnatural if spoken, like this one:

I   went   walk - ing   on   a   sun - ny   aft   -   er - noon

Extremely awkward rhythmic phrasing—it doesn't sound natural.

This rhythm sounds wrong because the accents are in all the wrong places. People simply don't talk like this; there's no reason they would sing like this, either.

Edit Accordingly

When you try to combine a set of lyrics with a given melodic line, they don't always fit perfectly together. A common mistake is to try to fit too many syllables onto a single pitch, which sounds more like chanting than it does singing. You may be able to work your way around this by adding some neighboring notes to hold the extra syllables, but truncating the lyrics should always be an option. The last thing you want to do is to sacrifice the curve of your melody for an awkward lyrical line; static melodies that spend too much time on a single pitch quickly become boring.

Sat - ur - day morn   -   ing   on   a   dark   and   dir - ty   street

Trying to fit too many words into a melodic line—notice the repeating tones.

Sat - ur - day morn   -   ing   on   a   dark   and   dir - ty   street

One solution: embellish the melody with neighboring tones to accommodate the extra syllables.

Morn - ing   on   a   dir - ty   steet

Another solution: cut some of the excess words.

Create a Sympathetic Contour

You also want the contour of your melody to match the flow of the words. For example, if the words ask a question, you probably want the melody to flow upward, to imitate the way a human voice ends a question on a higher pitch. And if the lyrics are extremely downbeat, you might want to introduce a descending contour to the melodic line.

A questioning lyric implies a melody with an ascending contour.

Match the Feel

In addition, you want the feel of the music to match the feel of the lyrics. If the lyrics are sad, you probably don't want to set them to a happy-sounding melody. There are exceptions to this rule, of course—mismatching words and lyrics can create a sense of musical irony that is appropriate in some situations—but in general, you want your melody to reflect the feel of the lyrics, even when played without vocals.

A minor-key melody for a sunshiny lyric? It feels all wrong ....

Better to compose a major-key melody to get the right feel.

Writing in the Proper Song Form

When you're writing popular music, there is a common song form that you probably want to work within. This song form can include some or all of the following components:

◆ A brief instrumental *introduction*

◆ One or more *verses*

♦ A repeating *chorus*

♦ A *bridge* or break in the middle of the piece

In musical shorthand, the verse is designated as section A, the chorus as section B, and the bridge (if included) as section C. So a typical song form without a bridge is A-B-A-B or A-A-B-A-B. (The chorus is typically used—sometimes repeatedly—as the last section of the song.) A song with a bridge might be in the form A-B-A-C-A-B.

The most common of these forms, generally called the *song form*, is the A-A-B-A form. That's one verse, repeated with different lyrics, followed by a chorus and a repeat of the first verse. When you're stuck for a structure for a new song, there's no harm in using this extremely popular form.

Some songs differ from these traditional "verse-chorus" structures by starting off with the chorus. Given that the chorus is often the strongest part of the song, it makes a bold statement.

Other songs differ by having only a single section, in the form of a verse that gets repeated two or three times (with different lyrics each time) in an A-A-A structure. A good example of this verse-only structure is Jimmy Webb's "By the Time I Get to Phoenix;" when done skillfully, listeners will never notice the missing chorus.

With these forms, in mind, let's look at the various sections you can use when composing your own songs.

Introduction

A song's introduction is typically some sort of instrumental lead-in. It can be of any length and doesn't even need to exist—a song can start cold on the first note of the first verse.

What to put in the introduction? The introduction may include a theme based on the song's main melody, played by one of the instruments, or maybe just a chord progression from either the verse or the chorus. In any case, the introduction is used to set up the first verse of the song and then is quickly forgotten.

Tip

If you're not totally sure how to start your song, keep the introduction short and then move on to the meat of the piece.

Verse

The verse is the first main melody of the piece. It's an important melody and often is repeated several times throughout the course of the song. Harmonically, the melody might end on the tonic chord (I), or it might end on the dominant (V), creating a tension that is resolved when you proceed to the chorus.

Each instance of the verse typically has a different set of lyrics, although the lyrics to the first verse are sometimes repeated in the final verse. In all cases, the verse should relate to and lead into the song's chorus.

Chorus

The chorus is the second main melody of the song and the emotional high point of the piece. The chorus should contain the main melodic theme, as well as any hook you might have to grab the listener. The hook can be in the melody, chords, rhythm, or lyric—something unique and memorable that sets this song apart from all others.

Your chorus should not be longer than your verse, and it's okay if it's shorter. Because the chorus is the heart of the song, it is repeated frequently through-out the piece—sometimes after each verse. You will almost always include the chorus as the final section of the song. You can end the song by resolving the chorus to a dead stop or (on a recording) by fading out while repeating the chorus. In any case, this repetition requires that the chorus be memorable, both melodically and lyrically.

Bridge

Some songs include a bridge, which is kind of a break in the middle of the piece. Most bridges sound completely different from the verse and chorus, and are often based on a different harmonic structure. (For example, a bridge might be based around the IV chord instead of the I chord.) Bridges typically are short, only about eight measures—which is why a bridge is sometimes called the "middle eight" of a song.

Keep It Simple

One final bit of advice for the aspiring songwriter: keep it simple. The popular song is not the best forum for experimenting with nontraditional harmony and tonality.

That's because most popular songs are relatively straightforward, music-wise. It's not unusual for a popular song to contain only two or three chords (I, IV, and V) or, at the most, a half-dozen chords (throw in ii and vi). Extended chords, with the notable exception of the V7, are typically used little. The melody stays within the confines of the underlying scale, often using the tones of the chord triads. Dissonance is seldom employed.

That said, some popular songs *are* harmonically complex, to a degree. Listen to the work of Burt Bacharach or Jimmy Webb, to name two notable examples, and you'll hear a fair number of extended chords, sophisticated melodies, and dissonances and suspensions. But this more sophisticated approach is accept-able only when it comes from experienced hands and, even then, is relatively unheard of in some specific forms, such as roots rock, heavy metal, country pop, and the like.

Bottom line when writing popular songs: use your compositional tools wisely and judiciously, and don't show off by complicating things unnecessarily. Work within the parameters of the form; it's okay to throw in some sophisticated techniques, but only when it adds to the composition.

Tip

In lieu of a bridge, you might include a short instrumental section or solo after the chorus. This section can be based on the chords of either the verse or the melody. When the instru-mental ends, you can return to either the verse or the chorus and pick up the lyric where you left off.

> **Note**
>
> Because this book focuses on composing music, I don't pretend to cover the art of lyric writing. For that, you can turn to Jimmy Webb's book *Tunesmith* (Hyperion, 1998), which deals with both words and lyrics (and a lot more). Other good lyric-writing books include Sheila Davis's *The Craft of Lyric Writing* (Writer's Digest Books, 1985) and Pat Pattison's *Writing Better Lyrics* (Writer's Digest Books, 2001).

A Final Word

This being the last piece of the last chapter of the book, I'd like to throw in a few parting words for all aspiring composers—songwriters included.

As you sit at your desk or piano and start sketching out your latest notes, remember that the advice given in this book is just that—advice. The only hard-and-fast rule of composition is that there aren't any hard-and-fast rules. You have to use both the skills you've learned and your own musical sense to express the music you hear inside your head. If that means writing a song chorus with nine measures instead of eight, or moving from a V7 chord to a iii instead of a I, or writing a duet in parallel fifths, then that's what you should do—even if all the "rules", guidelines, and advice say otherwise.

You see, all the techniques I've presented here are just tools for you to use as you choose. You can employ them as presented, do something similar but not exact, or ignore them completely. That's one of the joys of composing; it's what you create that matters, not necessarily how you create it.

The important thing is to keep at it. The more you write, the better you'll get. And don't limit yourself to one type of composition; try lots of different things, learn to stretch yourself, do everything in your power to grow as a composer. That's how average composers get good, and how good composers become great. It's certainly how you'll get better, over time.

And remember—you have only to please yourself. If a listener or critic doesn't like something you've written, that's just an opinion (which that person is entitled to, of course). You should seek out the opinions of others, of course, but ultimately you have to rely on your own final judgment. You have to believe in yourself—and continue to do the best work you can do.

Write, learn, and grow. That's what being a composer is all about.

The Least You Need to Know

- In a popular song, words and music should be of equal importance; melody should not be an afterthought.
- The melody of a song should fit the pacing of the lyrics; you may need to edit either the melody or the lyrics to make a better fit (and avoid too many repeated pitches).

◆ The contour of the melody should match the tone of the lyrics; upbeat lyrics dictate an ascending contour, and downbeat lyrics dictate a descending contour.

◆ Make sure that your melody matches the overall feel of your lyrics; use major- and minor-key melodies accordingly.

◆ Traditional song form includes an optional instrumental introduction, one or more verses, a repeating chorus, and an optional bridge in the middle.

◆ The popular song is a relatively simple, somewhat traditional compositional form; it isn't the best forum for introducing nontraditional harmonies and tonalities.

Exercises

Exercise 18-1

Write chords and a melody to fit the following lyrics:

> **The ship sails distant in the night,**
>
> **Sliding, slowly gliding.**
>
> **The moon glares off its fading sails**
>
> **Treasure, surely hiding.**

Exercise 18-2

Write a melody to fit the following chords and lyrics:

> F
>
> **I saw her outside today.**
>
> Dm
>
> **I told her my name.**
>
> Gm
>
> **She laughed as she walked away.**
>
> C7
>
> **It's all just a game.**

Exercise 18-3

Write a lyric that fits the following chords and melody:

Exercise 18-4

Fit the following lyrics to the following melodic outline, editing either the words or the music, as necessary.

> **They met under an old oak tree in the meadow in the moonlight.**
>
> **He liked her deep blue eyes and her long golden hair.**
>
> **And remembered how, on that warm summer night**
>
> **She first told him that she really, truly cared.**

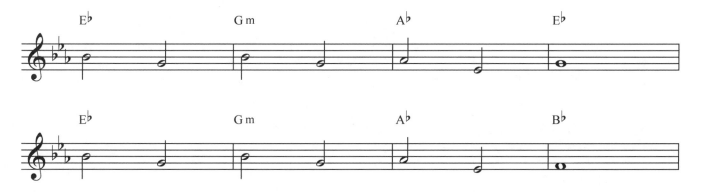

Exercise 18-5

Compose a song (with or without lyrics) that contains a short introduction, three verses, an eight-measure bridge, and a repeating chorus.

Glossary

accidental   A marking used to raise and lower the indicated pitch. Sharps raise the note a half-step, flats lower the note a half-step, and naturals return the note to the original pitch.

altered bass chord   A chord with some note other than the root in the bass. The altered bass note is typically notated after a slash, like this: Am7/D.

alto clef   A clef used primarily by the violà that places middle C on the middle line of the staff.

alto voice   The lowest female voice.

approach note   A note that leads up or down to a structural tone; an *approach note run* contains two or more approach notes.

arch contour   A melody that rises and then falls; in an arch-shape melody, the highest notes come somewhere near the midway point.

arpeggio   A chord that is broken up and played one note at a time.

arranging   *See* orchestration.

ascending contour   A melody that starts low and ends high.

asymmetrical phrase   A longer musical phrase that contains an odd number of shorter phrases of the same length, or any number of phrases whose lengths vary.

atonality   An approach to composition that is primarily or even completely chromatic in melody and harmony.

augmentation   A type of variation in which the melody is restated in longer note values.

augmented chord   A chord with a major third and a raised fifth (1-3-#5).

back phrase   The act of playing the notes of a melody later than originally written.

baritone voice   A male voice pitched between the bass and tenor voices; not always isolated in choral music.

bass   The lowest pitch of a chord (not necessarily the root).

bass clef   A clef used by lower-pitched voices and instruments that places middle C on the first ledger line above the staff.

bass voice   The lowest male voice.

bebop scale   A jazz-oriented scale that is essentially the Mixolydian mode with a major seventh added; in relation to a major scale, the scale degrees (not counting the octave) are 1-2-3-4-5-6-♭7-7.

big band   *See* jazz band.

blues progression   A 12-bar sequence of chords common in blues and jazz music, as follows: I-I-I-I-IV-IV-I-I-V7-IV-I-I.

blues scale   A seven-note scale (counting the octave) used when playing blues progressions; in relation to a major scale, the scale degrees (not counting the octave) are 1-♭3-4-♭5-5-♭7.

brass   The family of instruments, typically made of brass, that produce sound when air is blown through a mouthpiece. The brass family includes the trumpet, trombone, tuba, and French horn.

bridge   A short section that links two important sections of a piece of music.

cadence   A pause or stopping point, typically a short chord progression at the end of a phrase or piece of music. A *perfect cadence* results when a dominant (V) chord leads to the tonic (I), an *imperfect cadence* results when the dominant leads to the subdominant (IV) instead of the tonic, and a *plagal cadence* results when the subdominant (IV) chord leads to the tonic (I).

call and response   A melodic technique in which a phrase is stated in the first part of the melody and then answered in the second part.

chamber music   Music for a small group of solo instruments.

chamber orchestra   A smaller version of the full orchestra.

changing tones   A two-note pattern that functions like a neighboring tone, using both the upper and lower neighboring tones to surround a structural tone.

chord   Three or more notes played simultaneously.

chord leading   The concept that certain chords in a scale naturally want to move to certain other chords.

chord progression   A series of chords over a number of measures.

chord substitution   The art of substituting one chord in a harmonic progression with a convincing alternative.

chorus   In popular music, the part of the song (typically following the verse) that recurs at intervals; also known as the B section of a song.

chromatic   Pitches outside the underlying key or scale. The opposite of *diatonic.*

chromatic scale   A scale containing 12 equal divisions of the octave—on a piano keyboard, all the white keys and black keys within an octave.

chromaticism   (1) The use of chromatic intervals, chords, and scales. (2) A style of composing that employs chromatic harmony.

close harmony   Harmony in which the notes are close together; typically, all close harmony voices lie within the range of an octave.

coda   A short section at the end of a composition that reinforces the final resolution.

common tone   A note that is shared between two adjacent chords.

compound chord   Two chords sounded together. Typically notated with a vertical slash between the two chords.

concert band   An instrumental ensemble that includes virtually all the brass, woodwind, and percussion instruments from the larger orchestra, but without the strings.

concert pitch   The actual (nontransposed) pitch of a piece of music.

concerto   An instrumental work in which one or more solo instruments are contrasted with a larger orchestra.

consonance   Harmonious combination of tones. The opposite of *dissonance*.

contour   The shape of a melody, as indicated by the progressive upward or downward direction of the pitches.

contralto voice   The lowest female singing voice, lower than an alto; not used in all choral music.

contrapuntal   *See* counterpoint.

contrary motion   Two voices moving in opposite directions.

countermelody   An accompanying melody sounded against the principle melody.

counterpoint   Two or more simultaneous, independent lines or voices.

countersubject   A secondary theme heard against the main melodic subject. Also known as a *countertheme*.

countertheme   *See* countersubject.

decrescendo   Gradually softer.

descending contour   A melody that starts at its highest point and then descends to the end.

diatonic   Notes or chords that are in the underlying key or scale.

diatonic substitution   Replacing a chord with a related chord either a third above or a third below the original.

diminished chord   A chord with a minor chord and a flatted fifth (1-♭3-♭5).

diminished scale   A nine-note scale (including the octave) distinguished by alternating whole-step/half-step intervals; in relation to a major scale, the scale degrees (not counting the octave) are 1-2-♭-4-♭5-♭6-6-7.

diminution   A type of variation in which the note values of the original theme are shortened.

disjunct movement   A melodic line that contains much skip-wise motion and relatively large leaps—often of a fifth or more.

dissonance A combination of tones that sounds discordant and unstable, in need of resolution to a more pleasing and stable harmony. The opposite of *consonance*.

dominant The fifth degree of a scale, a perfect fifth above the tonic; also refers to the chord built on this fifth scale degree.

double Using a second voice or instrument to duplicate a particular line of music, either in unison or an octave above or below.

double-stop On a string instrument, playing two notes simultaneously.

duet A musical composition for two performers.

dynamics Varying degrees of loud and soft. For example, *forte* signifies a loud dynamic, while *piano* signifies a soft dynamic.

electronic music Music that employs computers, synthesizers, and other electronic equipment to generate, modify, and combine all manner of sounds.

embellishment Melodic decoration through the use of additional notes added to a structural tone.

enharmonic Different notations of the same sound; for example, F# and G♭ are enharmonic notes.

expansion A type of variation in which new material is added to the original melody, typically to the end of the phrase.

extended chords Chords with additional notes (typically in thirds) added above the basic triad.

form The structure or shape of a musical work, based on repetition, contrast, and variation; the organizing principle in music.

free atonalism A structured type of atonality that consciously avoids the use of traditional scales, major and minor triads, and any chord sequence that resembles a traditional cadence.

front phrase The act of playing the notes of a melody earlier than originally written.

half-step The smallest distance between notes in a Western chromatic scale.

harmonic composition Constructing the underlying chord progression of a musical composition. In harmonic composition, the chords are typically created first, followed by the melody.

harmonic rhythm The pace of a chord progression, or how often chords change within a composition.

harmonization The choice of chords to accompany a melodic line.

harmony The sound of tones in combination; also used to refer to the accompanying parts behind the main melody.

holistic composition The act of creating the chords and melody of a musical composition simultaneously.

hook A piece of melody designed to deliberately grab the attention of the listener.

imitation   Compositional technique in which a melodic idea is presented in one voice and then restated in another.

indeterminacy   A twentieth-century musical approach that leaves to chance various aspects of the musical performance.

interlude   A short piece of music that serves to connect two major sections, often blending themes contained in both sections.

interval   The distance between two pitches or notes.

interversion   A type of large-scale variation in which the order of complete motifs is rearranged within a longer phrase.

introduction   The beginning of a piece of music.

inversion   (1) A chord in which the bass note is not the root of the chord. The *first inversion* indicates that the third of the chord is played as the bass note; the *second inversion* indicates that the fifth of the chord is played as the bass note; the noninverted status is referred to as *root position*. (2) A type of melodic variation that starts on the same pitch as the original melody but then moves in the opposite direction—but by the same intervals. Also known as a *melodic inversion*.

inverted arch contour   A melody that starts high, descends to a low point, and then rises again toward the end.

isorhythmic   The art of repeating a rhythmic idea over and over, typically in multiple voices.

jazz band   A large jazz ensemble containing a mixture of trumpets, trombones, saxophones, and a rhythm section.

key   A combination of a tonic and a mode. For example, the key of F major has F as the tonic and major as the mode.

layering   A compositional technique in which multiple vocal or instrumental parts are layered on top of previous parts.

lead sheet   A piece of sheet music that contains a single staff for the melody, with the accompanying chords written above the staff.

leading tone   (1) The note that is a half-step below the tonic of the scale, that leads up to the tonic note.

major chord   A chord with a major third (1-3-5).

major scale   The most common scale, consisting of the following intervals: whole-whole-half-whole-whole-whole-half.

melodic composition   Constructing the melodic lines of a musical composition. In melodic composition, the melody is typically created first, followed by the chords.

melodic outline   The underlying skeleton of a melody, built from the melody's structural tones.

melody   The combination of tone and rhythm in a logical sequence.

meter   The organization of beats and their divisions.

microtonality   A twentieth-century musical form that divides the traditional twelve notes of the octave into more and smaller harmonic intervals.

microtone   An interval smaller than a semitone, prevalent in some non-Western music and twentieth-century art music.

minimalism   A twentieth-century musical style characterized by repeated simple melodies and rhythms employed with diatonic harmony and long pedal points.

minor chord   A chord with a minor third (1-♭3-5).

minor scale   One of three scales, each with a flatted third of the scale. Natural minor is identical to *Aeolian mode*; in relation to a major scale, the scale degrees (not counting the octave) are 1-2-♭3-4-5-♭6-♭7. The harmonic minor scale is similar to the natural minor scale, but with a raised seventh; in relation to a major scale, the scale degrees (not counting the octave) are 1-2-♭3-4-5-♭6-7. The melodic minor scale has both a raised sixth and seventh; in relation to a major scale, the scale degrees (not counting the octave) are 1-2-♭3-4-5-6-7.

mixed movement   A melodic line that contains both smooth (step-wise) and disjunct (skip-wise) movement.

modal music   A type of composition based on one or more modes.

mode   A set of scales, based on centuries-old church music that preceded today's major and minor scales. These include the *Ionian, Dorian, Phrygian, Lydian, Mixolydian, Aeolian,* and *Locrian* modes.

modulation   (1) A change of key. (2) A type of variation in which the original theme is repeated exactly, but in a different key.

motif   A brief melodic or rhythmic idea within a piece of music. Sometimes called a *figure* or *motive*.

motion   The upward or downward movement of a melody.

movement   Self-contained part within a larger musical work.

musique concrète   A twentieth-century musical form that employs recordings of everyday sounds, combined in various ways.

neighboring tone   A tone one diatonic step away (either above or below) a structural tone.

notation   The art of communicating musical ideas in written form.

note   A symbol used to indicate the duration and pitch of a sound, as in whole notes, half notes, and quarter notes.

oblique motion   Two or more voices, with one voice remaining on the same tone while the other voice moves up or down.

octave   Two pitches, with the same name, located 12 half-steps apart.

orchestra   A group of instruments organized for the performance of symphonies and other instrumental works, or to accompany a opera or other staged presentation.

orchestration   The art of scoring music for an orchestra or band. Also called *arranging*.

ornamentation   Notes that embellish and decorate a melody.

overture   (1) The instrumental introduction to an opera or other musical drama. (2) An independent single-movement instrumental work, typically used to open a concert.

parallel harmony   A harmony line that mirrors the existing melody line, at a fixed interval.

parallel motion   Two or more voices moving in the same direction by the same interval.

passing tone   A pitch located (scale-wise) directly between two main pitches; passing tones are typically used to connect notes in a melody.

pedal point   A note sustained below changing harmonies.

pentatonic scale   A five-note scale; in relation to a major scale, the scale degrees (not counting the octave) are 1-2-3-5-6.

percussion   The family of instruments that produce sound when you hit, beat, crash, shake, roll, scratch, rub, twist, or rattle them. Included in this family are various types of drums and cymbals, as well as mallet instruments (marimba, xylophone, and so forth) and timpani.

permutation   A type of melodic variation that completely rearranges the pitches of the original melody.

phrase   Within a piece of music, a segment that is unified by rhythms, melodies, or harmonies, and that comes to some sort of closure; often composed in groups of 2, 4, 8, 16, or 32 measures.

pitch   The highness or lowness of a tone. (In scientific terms, a specific frequency.)

polyphony   The mixing together of several simultaneous melodic lines.

polyrhythm   Two or more rhythms played simultaneously, or against each other.

polytonality   Employing more than one tonality simultaneously.

register   The specific area in the range of a voice or an instrument.

relative keys   Keys that share the same key signature but not the same root.

repetition   A technique that involves repeating all or part of a motif; typically used in conjunction with *variation*.

resolution   (1) Conclusion of a musical idea. (2) The release of a musical tension.

resolve   The act of moving a suspended or dissonant note down to a chord tone of the chord.

rest   A symbol used to denote silence or not playing a particular note.

retrograde   A type of melodic variation that plays the pitches of the original theme exactly backward.

rhythm   The organization of sound in time; the arrangement of beats and accents in music.

rhythmic displacement   A type of variation that repeats the original phrase, but at a different place in the measure.

root   The fundamental note in a chord.

SATB   Shorthand for soprano, alto, tenor, and bass. (Choral scores are sometimes called SATB scores.)

scale   A sequence of related pitches, arranged in ascending or descending order.

score   (1) The written depiction of all the individual parts played of each of the instruments in an ensemble. (2) To orchestrate a composition.

sectional form   A common musical form in which the composition is divided into two or more distinct sections.

semitone   The interval of a half-step.

serialism   The ordering of pitches, rhythms, and dynamics in a predetermined fashion. The *twelve-tone method* is one specific aspect of serial music.

side slip   The technique of repeating a motif either a half-step higher or lower, and then repeating it again at the original pitch.

similar motion   Two or more voices moving in the same direction, but by different intervals.

skip-wise motion   Melodic motion that moves from one note to the next in intervals of a third or more.

smooth movement   A melodic line that moves evenly from one point to another, typically in a scalar pattern without a lot of large leaps.

sonata   (1) Composition for solo piano or another instrument with piano accompaniment. (2) Specific musical form; *see* sonata form.

sonata form   A specific musical form, established during the Classical period, typically applied within a single movement of a longer piece (such as a sonata, symphony, or string quartet). The sonata form consists of three main sections: exposition, development, and recapitulation.

song   Short vocal composition.

song form   The structure of a short piece of music; usually diagramed as A-A-B-A.

songwriting   A particular type of composition with both music and lyrics.

soprano voice   The highest female voice.

stable tones   The strongest tones within a scale; in a major scale, the most stable tones are the tonic, the fifth, and the third.

staff   An assemblage of horizontal lines (generally five) and spaces that represent different pitches.

stationary contour   A melody that neither rises nor falls.

step-wise motion   Melodic motion that moves from one note to the next note one step away in the scale.

string   The family of instruments that produces sound when a bow is moved across a string. The string family includes the violin, viola, cello, and double bass.

string orchestra   A large ensemble containing the five instruments of the orchestra's string section (first violin, second violin, viola, cello, and double bass), sometimes accompanied by a piano.

string quartet   A form of chamber music for two violins, viola, and cello.

structural tones   The most important notes in a melody; the notes that remain when you strip a melody of all embellishments. The structural tones of a melody create the *melodic outline.*

subdominant   The fourth degree of the scale, or the chord built on the fourth degree (IV).

subject   (1) A motif, phrase, or melody that is a basic element in a musical composition. (2) The initial melody or phrase in a fugue.

suspension   A dissonant note used within a chord to create tension. The suspended note is often the fourth of the chord, which then resolves down to the third.

symmetrical phrase   A longer musical phrase that contains an even number of shorter phrases of the same length.

symphony   A large-scale instrumental composition, usually in four movements.

syncopation   An accent on an unexpected beat—or the lack of an accent on an expected beat.

tempo   The rate of speed at which beats are played in a song.

tenor voice   The highest male voice.

tension and release   A technique that builds tension in a melody or phrase until reaching a musical climax, at which point the tension is released.

theme   A recurring melodic or rhythmic pattern or idea; the main melodic phrase in a composition.

theme and variations   Musical technique involving the statement of a theme and then the varying of that theme. *See* variation.

tonal center   (1) The key in which the music is written. (2) A chord or pitch that establishes itself as a point of departure (and often a point of return) against which the other chords and pitches are heard.

tonality   The organization of musical notes around a tonic, or home pitch, based on a major or minor scale or mode.

tone   A sound played or sung at a specific pitch. (The term is also used sometimes to indicate *timbre,* or sound quality.)

tonic   The primary note in a scale or key; the first degree of a scale or a chord built on that degree (I).

transition   (1) Modulation from one key to another. (2) Short musical passage that acts as a link between two more substantial passages.

transpose   *See* transposition.

transposing instruments   Those instruments that are not notated at their sounding pitch.

transposition   Translating pitch.

treble clef   A clef used by higher-pitched voices and instruments that places middle C on the first ledger line below the staff.

triad   Three notes, each a third apart from the previous. Most chords are built on triads.

truncation   A type of variation in which one or more notes from the beginning or end of the original phrase are deleted. Also known as *segmentation*.

twelve-tone method   A type of twentieth-century atonal music developed by Arnold Schoenberg, in which the 12 tones of the octave are played in a predetermined order indifferent to their traditional tonal structure.

unison   (1) Two simultaneous notes of the same pitch. (2) Voices or instruments all singing or playing the same pitch.

unstable tones   Those tones within a scale that want to move to more stable tones; the least stable tones in the major scale are the second, the fourth, and the seventh.

variation   A technique in which some aspects of the music are altered but the original is still recognizable. Typically used in conjunction with repetition. *See also* theme and variation.

variation form   A musical form that incorporates a primary theme that is then reworked throughout the composition via a series of variations.

verse   In popular music, the first or A section of a song, preceding the chorus.

voice   Melodic or harmonic lines.

voice leading   The motion of a single voice in a musical composition or arrangement.

voicing   The way the notes of a chord are arranged.

whole step   An interval equal to two half-steps.

whole tone scale   A seven-note scale (including the octave), each a whole step part; in relation to a major scale, the scale degrees (not counting the octave) are 1-2-3-♭5-♭6-♭7.

woodwind   The family of instruments that produce sound when air vibrates a wooden reed. The woodwind family includes the clarinet, saxophone, oboe, and bassoon. Also included are the flute and the piccolo, which do not use reeds.

Answers to Exercises

This appendix contains the answers to several of the exercises found at the end of each chapter in this book. Only those exercises that have exact solutions are answered here. Many of the exercises are open-ended, meaning that there is no one single "right" solution. For those open-ended exercises (such as those that ask you to write your own melodies and chord progressions), apply the techniques you learned in that chapter—and trust your ears to judge the final result.

Chapter 3

Exercise 3-1

Most of these chord progressions can be completed in a number of different ways. I'll provide the most common solutions here, but other solutions are possible.

a: I	IV	<u>I</u>	V
b: I	<u>vi</u>	IV	V
c: ii7	<u>V7</u>	I	
d: I	<u>ii</u>	IV	
e: I	<u>IV</u>	V7	

Exercise 3-2

a: Key of C:	C	F	G	F
Key of F:	F	B♭	C	B♭
Key of G:	G	C	D	C
Key of B♭:	B♭	E♭	F	E♭
Key of A:	A	D	E	D
b: Key of C:	C	F	G	
Key of F:	F	B♭	C	
Key of G:	G	C	D	

	Key					
	Key of Bb:	Bb	Eb	F		
	Key of A:	A	D	E		
c:	Key of C:	C	G	Am	F	
	Key of F:	F	C	Dm	Bb	
	Key of G:	G	D	Em	C	
	Key of Bb:	Bb	F	Gm	Eb	
	Key of A:	A	E	F#m	D	
d:	Key of C:	C	Am	F	G	
	Key of F:	F	Dm	Bb	C	
	Key of G:	G	Em	C	D	
	Key of Bb:	Bb	Gm	Eb	F	
	Key of A:	A	F#m	D	E	
e:	Key of C:	C	Am	Dm	F	G7
	Key of F:	F	Dm	Gm	Bb	C7
	Key of G:	G	Em	Am	C	D7
	Key of Bb:	Bb	Gm	Cm	Eb	F7
	Key of A:	A	F#m	Bm	D	E7

Exercise 3-3

	Key		
a:	Key of C:	G	C
	Key of F:	C	F
	Key of G:	D	G
	Key of Bb:	F	Bb
b:	Key of C:	F	C
	Key of F:	Bb	F
	Key of G:	C	G
	Key of Bb:	Eb	Bb
c:	Key of C:	C	G
	Key of F:	F	C
	Key of G:	G	D
	Key of Bb:	Bb	F
d:	Key of C:	F	G
	Key of F:	Bb	C
	Key of G:	C	D
	Key of Bb:	Eb	F
e:	Key of C:	G	Dm
	Key of F:	C	Gm
	Key of G:	D	Am
	Key of Bb:	F	Cm

Exercise 3-4

The solutions presented here are just one way to complete each progression;
other solutions are possible.

a:	I	vi	<u>ii</u>	<u>V</u>	I
b:	I	IV	<u>V</u>	<u>I</u>	
c:	I	ii	<u>IV</u>	<u>V</u>	I
d:	I	vi	<u>V</u>	<u>I</u>	
e:	ii	IV	<u>V</u>	I	

Exercise 3-5

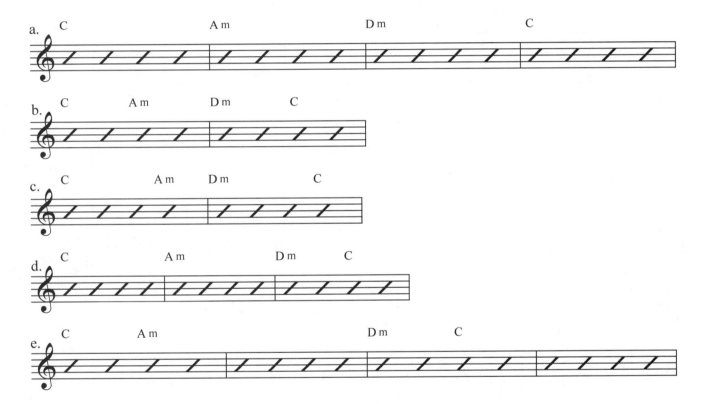

Chapter 4

Exercise 4-1

The solutions presented here are just one way to complete each progression;
other solutions are possible.

a:	I	IV	<u>iii</u>	<u>V</u>
b:	I	ii	<u>iii</u>	<u>IV</u>
c:	I	vi	<u>iii</u>	<u>V</u>
d:	I	V	<u>ii</u>	<u>vi</u>
e:	I	iii	<u>V</u>	<u>IV</u>

Exercise 4-2

a:	CM7	G7	Am7	FM7
b:	CM7	Am7	Dm7	G7
c:	CM7	FM7	CM7	G7
d:	CM7	Dm7	FM7	G7
e:	FM7	CM7	FM7	G7

Exercise 4-3

Exercise 4-4

The solutions presented here are just one way to complete each progression;
other solutions are possible.

a: Am   Dm   Em

b: Em7   CM7   FM7   Bdim

c: Em   C   Am   Dm7/G

d: FM7   Bdim   Am7

e: Am7   Dm7   Em7   Edim   Am   Em

Chapter 7

Exercise 7-1

Chapter 9

Exercise 9-1

a: Descending

b: Stationary

c: Arch

d: Ascending

e: Inverted arch

Exercise 9-3

a: Mixed

b: Smooth

c: Disjunct

d: Smooth

e: Mixed

Chapter 13

Exercise 13-1

a.

b.

c.

d.

e.

Exercise 13-2

a.

b.

c.

d.

e.

Exercise 13-3

a.

b.

c.

d.

e.

Exercise 13-4

a.

b.

c.

d.

e.

Chapter 15

Exercise 15-1

Exercise 15-2

Index

Find the ~~~~~
with thes~~~~
COMPLETE I~~~~'S GUIDES®

Music Theory
SECOND EDITION

1-59257-437-8
$19.95

Playing Drums
SECOND EDITION

1-59257-162-X
$21.95

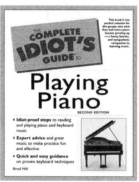

Playing Piano
SECOND EDITION

0-02-864155-8
$16.95

Playing the Harmonica

0-02-864241-4
$15.95

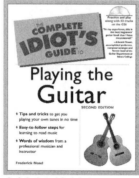

Playing the Guitar
SECOND EDITION

0-02-864244-9
$21.95

Singing

1-59257-086-0
$24.95

Starting a Band

1-59257-181-6
$18.95

Home Recording
Illustrated

1-59257-122-0
$19.95

Songwriting
SECOND EDITION

1-59257-211-1
$18.95

ALPHA